Uncommon Lives

Uncommon Lives

My Lifelong Friendship with Margaret Mead

Patricia Grinager

ROWMAN & LITTLEFIELD PUBLISHERS, INC.
Lanham • Boulder • New York • Oxford

ROWMAN & LITTLEFIELD PUBLISHERS, INC.

Published in the United States of America
by Rowman & Littlefield Publishers, Inc.
4720 Boston Way, Lanham, Maryland 20706
http://www.rowmanlittlefield.com

12 Hid's Copse Road
Cumnor Hill, Oxford OX2 9JJ, England

British Library Cataloguing in Publication Information Available

Library of Congress Cataloging-in-Publication Data

Grinager, Patricia, 1918–
    Uncommon lives: my lifelong friendship with Margaret Mead/Patricia Grinager.
        p.   cm.
    Includes bibliographical references.
    ISBN 0-8476-9378-3 (cloth : alk. paper)
    1. Mead, Margaret, 1901–1978—Friends and associates.   2. Mead, Margaret, 1901–
1978—Contemporaries.   3. Women anthropologists—United States—Biography.
4. Women anthropologists—Melanesia—Biography.   I. Title.
GN21.M36G75   1999
306'.092—dc21   99-21548
                                                                        CIP

Printed in the United States of America

♾ ™The paper used in this publication meets the minimum requirements of American
National Standard for Information Sciences—Permanence of Paper for Printed Library
Materials, ANSI Z39.48–1992.

CONTENTS

FOREWORD

Pat Grinager paints intimate vignettes from the life of Margaret Mead and provides us with a new portrait of America's quintessential human scientist. MM, as we called her, was a legend in her own time, eminent in her youth and significant throughout her life. She was the queen of the social sciences. She shaped the worldview of several generations with her insights about culture—the staggering differences among people and the equally astounding similarities. She awakened in people an awareness of global patterns of behavior. Grinager takes an anthropologist's look at this extraordinary person. Here we have a metafunction of observer watching observer. The author has raised the art of observation to a personal factual drama.

Grinager, willing friend and associate, with affection and great admiration, transported, hosted, coddled, and worked for Margaret Mead. But she did one more thing. She recorded every interaction, every phrase, every emotional moment—tired, hungry, bored, angry, alone—so that we have a remarkable picture of Mead's brilliance, her foibles, her humor, and her private reactions to friends and enemies.

In the process, we learn a lot about Grinager's life as well as about her brand of observation. She admits the work experience with MM was no picnic. There were some heavy times and heartbreaking experiences, but she carried on through adversity, mellowed by a perceptive humor that spoke volumes about their relationship.

Margaret Mead was always striding onto the world stage. She was a major figure in the development of interdisciplinary studies and linkages across traditional academic lines. She advised presidents and first ladies. She presided over the "science establishment" and influenced the thinking of everyone she met, from government figures and academics to national and international leaders to students to PTA members. Her breadth of topics, from food to culture, health to education, sex to space travel, as well as her remarkable memory, were legend. If it concerned people, it concerned her. And Grinager paid close attention.

The participants in some of the moments Grinager describes report that she captures the sense and the feeling of those times and the interactions we had with her. Her account of MM's illness and death is amazing, but to the end MM was amazing. One day I entered MM's hospital room to find her in a comalike state. She woke briefly, recognized me, and in reference to her long-term affiliation with the Human Lactation Center, which I direct, she asked, "Dana, what do you have that I should sign?" Then she lapsed back into unconsciousness.

Grinager obtained much of the information by researching intensively, conducting dozens of interviews, and making several trips to the Library of Congress, which houses Mead's lifetime output of writings, correspondence, calendars, films, and photos (the largest personal collection in the world). With the support and encouragement of curator Mary Margaret Wolfskill, she plowed through thousands of documents.

Margaret Mead's indomitable spirit, despite the pain of pancreatic cancer and the realization that her life was ebbing, amazed us. Grinager writes about MM's time with Carmen de Barraza, healer of extraordinary powers. Imagine, Margaret Mead recording their time together so that someday we would have a complete lesson in nontraditional assistance in dying.

Grinager has captured the anthropologist as subject and object. She takes us through the early years of anthropology with a penetrating personal journal while in the presence of one of its pioneers, and we gain new insight into the pivotal role Margaret Mead played in the development of this human science.

Dana Raphael

PREFACE

M argaret Mead began teaching during her seventeenth summer. Her students were young Philadelphians who wanted to learn more about the Bible. Exactly sixty years later she completed teaching her spring classes in anthropology at Columbia University when she was seventy-seven years old. She influenced over 10,000 students. I was one of the multitude.

After her death I drove 56,000 miles, crisscrossing the United States, tracking down memories of her by interviewing more than two hundred people in what I came to call "sleeping bag interviews." They usually began with a postcard warning of my impending approach a week ahead of time. I phoned for directions to their place of residence, and then I usually came loaded with goodies from some farm stand or grocery store. Since most of the interviewees were older, I deliberately planned not to cause any extra work before or after my visits. I was, nine times out of ten, invited to stay the night. I put my blue sleeping bag on any horizontal surface, although usually a sofa or a couch. Before I left the next morning, I obtained each person's birth date, which I filed on cards in the trunk of my car. Over the years I sent some three hundred greetings to my new correspondents. Many invited me to come back next time I hit town, but those stories would fill another book.

Patricia Grinager

ACKNOWLEDGMENTS

I wish to thank Senta Essenfeld, who rounded out our very special teacher–student friendship when she flew from her home in Caracas, Venezuela, to help me achieve closure on this twenty-year endeavor.

I also thank Virginia Finch of Burringbar, NSW, Australia, who saw to the publication of the book for the first time.

My heartfelt gratitude goes to my daughter-in-law, Vicky Sinsley Powers, who undertook all my computer communications for many months prior to publication.

P. G.

1

TWO WOMEN MEET

M argaret Mead charged into her first class of the 1953–1954 semester at 8:10 sharp. She believed in being on time. She looked us over. We stared back at her. A mutual anything-can-happen expectancy filled the lecture hall.

"I'm standing in front of a group of individuals who I never was. You're facing a person you'll never be." She seized the attention of moonlighting students in the School of General Studies at Columbia University in New York City.

"We're like immigrants to strange new worlds where changes never stop. In my lifetime, I've seen the people in this country go from horse-and-buggy transportation to jet airplanes. From listening to weekend afternoon concerts in the park to watching television. From wearing petticoats and celluloid collars to short socks and blue jeans. From frequenting outside three-holers equipped with pages torn from a mail order catalog to tiled bathrooms with scented toilet tissue. No one of us has ever experienced a stable culture and I doubt if we ever will."

She addressed us on the last possible class period of the first week of a new semester. She scheduled her big evening class at that late hour so as to squeeze in every minute of extra time for her between-term lecture swings around the country.

Without any further introductory ado, she plunged into the business at hand. "Biographical cards will be distributed next week," she announced. "They are to be filled out in duplicate. I want you to attach a small photograph to each one. Turn them in as soon as possible. These cards will tell me something about the composition of this group—whether it's older or younger, more female than male, more single than married, and whether more of you are anthropology majors or what.

"My classes are too heterogeneous for a normal curve. I mark in this course against your own experience or lack of it. If I have your examination blue book and cannot find a biographical card for you, your paper will not be corrected. Get that? No biographical card? No grade! Consider yourselves lucky that I use them. In how many other courses do you get a chance to be individualized?

"A biographical card is just a technical device I've invented to give me some idea of your aspirations. It also helps me to find you in case I need to. Besides, I've something solid to go by when you call me up in five years and ask for a reference. You have no idea how fast teachers forget."

Those of us wedged into the small seats of the large lecture hall hunched forward or sat back. We had seen this woman on television, heard her on the radio, read something by or about her. Here she was in the flesh, a prickly little butterball, that's for sure.

"All tests should be related to the culture in which they are given so, yes, there will be a midterm and a final. Both essay-type. The midterm is my way of finding out where you are and where you are going. I don't give exams to find out what you don't know, nor do I ever make assumptions about what you do know. I take the trouble to find out. I read each exam myself, so consider the midterm a chance to express yourself intelligently as to what you've read and what you plan to read. You're supposed to demonstrate that you've listened to lectures, so mention them from time to time. If you parrot or memorize, you're lost. And remember, I can't grade you for your interesting opinions or passionate regrets. You can get into graduate school for being interested or passionate but you can't . . . get . . . out.

"In lieu of a final, I do accept projects. Any study which helps us understand any aspect of this course is relevant. Projects which involve working with the human body are safest. Everybody's got one."

She hesitated long enough to let random chuckles subside. "I spent years recognizing projects rather than people. Now I more or less like to connect people with projects. Only graduate students and those of you with special qualifications should elect to do one. Submit a written proposal in duplicate. Requests need be no special length, two pages or more. Anthropology doesn't operate in fixed categories."

Her mouth snapped shut. Her chin jutted out slightly as she poured herself a glass of ice water. She sipped from it and watched us exchange glances with responsive strangers from a sea of faces. The lecture hall was as full as a hit Broadway show.

"A huge variety of students sign up for this class," she said, recapturing our attention. "Generally, you fall into three main groups: Those who don't expect to use what you learn but want to know what is meant when someone says, 'Don't forget the culture.' Those who have to pass a course in something somewhere and must be accommodated. And then, heaven help them, those who aspire to be professional anthropologists.

"No matter which category you fit into, I teach with the assumption that you deserve an education rather than a temporary treatment. So be prepared to do some thinking on your own. I welcome questions. They indicate that you've thought deeply enough to have some. I don't care how long it takes to answer them either. There's never one explanation for the behavior of human beings, or Homo Sap if you like that term better."

She paused to pick up her copies of the two bibliographies. "There is no textbook in this course. The smaller book list which you took off the table at the doorway will give you the basic clichés of the field. The larger one is extensive enough to include your special interests." She flipped through the first few sheets. "There're plenty of suggestions to get you started. Plan on reading at least twelve hundred pages. Set your own pace. Just know what you're doing and why. If you'd like to read something that isn't here, say so on the back of your biographical card."

She looked up from the papers in her hand, scowled at her latest batch of students. She dropped her voice an octave. "One more warning: I get tired of people who read too many of my books. I know my work so well that it is much more hazardous."

So began my first encounter with anthropologist Margaret Mead. A scant eighteen and a half months before she spoke to us on that October evening, I didn't know an anthropologist from a Zoroastrian. A series of serendipitous happenings led to my enrolling in her class.

My number four son, Kent, could pull his pants up and down but could not tie his shoes when I chanced upon a notice in the Easter 1952 issue of the Northport, Long Island, weekly newspaper that New York University Extension would be offering a two-semester course in social anthropology at the local library to begin in the fall. The class was to meet every other Thursday at 4:30 in the afternoon, run through dinner, and end at 10:30.

Social anthropology? What's that? The dictionary didn't mention the term but it defined anthropology as "the study of man." Hmmm. That kind of definition left me as ignorant as I was before I looked it up. Oh well, it could have been that at thirty-four years of age I needed to step off a treadmill of dishes and diapers. The four babies who changed my life in the first eight years of marriage convinced me that each one deserved an individual mother, nonstop. Year after year, my days and nights—365 twenty-four-hour stretches of them—were stuffed full of attending to others. The whole rigmarole buried the "I" in me alive. Hardly anyone in my everyday world reached above my navel. I starved for *materia intelligentsia* meatier than "Seventeen Ways to Fix Hamburger" or "How to Pull Your Child through Teething."

Over the years, I had taken a number of evening courses off and on at the local high school or at the "Y." Whatever I learned outside of our home bounced back into it. A Chinese cooking class chopped our food bills by a third. Bookbinding lessons taught me how to keep storybooks together longer. I sketched the kids' faces while they slept, painted oils and watercolors of barns or trees, and eventually plunked out "Lavender Blue, Dilly Dilly" on the secondhand piano.

How-to courses, alas, do not always answer who, what, why, when, and where questions. After caring for a quartet of infant personalities from birth, I wondered about the development of babies into children and of children into adults—all over the world. What do other mothers feed their infants? How do they teach them what they teach them and why? Do youngsters everywhere begin to talk by salivating "goo goo" and "da da"? Do they always crawl, either backward or forward, before balancing precariously to risk their first steps?

I puzzled over the role of women too. Were there any people who allowed grown females to be persons, really? When a woman becomes a wife and mother, where does the person go? Who was I? Where had the "me" of my childhood and premarriage adulthood gone? Long before women's liberation gained any momentum, young mothers asking questions like these must have provided a wellspring that nourished some of the rootlets of the women's movement.

I checked various reference books and discovered that a course called Social Anthropology would be about culture and that culture is to anthropologists what water is to fish. If fish were scientists, the last thing they would think about studying would be water, the very medium in which they live. So obvious. So ever present. So all-pervasive that it's hidden from casual view. So too with culture. Anthropologists are the scientists who study it. Culture is the stuff of life, the life of stuff, the whole bundle of attitudes, beliefs, customs, knowledge, law, and rules that people live by and take for granted. It's everything to everybody everywhere all together or in pieces. I read that you can systematically observe how people involve themselves with any practice, idea, or artifact from breathing to fornicating; from postures to hairstyles; from chickens to safety pins and presto! You've got a mini-anthropology of that.

Along with an assortment of curious homebodies and credit-seeking teachers who also read the announcement, I mailed in the $5 deposit. After all, I thought, who could miss signing up for a course with such humanistic potential?

Simone de Beauvoir's book *The Second Sex* had recently been translated into English from French and distributed for sale in the United States. I chose to read it for one of my book reports. Until then, men had written all the books I ever read about women. I always wondered why. So *The Second Sex* made more sense. At last, here was a scholarly book about women written by a woman.

"How can she know so much?" I marveled as my eyes leaped through the pages. One paragraph in one of her chapters startled me. In it, de Beauvoir accused those who dutifully bear babies of being "institutionalized abdomens." As I pondered her description, I realized that she was right. As a member of the "second sex," a woman was a thing, a possession, a piece of property until she worked her way out of such biological programming to become a professional person capable of self-support. At the time, the author's message was too revolutionary for me to do more than let it simmer on the back burner of my consciousness.

Shortly after Thanksgiving, the instructor of the extension course informed us that it would be followed by a social anthropology workshop in Peru in July and August. That announcement was the closest I had ever come to a chance to travel abroad. My desire to go seemed preposterous enough to be possible.

What about the money? Money is only as powerful as we let it be. I volunteered my services as a secretary and Jill-of-all trades for the workshop. As the oldest of five and mother of four, I had already tackled a variety of jobs, including scriptwriter, secretary, storekeeper, teacher. I could type, take shorthand, write, and talk effectively. I'd read enough about the contrasting roles of women on the North and South American continents, as well as about the agricultural heritage that ancient Peruvians bequeathed to the world, to do double duty as a part-time lecturer on these subjects as well.

What about the kids? I would take the oldest with me. That left three to farm out. To whom? Our nearest relatives lived too far away. I asked each of my younger sons to name his favorite schoolboy chum. On three separate afternoons I drove to a different home, parked opposite the front door, and agonized over how to broach my request to yet another set of surprised parents.

"Just go in and be amiable and warm into it somehow," I coached myself, "and then jump at the first chance to lay the proposition on the line: If they'll adopt Kent or Laird or Neal for the six weeks that Miles and I will be away, I'll take their Leif or Bobby or Alan whenever they want to go somewhere." Primitive barter, pure and simple, and audacious enough to intrigue some mothers and fathers.

"An insight I got from studying the Hawaiian kinship system in this anthropology course I'm taking," I explained to the couples, "is that children grow in tolerance and understanding when they are exposed to households other than their own."

One of the fathers identified himself as an aircraft employee; another, a psychiatrist in a veterans' hospital; a third painted houses and built fiberglass boats.

One of the mothers wrote and broadcast book review spots for libraries; another was a nurse; and the last one sewed on a freelance basis. They all had daughters too. What a magnificent opportunity for the six little boys involved to live in somebody else's home, a miniculture, and experience another lifestyle firsthand. The prospect delighted the children. Each couple, though unprepared for the idea, either agreed to it on the spot or wanted to talk it over and let me know later.

Six weeks before the group was to depart, the experience nearly ended before it began. A call came from New York University saying that Miles, who would turn ten on the trip, could not go because he was not a registered student.

"Then enroll him," I retorted without giving myself time to find the money. Preparations had gone too far to let a minor detail like another academic fee deter us. "After all," I endeavored to convince the university caller, "Nicholas Murray Butler went to college when he was nine. This way Miles will have credits ahead when he needs them in another seven or eight years." As plans and policies for the overseas course developed further, the university agreed to permit Miles and someone else's daughter of the same age to accompany the group without paying tuition.

Whatever the focus of a tour, be it academic, business, professional, religious, or sheer joy, each traveler takes two trips: one, official, and the other, individual and private. Although the behavior of some registered full-time students in the social anthropology workshop in Peru indicated that they never got past the word "social," I personally took the trip with the awe of a peasant on a pilgrimage. On a personal level, I needed to distance myself in space and time from a marriage to an alcoholic. If our merger continued to wobble, and I indeed should be left to raise the kids alone, wouldn't it be prudent to persist in collecting credits in the meantime? What better way to roll up points toward a university degree than by studying the mountain Inca and the coastal Mochica Indians of Peru in Peru?

Workshop members arrived in Patchacamac to study and travel throughout the country. I admired these hardworking Indian people. I admired their ancestors who carved in stone as though it were laundry soap, modeled pottery, and wove cloth unmatched by machine. In their equivalent to our "hello" they declared, "I do not lie, I do not steal, I am not lazy." They didn't even need police. I felt so at home among these Quechua language speakers that I might have been a reincarnated prehistoric Peruvian myself.

On a jitney excursion to the magnetic equator one Sunday, someone handed me an article from the magazine section of the *New York Times*. In it, the School of General Studies in Columbia University advertised courses available to mature adults for the fall of 1953. There were to be day, evening, and Saturday morning classes. One of the night offerings would be taught by Margaret Mead.

Margaret Mead! No other single person did more to lift anthropology out of dry textbooks or even drier research reports and make it real to ordinary readers. She wrote articles in *Parents' Magazine* about how people on Pacific islands raised their children. She had lived in at least half a dozen South Sea societies long enough to learn their languages. She recorded how infants, youngsters, and adolescents became functioning members of their own groups; where they played; why they were disciplined; how they assumed culturally defined sex roles. Her accounts were down-to-earth, witty, and well illustrated. The idea of my being able to take a course taught by such a woman seemed absolutely impossible. But life is full of impossibilities that materialize somehow and astound the most skeptical. If I wanted to study under her seriously enough, maybe, just maybe, I would.

I jounced up and down in that dilapidated bus and puzzled over the logistics of attending Mead's classes. We lived an hour away from New York City by Long Island Railroad. It would take another thirty to forty-five minutes by subway from Grand Central Station to Columbia University. My husband wouldn't be home to take over because he worked evenings. How could I ever feed the kids, bed them down, and make it by 8:10 p.m. once a week? The Mead lectures would last approximately two hours. If I missed the 10:30 train, it would be midnight before the next one departed for home. Still, an exposure to her insights on motherhood, wifehood, and womanhood was too pregnant to let pass.

I airmailed one letter to the School of General Studies at Columbia University applying for registration as a transfer student and another to Mead herself, requesting permission to be in her class come the fall. I hoped she'd pay more attention to an envelope with Peruvian stamps on it.

We returned to the States in mid-August, a month before the beginning of the next semester. A letter of acceptance from Columbia awaited me. One morning I traveled to the city for an interview with her graduate assistant before being allowed to sign up for her class, General Studies, Anthropology R 133, the Study of Cultural Character. I left the children in the care of a motherly woman who lived across the street.

Huldah Antwerp immigrated to this country from Belgium with her husband, Alphonse. They were middle-aged and childless. She gathered neighborhood youngsters around her like Santa Claus. He avoided them like Scrooge. Everybody on the block knew that he bought a new Plymouth for himself every year. She told me that he drew the line on spending one red cent of his hardearned cash on such an American frill as a washing machine for her. We owned an extra one in good condition.

On the train returning to Northport, I shivered in excitement over being accepted into Mead's course even as I shuddered over the complications involved in arranging for baby-sitting services during my absences.

Sometimes the neatest solutions lay closest at hand. I decided to try making a deal with Mrs. Antwerp: If she would referee the boys' meals and oversee their getting to bed on one evening a week between September and mid-December, she could have our extra washing machine. No haggling with Alphonse over money to pay for it. It would be hers, free and clear, come Christmas.

Even though I frequently heard the Antwerp roosters crow when I crawled into bed after hours of study, the lectures and readings for Mead's class switched the rest of my life around. Taking her course was like emerging from twilight into sunlight. I began to become a more patient mother to our bouncing band of four frisky natives, and a wiser wife. So the same behavior stereotyped as "proper" for females in one culture belongs to males in another? So a culture is learned and any baby anywhere could grow up to become an Arapesh as easily as an American? So a Manus parent in the wilds of New Guinea consistently rewards all the right things a child does and overlooks wrongdoings? What a change from the way we rub our children's noses in their mistakes and rarely mention their good deeds! Insights like this expanded my perceptions. I didn't want the course to end.

Desiring more exposure to Mead's anthropological lore, I next hatched a scheme to go to her office in the American Museum of Natural History and offer my secretarial skills to her for free. She had been a wife, yes, and she was a mother too. But she didn't let these traditional roles bury her alive. She took field trips. She wrote books. A half century before most of us dared step out of bedroom or kitchen, she proved that a wife and mother could also be the kind of professional person that Simone de Beauvoir wrote about. A female human didn't have to settle for being just another anonymous member of the second sex, an "institutionalized abdomen," a thing, a dependent, a piece of property.

"I bargained a washing machine to take this course," I wrote in my blue book at the end of an essay for the midterm, "and the neighbor who is working for it would come over early any afternoon before class when you say I might have an interview with you."

"I'll save 4:30 in my office next week," she scribbled so cryptically that I focused a magnifying glass under a floodlight to decipher the words. "Come and see me." Margaret Mead actually agreed to take some time out to talk to me? Me? A Long Island housewife–mother, one of Emily Dickinson's nobodies? How should I prepare for such a meeting?

Every day for the next week, I dragged the kids to one library after another as I searched for morsels of information about her or any other Mead who might be remotely related. I copied what I found on 7-by-11 cards, organizing and memorizing as I went, so that whatever I wrote down would have a better chance of being between my ears when we sat face-to-face.

She pounded on a typewriter with her back to a window in a storage room away from the phone outside of her office at the American Museum of Natural History. She glanced up as I entered and smiled toothily. Frowsy bobbed hair fringed her glasses. A large crystal pendant dangled from her neck. She wore a gingham smock over a street dress. She didn't look too different from many a dumpy little hausfrau who had stood in front of me in checkout lines at the supermarket.

I drew up an old wooden chair, sat down, and leaned toward her. "You know," the words bumped into each other in my excitement, "we're a lot alike. We're both the oldest of five with a brother next to us in age. Our parents went to college. Each of us graduated at the top of our high school class; you, the week I was born. We've married at least once and given birth to at least one child apiece. Both of us can trace deep family roots in the Midwest. We teach and we're hooked on anthropology."

An approach like this might antagonize or amuse. It piqued her fancy. She cupped her chin in tiny hands. Her eyes glistened as she listened to my spiel. I grew bolder and divulged a wish to work for her as a volunteer. "All I can offer for the rest of this semester is thirty minutes before class each week," I apologized. "A mere snippet of time really. Still, women have been hand crafting heirloom quilts out of snippets of cloth for centuries. Who can tell what might come out of my helping you here at the Museum if you just let me start small?"

"Your enthusiasm pleases me," she smiled. "You're raising a family, substitute teaching out on the Island, and taking my course. Now you say you want to be a volunteer. For a transfer student, that's taking on too much too soon. Finish this and next semester. Sometime later in the spring, if you still want to come in and help here at the Museum, drop me a line."

She didn't wait for me to contact her. Shortly before final exams in May 1954, she sent a one-line postcard to my address at 36 Burt Avenue in Northport that read, "Do you still want to work for me?"

Work for her? I restrained my excitement and sent two letters off immediately. The one to her read, in part, "In the same mail as this, you will probably find a letter to your secretary, Martha Held, pertaining to my availability as a volunteer.

Your card thrilled me. I do indeed accept your invitation to work and will come in next Tuesday long before class."

Between sending those letters and receiving a bachelor's degree in anthropology three years later, I stopped by her office at the Museum whenever I went to town. A friendship developed out of our working together and continued for the rest of her life.

She knew I wanted to write a book about us someday. "Now don't put that in the book," she admonished so often I wondered whether there would be anything left were I to permit her to edit every line. So I decided to postpone the effort until she died. When she reached her seventy-fifth birthday and was still going strong, I began to doubt that my sixteen-and-a-half-year age advantage would be sufficient after all.

"How old was your father when he passed away?" I asked her as I knelt to nurse a fire in the hearth of my Wisconsin home one of the last times she visited me.

"Eighty-two, the same age as his mother when she died."

"And your mother?"

"Seventy-eight, but both of her sisters are still alive and they're in their nineties."

"Ye Gods," I coughed on a puff of misdirected smoke, "my book might never get written if I hold off until you cannot check it out anymore."

Her voice softened. "A long time ago my mother published a study of Italian immigrants in a little town near the New Jersey Pine Barrens. Even though she didn't think of it in those terms, hers was one of the first, if not the first, anthropological study of acculturation made in the United States. We moved to that town when I was a year old. The people in her book were our neighbors. I remember the ostracism we suffered after the U.S. Department of Agriculture published my mother's book in 1907. Although most of them were illiterate and couldn't read what she wrote, they turned against us and we moved away. That experience taught our family that people don't like to be studied. I've tried to write so discreetly about the groups I've studied that they'd not be angry if they ever learned English and were able to read anything I wrote."

"A book about a friendship involves two people," I responded as I pushed the wood further back in the fireplace. "The survivor selectively perceives. I'd neither blacken nor whitewash you. I'd strive to pile up word pictures of you and leave readers free to recreate you in their own terms. They'll do it anyway."

"That's right, readers remember what they read by hanging new information on familiar hooks."

"I identify with you in lots of ways. And the older I get, the more I see how much the experience of childhood influences our personalities and careers. My parents raised me as effortlessly as they groomed their fingernails. Yours seem to have deliberately set out to develop fearlessness and self-confidence in their offspring."

"So?"

"I'm curious to learn more about how they did it and what made the girl you were become the woman you are. The community's reaction to your mother's study, as well as your family's response to community behavior, would be an example of the kind of experience I'd look for."

"You'd be crazy to do it. Too much work."

"Crazy and dedicated. I remember your claiming that your teacher and friend Ruth Benedict was the only person who ever read everything you wrote. A generation later, you're my teacher and friend. You salt and pepper your writings with recollections all of the time and I'm going to read everything you've written with the express purpose of collecting those memories."

"You won't live long enough."

"If my luck holds out, I will."

I straightened up and stepped back to sit beside her in a companion easy chair facing the fireplace.

We sat in relaxed silence.

"I don't think I'll ever tire of watching flames flicker in a fireplace," she reminisced after a while. "Almost all the houses I lived in as a child had at least two of them. Now I live in an apartment and I don't get a chance to look into firelight much."

"I love fireplaces. Some people don't like to be bothered with the ashes, but I don't mind. Summers, I spread ashes on the compost pile; winters, on the driveway."

During another visit on Valentine's Day in the mid-1970s, she and I gambled on a drive through a blinding snowstorm from Milwaukee, where all planes were grounded, to Chicago, where some might still be departing, so that she might make a lecture commitment in Buffalo. En route, we discussed her newly published autobiography, *Blackberry Winter*. She was already trying to think of a name for its sequel.

"I'd like to call it 'Indian Summer,'" she confided, "but I can't because people will think it's about Indians, so I'm considering, 'Bright Blue Weather' instead."

"Helen Hunt Jackson used those very words in her poem about October, which I remember reading in a schoolbook in the 1920s."

She shot a pleased glance my way.

"Buh buh wuh tur," I tolled the consonants twice over. "Both *Blackberry Winter* and 'Bright Blue Weather' have the same sound pattern."

She flashed another lightning look at me as she squinted through the windshield and complained. "I can't see a thing out there."

"I haven't given up on my idea to do a book about you either," I bent over the steering wheel and peered through the storm at shadowy cars slithering and slipping all around us. "I'd like to drive to places you've mentioned like Hammonton and Lavalette in New Jersey; Doylestown and Swarthmore in Pennsylvania, and seek out some of the neighbors, household help, and teachers who were important to you when you were the same ages as the various young people you've studied."

"There's no reason to do that. They've been bothered enough already and they're tired of being asked about me. As long as I'm alive, I want to do whatever books come out about me, myself." She stared straight ahead into blank whiteness.

"I respect your preference," I humored her, "but you won't be able to keep biographers off forever. Writing's not easy. Only the fittest survive. You know as well as I that most of the books most hopesters say they're going to write never hit the presses."

"If I were you, I'd not plan to do anything beyond a magazine article for something like *Psychology Today* or a metropolitan Sunday supplement," she suggested. "And promise to let me see whatever you write before you submit it."

"Okay, but I'm one of those readers who spends more leisure time on books than magazines or newspapers. A book is what I'd rather do. If it gets done in time, you'll be the first to see it." I touched the black embroidered edge of her red cape. "You probably haven't forgotten what I said about an heirloom quilt when I came to the Museum to ask to be a volunteer. Over twenty years ago, you encouraged me to keep a daily log. So I've got enough snippets of memory for a solid start."

So here it is, a storybook quilt with pages instead of patches, gathered and seamed with multitextured strands. It tells of a friendship. Margaret Mead and I became acquainted in the early 1950s. She taught anthropology courses in a university-connected evening school designed for adults who wanted a second chance to complete a bachelor's degree. I was a young wife and mother who returned to college to pick up the threads of formal learning that I had impetuously dropped to marry and propagate.

Mead tended to say yes to students like me when we reached out to her. She made friends of many of us. Partly because of her missionary zeal to spread everyday insights from anthropology to everybody during the sixty-odd years of her career, her name became familiar to sophisticates around the world. Many women made her success a model for their own. "She's my absolute ideal," they've told me. "If Dr. Mead could get to the top in her profession, so can I in mine."

I grew up in Fergus Falls on the Minnesota side of the North Dakota boundary. When the wind was right and our mother chastised her offspring, you could hear her in Chicago. Margaret's stormier moods reminded me of my mother's. Margaret admired the flint-hearted few who stood their ground and answered back. I had had plenty of practice in that department. We took to each other and sparred with the affectionate defiance of sisters from the start.

2

WORKING AT THE AMERICAN
MUSEUM OF NATURAL HISTORY

The weakening rays of midafternoon winter's light silhouetted the head and shoulders of the tiny, tousle-haired woman at the phone. "You sent me a reprint of your paper on the swaddled soul of the great Russians," I overheard her tell somebody as I strode closer to her cluttered desk in the far corner of her office, "but we've misplaced it. Would you rush another to me here at the Museum as soon as possible?"

Klunk! She banged the receiver back on its hook without a please, thank you, or good-bye. Floor-to-ceiling shelves crowded with books and boxes dwarfed her figure. She pushed the phone aside and looked me in the eyes as though she sensed I brought a message.

"You didn't have to hang up," I protested. "It won't take but a minute to report that I just came up to the fifth floor on the same elevator as Dr. George Gaylord Simpson. He's tried to call several times. Claims it's more difficult to catch you on the phone than it would be to climb up here in person. I promised to tell you that he'd like you to call him."

"Okay."

I glanced down at the rooftops overlooking the west side of Central Park as she straightened a stack of letters that awaited signing. "Isn't he the head of this place?" I asked.

"Yes, he's the president so I'll call him right away," she answered. "The administration of this Museum thinks of me as a kind of tumor. That's how I want to keep it. As long as I'm only a tumor, I'm safe. The day too many administrators get around to considering my presence up here a cancer, I won't be."

We were high in one of two citadels that distinguish the architecture of the American Museum of Natural History. For twenty-odd years, Margaret Mead had headquartered in this tower of the old 77th Street building. Because it served as her most reliable address for her half-century-plus career, her record indicates

15

that she did indeed manage to maintain her preferred tumorhood with the Museum's passing parade of powers.

She began using the American Museum of Natural History as her base as soon as she returned from her first field trip in the summer of 1926 at the age of twenty-four. On the recommendation of Franz Boas, her anthropology professor at Barnard College, Museum curator Pliny Earle Goddard offered her a job. Goddard, who specialized in the Indians of the American Southwest, put Margaret Mead in charge of the preservation and display of artifacts from the South Pacific that no one knew how to make any more. Her analyses of these materials dovetailed with her writing an 85-page dissertation, "The Question of Cultural Stability in Polynesia," as well as with its 175-page spin-off, *Coming of Age in Samoa*. Because of space limitations in the building at the time, Goddard gave her squatter's rights to a former custodian's apartment on the seventh floor. To get to it, she trudged down a windowless hall lined with glass cases stuffed with specimens and up two flights of narrow steps beyond the last elevator stop.

During her childhood, her family moved two times a year: into and out of whatever they rented in Philadelphia, winters; into and out of country places, summers. Except for an apartment at 310 S. 10th Street, which housed the family entourage prior to sister Elizabeth's birth in 1909, the Meads chose spacious and sprawling nineteenth-century three deckers. Grandmother Meade usually got the first choice of a room; Margaret's parents the second.[1] The children and live-in help divided up what was left.

The Meads allowed each child to express a preference. Margaret, the eldest, invariably chose a room at the top. It was remote. You could be your own boss up there and get away from everybody else. You could hear approaching footsteps on one set of stairs and duck down the other. You could spill out over an attic and spread around. It's hotter in the summer and colder in the winter, yes, but nothing's perfect.

So her space assignment in the Museum was just like home. Bit by bit, family, friends, and students transformed the former building superintendent's living and sleeping quarters into offices and workrooms. They adapted sink, tub, and jet-fitted tile fireplace for storage. Space outside the original apartment yielded crannies and cubbyholes for surplus books, files, films, notes, and student project papers. The tower also provided windowed nooks aplenty near which to wheel her typewriter table for protracted writing sessions. When offered a regular office after the completion of her Samoan books and Goddard's death, she declined to budge. Why settle for four walls and elevator service when the alternative was the whole floor of an entire tower?

She appreciated the fact that a museum is one place in our society in which time stands still for people, as well as for things. Her South Sea Island speakers of pidgin English call a museum a "house look look belong all." She grew up in the neighborhood of Philadelphia's University Museum, which began sending expeditions to exotic places during her parents' childhood. During her own, she spent many a happy hour in its palatial halls look-looking at anthropology exhibits that belonged to all. As a student at Barnard College, the women's counterpart to the all-male Columbia College, she would find illustrations of these same artifacts on the pages of her textbooks. And she knew from years of listening to family table talk that museums didn't oust septuagenarian curators as universities do professors. Once you acquired a foothold in a museum, you could stay safe for the rest of your life.

"I'll be able to come and go and do the kind of work I most want to do," she told herself at twenty-four. "I'm going to continue working here as long as I can walk up the steps to this tower."

Some time after my assistantship, the Museum became even more like home when former Barnard classmate Marie Eichelberger and fellow anthropologist Rhoda Metraux joined her there. Through the institution of godmotherhood, Margaret incorporated each of these women into her own extended family. The pair stayed on some months after Margaret herself last climbed the steps.

Permanent as Marie's and Rhoda's berths turned out to be, such was far from the case for the rest of Margaret's handmaidens. "I never go looking for help," she declared on occasion, "help comes to me."

Ex post facto, I realized that I too was one of a legion whom she enchanted in the courses she taught by moonlight in the School of General Studies at Columbia. Evening students seldom run into teachers as approachable and energetic as Margaret Mead. In a classroom or lecture hall, she radiated a special mana. We gravitated to her. She welcomed us on the assumption that the experience of working for her, no matter how fleeting, was better than no such contact at all. One by one, lots of new brooms sweeping clean, we volunteers came, we labored, we left.

To her superiors downstairs, Margaret may have seemed like a tumor in situ, out of the way and spreading unobtrusively. To her subordinates upstairs, she behaved like a tempest, wildly in the way and intrusively distracting. She preferred females because "they stand up better under pressure." By word and by deed, she was her father's daughter and she ruled in the manner of a benign despot. What she perceived as ineptitude or stupidity frequently frustrated her to the point of fury. She never physically abused anybody, but the combustion level of her verbal invective could have set the place afire without a match.

Random family members and volunteers perform more efficiently when at least one paid office person manages the minutiae. Margaret vacillated between hiring real secretaries who were trained to delegate and do office work and anthropology majors who weren't. Even though they never stayed long, she favored the latter because they were more interesting. She found the former more capable but anthropologically illiterate. Occasionally, she lucked into a secretary who was taking courses at General Studies with the hope of becoming an anthropologist.

Two ironclad rules coordinated the efforts of her succession of employees and volunteers through the years: (1) date every piece of paper coming into the office and (2) keep a copy of every piece of paper going out.

So far, so good as rules go. But as far as rules go, these went. No two paper handlers, hired or volunteer, agreed on precisely where dated and copied material should be put. Nor was there much formalized meeting of minds on these matters between predecessors and successors. As time passed, everyone knew less and less about where to look for more and more.

A generation before Margaret, her father asked an out-of-town student turned into town secretary to go on an errand for him. Since she was a stranger to most parts of Philadelphia, she asked for directions. "Details are thine," he scowled, leaving her to bumble through the errand in twice the time with half the satisfaction.

Details were "thine" for those who worked in his daughter's office too. Margaret tended to behave as though she expected us to know whatever we needed to know by osmosis or divine revelation. She alone knew the full range of projects, governmental or otherwise, in which she or Ruth Benedict, a predecessor whose papers and projects Margaret inherited, involved themselves. She alone possessed the continuity necessary to answer a neophyte's questions about them and she was much too busy to be bothered. We picked up information in seconds and on the spot.

I walked into the office one morning and caught two volunteers and a secretary prancing like reluctant Bombay fire walkers. Higher and faster they hopped, first here, then there, as Margaret slashed the air with a mittful of papers and raged about some photographs for her forthcoming book, *New Lives for Old.* "They were supposed to have gone over to the William Morrow publishing house yesterday. I saw them on my desk the last thing last night," she yelled. "Where are they? Who moved them?"

I put down my books. The din was too distracting to tackle the task that prompted me to stop by. When she looked for anything, she pulled almost everyone within earshot into her act. Those working on the floor below stayed out of sight and thought, "Those poor girls up there."

"How many pictures are there, Margaret?" I attempted to orient myself. "What size are they? Are they in a bundle or are they loose?" Her nostrils flared like a storybook dragon's. Her eyes emitted sparks. She caught the tip of her tongue between her teeth. I got the unmistakable impression that details, alas, were mine. A frantic search unearthed an item we had sought weeks before, but not, not, not the photographs she demanded now.

I marched into the main office and confronted her. "Unless they've been deliberately hidden, which I doubt, I've looked everywhere they could possibly be and they're not there. If you had them on top of your desk when you left last night, as you say, then they've got to be nearby. Let me leaf through the sheaf of papers you're holding, please." She handed it over. Sure enough. There they were, at the bottom of the batch she'd brandished for half an hour. Her temper blew by like a spring tornado.

"I've got to spew adrenalin out of every orifice, or nothing ever happens around here, Pat," she justified her ire. She recovered what she sought, but I departed that morning filled with an uneasy restlessness. During my undergraduate years, I never left her office when she was present without the conviction that all of us lost much too much time looking for things and that setting up an organized system for her total operation would merit whatever effort it might take.

We learn about ourselves in living. This job reinforced my conviction that a stitch in time does indeed save nine. And I'll put myself out to put in those initial stitches.

"Where's the box with the interviews that Ruth Benedict collected from people who grew up in China?" she stopped two or three of us in our tracks at closing time one afternoon.

Our mouths dropped open. We looked at each other wordlessly. The same thoughts sped through our heads. "Ruth Benedict died five years ago. Only God and Ruth Benedict know where those interviews are now and neither of them is likely to give us a hint."

The threat of missing out on an unhurried meal between work and evening classes spurred us on to superhuman ferreting. We found the interviews in an unlabeled cardboard box out of reach above her head on the top shelf of a bookcase on the wall behind her desk. Pixies must have put them there.

In another commotion, she discovered that who knows which one of possibly scores of volunteers in an effort, no doubt, to condense space, had planted a padlocked silver-painted wooden footlocker atop a silver-painted radiator next to the secretary's desk. In most offices, the secretary sits up front and the bigwig sits out of sight somewhere. Not so here. Strangers walked directly into the more pretentious office in which a definitely more pretentious officer faced them head on. The desk of the always temporary secretary stood out of sight behind the wall at Margaret's back. Because of this arrangement, she rarely invaded the secretary's space. So it was anybody's guess how long the aforementioned mysterious receptacle had roasted on the radiator.

It was my misfortune to be at her elbow when she spied the box. I took the heat of her initial blast—hot, loud, and splenetic. "If it were a baby, you'd not stick it on a radiator! How stupid can you get? What *do* you people do with what's on the top of your necks anyway?"

"Wait a minute, Margaret!" I jumped into her shout fest. "You can call me lots of things and not get a rise out of me, but I absolutely refuse to let anyone call me stupid."

"Pat Grinager, you couldn't even plan a field trip."

"Plan a field trip? That's kindergarten stuff compared to keeping house for six people, substitute teaching, taking courses at Columbia, and volunteering here."

A look of admiration glazed her eyes. She liked it when you answered back.

"Besides, you're changing the subject." Her look emboldened me. "What's in the box to get you so fired up anyway?"

"Hand-painted glass slides from the days of celluloid film; heat can destroy them," she sputtered.

"Then why isn't the container labeled with instructions to that effect? There's no way in hell any of the rest of us could guess what's inside a locked box. We weren't born with X ray eyes, you know."

Hers were not the only overwrought adrenal glands. She passed the malady along. Were it not for the fact that she absented herself almost as much as she showed up, her staff might have changed hands more often than it did.

Three or four of us exhausted ourselves one morning preparing her for a 1:30 p.m. send-off to Whereverland. With suit and briefcases bulging, she allowed us to shove her into a taxi shortly before noon. Coast clear, we sallied forth to a nearby deli. We tripled our lunch hour that day, illegally indulging in extended laughter and dark ale, the sparklier the better. It was such a relief to be rid of her. Work could wait.

The telephone's impertinent clang pierced our ears on our return. Nobody hastened to silence it. Whoever it was could call back tomorrow. Or the day after. It didn't make any difference. Chiefly for the peace and quiet we craved, one of us finally took the receiver off its hook. She held it out at arm's length. We heard Margaret steaming like a pressure cooker. She'd forgotten something. Thought of it in the taxi. Burned up the telephone lines at LaGuardia airport trying to reach us.

She was phoning from a refueling stopover in an airport halfway across the United States.

"Why did I have to hang on for twenty-three rings before one of you answered? Where in the world have you been for three and a half hours?" she seethed. She caught her breath and erupted in a new rule. "At least one person should remain in the office every minute between nine and five no matter what." We glanced at each other in carefree camaraderie, amused by the vision that her anger could have recharged the batteries of the plane that readied itself for takeoff.

The less I was able to accomplish in the flurry of Margaret's presence, the more the notion grew on me to labor in her absence. During the six months preceding my graduation, since volunteers can choose their hours of service, I limited my Museum forays to weekends. The four sons usually came along. We boarded an early morning Long Island train for New York City and flipped a seat back so that the five of us might face each other. At Penn Station, we caught a subway that stopped at the Museum's lower level entrance.

Once inside, the youngsters fanned out or banded together to ogle exhibits. They marveled at a sky full of stars in the planetarium. They made friends with the two watchmen, Mr. Nulty and Mr. Carrol, who gave them private tours of the storerooms. The men gave the boys a chance to admire the taxidermied dogs that pulled Admiral Peary to the North Pole; to sniff fish-skin boots from Siberia; to heft flintlock guns from the Old West or poisoned darts with which tiny people on the Malay Peninsula hunted down their dinners. They also introduced them to the last five-cent coke machine in New York City. The children plied it with nickels. They helped me help Margaret.

We took over her tower. Because so few knew the proper sequence for the six-step ritual necessary to gain entry, no one interrupted us on Saturdays or Sundays. The boys vied with each other to perform the sacred opening rites. Concealed in a fuse box above eye level and to the left of the main door hung a small key that unlocked a glass cabinet containing loosely stacked Indian paintings by George Caitlin. Inside that case, to the left on the floor, and in the dark, sat a four-by-three-inch topless box that hid yet another key that fit the lock to her door. At the end of a work session, one of us reversed the ritual and returned each key to its separate hiding place for the next entrant.

Margaret frequently unlocked the door on Monday morning. Although she rarely saw me at the Museum during my final undergraduate semester, changes in the general appearance of her work space revealed our having been there.

A few weeks after these forays began, the School of General Studies inadvertently provided her with a chance to express her appreciation. She received an interoffice memorandum requesting members of the faculty to endorse one student from a list of top-ranking June graduates for a special prize of $100. Margaret circled my name and typed a recommendation to the nominating committee that read,

> Patricia Grinager has unusual ability, energy, imagination, and drive. She is mature, yet flexible; enthusiastic, yet practical; ambitious, yet balanced. She has maintained honor grades against very great odds of a heavy load of domestic, teaching, and volunteer responsibilities. I take pleasure in recommending her for this award.

In reality, this recommendation describes Margaret Mead. No matter who we are, we do indeed consciously or unconsciously outline images of ourselves whenever we attempt to describe another.

General Studies awarded somebody else the $100. On Margaret's recommendation, the school gave me a job. "How would you like to be my graduate assistant?" she asked after class one evening.

"Wonderful. Thanks, Margaret, that's better than an award," I exclaimed.

"One of the side benefits of my appointment as adjunct professor includes a graduate student assistant," she said. "You'd owe me fifteen hours, minimum, of miscellaneous service per week and for that, General Studies would grant you full tuition plus pay you $125 per month."

"Could the appointment begin as soon as July?"

"The appointment would begin the day you graduate. Why?"

"The summer school bulletin's out. It's full of super courses. Everything I've taken so far has been required, so this summer I'm going to choose something I want for a change."

"You'll like that."

"A prof named Herbert Elftman is going to teach human anatomy at the College of Physicians and Surgeons. He'll pack a semester's work of information into six weeks. I can't get the notion of registering for his course out of my mind."

"Why take Elftman's course? It's geared for future physicians and surgeons, you know."

"Yes, I know, but medical school–level knowledge of human anatomy would come in handy in the field. I remember you said you spend half of every morning just fixing people and that it's a perfect way to establish rapport with them."

"That's right." Her eyes glistened. "My mother and I took a first aid course in Doylestown, Pennsylvania, in 1919. A Dr. Felix Murphy taught it. We used the Red Cross first aid book for a text and I've applied every page of it ever since."

"Do you think six weeks would be too concentrated a dose?" I feared she might say yes.

"Not if you don't," she tilted her chin upward. "If you think you can do it, do it."

"I wanted to register for it last night," I confessed, "but the price deterred me. It costs double what other courses do."

"Don't worry about the money. Your assistantship covers the tuition no matter what it costs." She leaned forward in her chair. "Except for one week late in August, when I'll fly back to the States for a few days, I plan to shut the office down until mid-September. I'm going to visit my daughter, Cathy, in Israel and attend several conferences in Europe and Saudi Arabia. For thirteen weeks, you'll have nothing more to do than the mail."

"That shouldn't take any fifteen hours."

"Use the extra time to study. It'll be quiet here."

I signed up for human anatomy.

The afternoon we turned in the final grades for that spring semester, she briefed me on my summertime duties. "Send all bills, checks, and receipts to Marie Eichelberger," she commanded. "Type out a list of what you enclose each time you send her anything and keep a carbon. I find it extremely aggravating not to have an exact record of money that comes in or goes out.

"If anybody writes for a recommendation on a former student, find the folder of recommendations and see whether I've ever written one for that person. If so, answer the request by saying that I'm away and that you've found a letter of such and such a date recommending so and so and then copy my letter.

"If anybody wants to know my whereabouts, you have no idea how to reach me. Be ignorant but be helpful initially. Just stall. Pretend that you don't know anything on God's green earth. Say that the office is closed and that everyone who knows anything is away." I smiled in spite of myself as she watched me transcribe her instructions.

"Under no circumstances give my address to a living soul," she ordered. "No matter what it is, don't forward any mail. Open every piece that comes in and read it. Call Rhoda Metraux on anything that looks like it needs urgent attention. Compile a weekly résumé of everything else you think I should know about and send it to me directly."

I looked up from my notes and tucked the eraser end of the pencil under my front teeth. "How would you like it if I were to condense each letter that I report on to you in a numbered paragraph headed by the name and full address of the writer? That would give you enough information to answer the person from wherever you are, or you could cable me and refer to a paragraph of this or that date by its number."

"Okay."

Neither of us took much time for idle talk. And besides, I fumbled over how to broach an idea that had been incubating since she told me her travel plans. I wanted to use the spare time available to clean out her office and set up a filing system. I saw the summer as a rare opportunity to create a place for everything with everything in its place. A permanent reminder that I too once toiled in her tower.

Nobody has ever documented what a housewife–multiple mother can do with bits of time if you leave her alone and stay out of her way. Circus performers who juggle hoops on their shoulders, elbows, hands, knees, feet, ears, and eyebrows have nothing on her. With neither fanfare nor publicity posters, she keeps that many hoops going around her all the time. And whoever benefits from her amazing dexterity takes her performances for granted until she dies or leaves.

My mother was no such housekeeper. She conducted a household as Margaret ran her office: from crisis to crisis. Pilley's grocery store stood a block away from our house. I can't remember a meal without various of the five children running relays back and forth between our kitchen table and Pilley's store. So far as food was concerned, mother never knew exactly what she wanted until she reached for it and it wasn't there. The same was true of Margaret and the instant service she demanded for papers that weren't at her fingertips when she grabbed for them.

Perhaps growing up in my mother's household addicted me to organizing spaces. I told Margaret about my daydream. She yanked me awake with an impatient snort. "You're being totally unrealistic. Setting up a filing system will only waste time. It'll never work."

I stood my ground. "I don't believe it won't work. Too often we have to stop whatever we're doing to hunt for something. That's what wastes the time, if you ask me. We need systematized places-to-put. When we have them, old-timers and newcomers alike will be more likely to put papers in their places."

Even though I promised to use devices no more expensive than one, two, three, primary colors, room assignments, and the ABCs, she doggedly resisted the changes that loomed ahead. "No matter how simple your system, nobody'll ever put anything back. Filing involves far more secretarial help than I can possibly afford. I keep information for long-term things in my own head and in my secretary's head for short-term things. We're getting along all right as we are.

"The office does suffer sometimes from the private lives of a series of secretaries, plus the fact that my life is rather different from most people's, and is going to continue to be." She battered at a few more keys on her typewriter. "Frankly, I don't like the idea at all. If you do, then that's the housewife in you!"

"Housewife be dammed," I defended my stance. "Cleaning out the files we do have and setting up some new ones makes sense. Whether you like it or not, I'm going to do it. We can't find out if it works until we give it a try. The alternative certainly doesn't work."

She shrugged her shoulders as she rolled the last page of an article out of her typewriter. "Is it more important to run an efficient office or one in which human values are taken into account?" The remark sounded exactly like her mother and the look in her eyes indicated that she doubted I caught the deeper meaning in her question even as she asked it. "Think it over."

"I've been thinking it over for three years now." I halfheartedly plunked at a thumb harp from a collection of primitive musical instruments being readied for display.

"Let the stuff pile up." For all my sales pitch, she hadn't altered a note of her solo. "We'll have a new secretary in the fall. Let her tackle the stuff when she comes. That way she'll get the hang of things."

We did not know yet whether or not a real, live graduate of the Katharine Gibbs Secretarial School on Park Avenue, who was taking anthropology courses with me, would accept Margaret's offer of a position. "The more organized things are around here, the less snowed under the new secretary will be as she does try to get the hang of things," I persisted.

Neither one of us gave the other an inch.

Margaret slipped one last paper into her briefcase and one more stopper into my summer. "Take the six weeks between the end of summer school and the fall semester off. Don't try to do too much. Go easy."

She left by taxi for her apartment in Greenwich Village where Rhoda was probably already folding her travel wardrobe in tissue paper so as to keep suitcase wrinkling to a minimum.

Margaret well knew that I couldn't relax while work waited. If anything, she probably envisioned my stewardship as that of a new broom metamorphosed into a vacuum cleaner with attachments. I brought the boys, all of school age at last, in with me. Already familiar with her place, they pitched in like stevedores. They got the big lifting and moving jobs out of the way and left the finer filing for the afternoons I labored alone. They grouped boxes together, Margaret's as well as those inherited from Ruth Benedict, and labeled them with black crayon on five sides by research project or teaching endeavor. They arranged books of her authorship by year of publication inside a glass enclosed bookcase across from her desk. They lined the other books in the place alphabetically by author's last name.

We delegated the writings plus various odds and ends associated with each of her marriages to three large drawers in the main office. She cancelled appointments when any of her former husbands visited New York City, so it seemed wise to keep their memorabilia within easy reach. We found very little to put in the drawer of her first mate from Pennsylvania. Not much more for the zesty second from New Zealand. The drawer assigned to the lanky Englishman who fathered her only child overflowed with so many reprints that I wrote her for permission to discard the excess.

"No," she denied me the pleasure, "we can't throw any of them away. I have to keep all Gregory's reprints for him. They'd get lost otherwise. He can't keep track of anything."

I puzzled over which drawer two handguns should be stored in. As I saw it, her three husbands represented three facets of her personality, three stages of her life in which one or the other side of her was dominant. Since the literary outpourings in Gregory Bateson's drawer, symbolically enough, almost kept it from closing, the decision lay between the drawers of peaceful preacher Luther Cressman or hot-tempered ethnologist Reo Franklin Fortune. I told her about my quandary later and cannot recall whether she said assigning the guns to her middle man was right or wrong.

If Margaret felt that she was going down in history, far be it from her to shortchange posterity for lack of data. She was a pack rat for personal papers. It wouldn't have surprised me to come across a childhood fan letter to someone who wrote stories for *St. Nicholas* magazine in 1912. "Save everything," she used to say, "so that we have it to study when we know more than we do now."

Although the volume of her papers tired me, she grew in my consciousness as a very human, human being. In order to decide where to file each piece, I hesitated long enough to skim over most of her letters from the field; to read a few from salutation to signature. For all her accelerating fame, deep inside, she was still the young woman one of her native informants referred to as "Missy Makarit." The sobriquet charmed me. I used it thereafter as a term of endearment in speaking of or to her.

Put in the same circumstances, any of us could have written the letters she sent home from the Sepik River in New Guinea not too long after she and Gregory Bateson married in Singapore (she, for the third time; he, for the first of three times) and honeymooned/worked in Bali. She told her family about their nightly fights with cannibal mosquitoes, typing up field notes, developing film, and trying to start a family. Time came to think about going home and she schemed to get across the United States as cheaply as possible. She wrote to her mother about the chances of staying with relatives in strategically spaced cities between the West and East Coasts. How about the Lockwood kin in California? Had they heard about her third marriage? What did they say? Might the newly-weds risk staying overnight with them? How did the relatives in Chicago feel about her latest merger? How welcome might they be with the Kirkpatrick cousins in Columbus? Margaret told me later that these were the years when she and Gregory rarely netted more than $2,500 between them.

Like many another doting parent, she hoarded smudgy pencil compositions by her daughter, Cathy. One described a dream with maximum movement and brilliant color. Another, the trip she and her mother made to Philadelphia in January 1950 when Margaret's mother died. The ten-year-old had just enough of an under-the-chin view to remark about how tightly her mother held her jaw at Emily Fogg Mead's memorial service. Margaret also saved an account Cathy wrote of a picnic with her parents in a large park near a wooded area. The radio in the next campsite blared forth play-by-play events in a baseball game as Margaret Mead and Gregory Bateson together broke the news to their daughter that they planned a divorce; that people do get divorced; that the world continues to turn anyway; and that it was not the child's fault.

I kept myself from spending too many more minutes on any one item. There were too many of them. The boys uncovered cache after cache of papers probably whisked out of sight by inundated volunteers swamped by the flood of them. What a mess! One box, for example, contained a month's worth of four-year-old unopened mail. The note taped to the foldover flap read, "For MM to read sometime." Who knows? That note could have represented the moment a predecessor gave up and walked off.

Part of my maintaining my own dedication to a self-imposed assignment depended on more filing containers. We ran out of storage space before Margaret left Saudi Arabia, the first country on her itinerary. I sent an SOS off in time for her arrival in Tel Aviv:

> We need more file drawers. Existing files are stuffed so full it takes a crowbar and a prayer to pull one out. Miles made a telephone canvass of office supply houses the other day. Something called transfiles are the cheapest files available. They're cardboard but they're the same size as regular metal file drawers.

They can be stacked four high. When purchased in quantities of six or more, they cost less than $4 apiece. Would you skin me alive (verbally, that is) were I to order a dozen? If you object to putting out the $40, I'm going to go ahead and buy them anyway. Give them to you for an early Christmas present. We need them that much. Forget that I've got four bottomless pits to feed. I'm ready to dip into my own meager funds to get this job done right, once and for all.

She responded from the Hotel Atlanta in Brussels on Accadia Grant Hotel, Tel Aviv, stationery. "Certainly order the transfiles. But remember my question, 'Is it more efficient to buy files or to help students who need money?'"

Her reply tickled me. Obviously, she didn't make the connection that none other than a needy student offered to take grocery money out of her own family's budget to pay for those transfiles. When they arrived and provided the retrievable places to put for which I so hungered, I didn't spend five seconds worrying about distributing loaves and fishes to mythical starving students.

Attention to endless human factors does make for endlessly interesting variety all right, I thought as I fingered through papers with one hand and held a sandwich in the other, but how the consequent interruptions jam the intricate piece of machinery that a smoother-running office could be. Whether I welcomed interruptions or not, they slowed down my progress in her office daily. For the first two weeks, the telephone rang constantly. The ten to fifteen pounds of mail that arrived each day brought messages of varying legibility from people just like her all over the world. The living greats of anthropology, many of whose books I'd read for class assignments, scientists in a dozen disciplines, acquaintances, editors, organizers of conferences, relatives, former students, friends, or friends of friends, all writing to ask for or give her favors, jobs, or information. They wished her well. They thanked her. They loved her.

As she had requested, I compiled weekly summaries of important letters and airmailed them off. I didn't take the time to tell her about fan mail from admirers who enjoyed her speeches or her books. She could skim through them later.

Reprints of published articles sent to her by colleagues or students weighted down her mail the most. For decades, what undoubtedly began as a trickle of reprints welled into a river, but she had slightly more than a score of years, brimming over with ever more of them, ahead of her. The flood of reprints left me feeling as futile as Sisyphus. The more I put away, the more came. It was like plowing the sea.

I wrote her at the Hotel Post in Ghent:

I have begun to pile all the reprints you receive in one spot. When you see the quantity of them, and multiply that by four to get the annual accumulation, then multiply that by how many years of mail has brought and will continue to bring you like amounts or more, you will have to face the possibility that they may some day have to be indexed.

That is, if you really want to hold onto each precious one of them. Then, when someone like Rhoda calls someone like me, as she did the other day, for the "Arden papers" or "themes in French culture," someone like me doesn't have to get apoplexy wondering where to hunt.

I would be long gone before that day came and, in the meantime, I inadvertently joined the series of assistants and secretaries who shared some troubling aspects of their personal lives with her. She knew that my husband and I, estranged since Christmas, had reconciled a few weeks before graduation. "He says he'll quit drinking," I confided to her before she departed.

"They never do," she shot back with such finality I wondered who were the people in her own history who'd left her with that firm a conviction.

"This case might be the exception," I assured myself, even though in my heart of hearts I knew that only the details differ from case to case. The overall patterns of alcoholism's effect on families are remarkably similar.

Midsummer, my husband accepted a position in Chicago. Would this move to Illinois be a glorious opportunity to start all over again from scratch? A new life with new neighbors, new friends, new networks for each of the six of us? Or would it be the same old life in a different place with no friends and no support networks? And what about the graduate assistantship with Margaret Mead that I'd worked so long to merit? Should I dump the certainty of that to take an uncertain chance on a rerun romance?

At the end of a weekly report on her mail I mentioned the dilemma facing me. "PLEASE FEEL FREE MOVE CHICAGO IMMEDIATELY," she cabled from the Hotel Gherhus in Berlin.

A few days later, the mail brought further word:

When I got your letter about the possible move to Chicago, I decided it would be best to cable you so you would feel free to make plans. I couldn't tell from your letter whether your comment about moving, when your commitment to me was over, was a statement about the whole year at Columbia or whether you felt bound to fill out the year simply because of the appointment for me. There is no need for the latter, if you find it advisable to go, but I should prefer that you try to set a move up in terms of the university semester.

Thanks very much for all you've done.

Yours, MM

Columbia University semesters began in October, February, and June. I chose June and wrote her to that effect:

I appreciate your generous releasing me from my commitment but, really, I have waited a long time for the opportunity I have now and I just don't want to let go of it. With husband off in Chicago I might even be able to complete the requirements for the master's degree. The ten months will fly by. Next June will also be better for the oldest boy who will be ready to enter high school then.

I have a train to meet. Stay busy as always but don't forget to stop to sniff some flowers now and then.

Best, Pat

At the same time that I chose to stay with Margaret at the Museum and at Columbia, my classmate Nora Holland resigned as secretary for an indulgent boss in the suburbs to assume a position with a demanding one in the city. Nora traveled to Manhattan a bit before Margaret's first return in August in order to register at the personnel office, pick up a Museum pass, and have a cook's tour of the tower.

In my last communiqué before Margaret flew back briefly between conferences, I told her about our lunchtime conversation in the Museum cafeteria and added:

Assistants and secretaries come and go. Nora and I are both in our thirties. We're older than most of the students who work for you in return for tuition at General Studies.

There's still a lot to catch up on in your office. Everything takes so much more time in the doing than the planning. And time can only be collected hour by hour. For our next year together, we ask of you the same kind of patience that shines out in your field photographs when you are dealing with natives in the South Seas. You have it. You've just gotten out of the habit of using much if any of it on us primitives here in the USA.

One of the handwritten letters piled on her desk came from her father, the very relative through whom she inherited her Ramsay temper. With his wife dead and his children grown and gone, he lived alone in the City of Brotherly Love. He had moved from a bungalow on McAlpine Street to a room in the Harris Hotel at 114 S. 40th. As far as I could decipher, he was comfortable, thankful, and well.

During his final, fitful hours he may have been aware that Margaret was winging her way across the ocean for a week of professional commitments before returning to Europe for another month. Dr. Edward Sherwood Mead died at 10:04 a.m. on August 21, 1956, the morning she landed. His funeral at 12:00 p.m. three days later, on what would have been his wife's eighty-fifth birthday, cut into his oldest daughter's already too tightly scheduled interval in this country. Could it have been ordained that Margaret Mead be on her father's side of the Atlantic precisely then?

"My father defined for me my place in the world," Missy Makarit was to write about him one day. And now his death redefined her place in an extended family. It jockeyed her into the position of next in line for ancestorhood. Family matriarch. She who keeps track of everybody. The strong one to go to for help in time of need. Margaret's father's death also bequeathed two human moles another month of time to burrow undisturbed through the backlog in her attic.

NOTES

1. The family name was Meade until Margaret's father, Edward, amended it to Mead at about the time of Margaret's birth. For clarity, "Mead" will be used throughout for Margaret's immediate family and "Meade" for her antecedents.

3

MARGARET MEAD, TEACHER

"We're have-ing break-fast in the moh-hor-ning," I sang to myself as I gathered together the materials that Margaret asked me to bring the first morning after her return from Europe and the Middle East.

Margaret Mead herself has invited me to break bread with her, alone, in the privacy of her apartment! Such invitations don't come every day. What a gracious way to acknowledge the transformations she saw in the office when she stopped by en route home from the airport, I thought as I preened myself for what I assumed to be her delight with my housecleaning. Short of our inevitable funeral orations, which we never hear anyway, how many mere mortals ever experience the inner glow of hearing our efforts appreciated?

At dawn, I shared seats with commuters on the train to the city and in the subway to Greenwich Village. Most of them already looked pooped. I, on the other hand, radiated jubilance. I smiled to myself so much that another anthropologist might have suspected me of sniffing laughing gas in the commotion at each stop. Why not? This was to be my first encounter with Margaret since she left for Saudi Arabia in June. After scanning so many of her old letters, I thought I knew her well enough to interpret her invitation as her way of conveying undying gratitude for my summertime labors of love.

"Actions speak louder than words," I would declare demurely were her praises to become embarrassingly rapturous. "The cleaning was just my way of saying thanks for your having given me a chance to work with you in the first place."

I knocked on the door at 193 Waverly Place. Tulia, the soft-spoken Haitian maid, opened it immediately. She showed me to the dining room, where a table was set with toast, orange juice, and coffee. She pulled a chair out for me that was directly across from Margaret. I was fifteen minutes late.

My hostess's eyebrows telegraphed displeasure. She must have gotten out of the wrong side of the bed again, I thought as I nervously made innocuous remarks about how well she looked after such a long trip. Tulia disappeared and returned with the plates of scrambled eggs and bacon that she had kept warm.

"Harrumph," growled Margaret when Tulia had left us alone. "Think back. I never told you to do that filing, remember?"

"But I did it all for you, Margaret." A lame excuse to be sure, but it was the only one available on short notice.

"Pat, don't blame anything on me. You were entirely on your own. All I asked you to do was sort out the mail," she yapped.

"Who only does what she's asked to do?" I countered. "The filing needed doing and I've done most of it. Didn't you *feel* the difference when you stopped by yesterday? I think the office even *smells* cleaner."

"It smelled and looked the same to me." She tore a piece of toast in two. "Nora's a natural. She'll do the work of three in running the office no matter what condition it's in. You're lucky. That leaves you free to move to Chicago as soon as you can get packed."

My insides marshaled ancient defenses for flight or fight. My heart beat faster. Digestion stopped. The palms of my hands turned clammy. My backbone chilled as the tiny hairs along it rose to attention. I chose to stand ground and fight. "But . . ."

"But, nothing!" she crumpled a paper napkin in a white-knuckled fist. "My mind's made up. If my father had not died, I'd have told you this a month ago, but there's absolutely nothing to stop you from moving to Chicago now."

"But, Margaret, there's everything to stop me from moving to Chicago now. My mind's made up too," I swallowed some coffee to moisten a mouth gone dry and continued in tones stern enough to scare off a rapist. "Columbia University has appointed me your official graduate assistant and I'm going to stay that way, come hell or high water." Our angry eyes met. Hers had as much compassion in them as a pair of glass marbles; mine, probably less. "I'm flabbergasted," I heard myself say. "I can't believe you're trying to get rid of me after all I've done for you this summer."

"I don't know what you've done for me all summer," she boomeranged back. "I didn't see you do what you say you've done, nor did I want you to do it in the first place." She pounded on the table to emphasize her point. One thing about working for a surprise artist like Margaret Mead—she's never dull. The words streaked through my mind. The minute I think I've got her pegged, she pulls the pegs.

"If you think what I did is nothing, Dr. Mead," I defied her aloud, "then it's darn funny it's taken every free minute from school and family since you left. It's not done yet and, for all I care, it won't be. Good-bye, Museum. Hello, Columbia. I'm going to earn that master's degree while I have the free tuition."

"Pat, how many times do I have to tell you that you don't need the master's?" She jabbed at her eggs with her fork. "It'll only waste time."

"My case is different," I argued as the eggs and bacon on my plate grew colder. "How many women candidates have four little kids? The master's degree will be a more marketable packet for me to present to hard-boiled school board members somewhere than a soft-boiled claim that I'm working on a doctorate. You know yourself that over half of those who say they're going for a doctorate never get there. And most of those who don't make it are women. Women let themselves get talked out of their goals. You didn't let that happen to you and I'm not going to let it happen to me either."

"I never wasted any time on a master's. Neither did my father, nor my brother, and each of us got a Ph.D."

"But Margaret, the surest way for anyone in my situation to earn all three degrees is by degrees," I persisted. "A master's makes a nice flat stepping-stone to stand on while I reach out for a doctorate."

"You're not listening to me, Pat. Go to Chicago now and get a head start under someone like Sol Tax or Bob Redfield. As I said before, Nora's eminently qualified to finish up whatever you leave undone at the Museum. And there are lots of needy students who'd like to take your place as my assistant at Columbia."

"You're not listening to me, either." We bucked each other like a pair of mountain goats with locked horns. "I worked as a volunteer for three years in order to be eligible for graduate study assistance and I'm not going to let it go."

I stirred the food on my plate around without eating any. Our deadlock inspired me to try another tactic. "Something else is bothering you, Margaret. Tell me what it is because I'm simply too upset to guess."

"All right, I'll tell you then. I don't want anybody working for me who thinks I'm cheap."

"Who says you're cheap?"

"You! I wanted to fire you when I got the first letter you sent to me in Tel Aviv. That letter made me very angry and I was half the world away."

"I don't understand. I remember asking for permission to buy some files in that letter. How does our needing files say you're cheap?"

"You said I was too cheap to buy them."

"That wasn't what I meant to say. Honest. Papers were piled to the window sills when you left. You know that. There was no retrievable place to move anything unless and until we got more containers. Cardboard ones offered the cheapest solution. They were cheap, for gosh sakes, not you. Accusing you of being cheap never entered my alleged head."

"That's not the way the message came through to me, Pat."

"If I hurt your feelings, I'm sorry. Please accept my apology."

My voice softened and so did her eyes. My pulse slowed down slightly even though I didn't know if I still had a job or not. "You surprise me," I avoided putting the fear into words. "I thought you were much too tough to get your feelings hurt."

"Nobody is," she bit into her last piece of bacon. She could have had mine too if she wanted it, but I didn't dare say so, given the circumstances. "Being called cheap is one thing I cannot tolerate. I'm not a penny pincher. My mother was and it never got her anywhere."

"I think most mothers pinch pennies, especially those who try to do something else, like go to college. And I remember yours did. Mothers wouldn't be able to do half the things they do if they didn't pinch pennies. In fact," I winked at her, "pinching pennies is probably most mothers' most favorite sport."

She smiled in spite of herself and her smile heartened me more than anything which had passed between us since my arrival. I reached for the coffee pot to warm up whatever remained in her cup and in mine. As I did so, I thought, If we ever need anything after this, no matter what it may be, I'll buy it and give it to her as an unbirthday present.

I put down the newly emptied pot. "Well, back to business. Veronica Sharpe, who's still girl Friday for the School of General Studies, tells me that we have until this afternoon to get the revised bibliographies over to her if we want them printed up for next week. If you can make your corrections on the bibs for last semester and bring them back to the Museum later this morning, I'll deliver them to her myself. I'm going to be up at Columbia all afternoon again anyway, to interview students who need permission to register."

I pulled the bibs out of the satchel at my heel and handed them over to her. "Okay," she answered as she drew a soft-lead pencil from her pocket. As I watched her add and subtract entries on the paper, I sighed with relief. "I'm darn glad you and I are tough enough to bang our differences together and stay friends," I said.

"I still wouldn't mind if you packed up and went to Chicago," she answered without looking up. "You have to go sometime. If you went now, you'd be a whole year ahead next September. I'm doing you a favor by letting you go. You're crazy to refuse it."

"That's only one opinion," I put my elbows on the table. "Moving now could stop me from ever getting any more degrees. My husband, Ray, left for Chicago six weeks ago. Selling one house and finding another will take months. For the first time in history all the kids are in school all day. And the simple truth is that I don't want to budge until I finish here."

I hesitated a moment, interlaced my fingers, and added, "I'm not even going to ask you to be my thesis adviser, so you'll save time there too."

"What?" she stopped writing and tapped her pencil on the edge of her coffee cup.

"I'm not so sure the move to Chicago will pan out. If it doesn't, I'll need a thesis practical enough to help me land a job. The idea of teaching young people international understanding through a study of known culture change in an early American society like the Moche' Valley of Peru appeals to me very much."

"Oh?" She scrutinized my expression as I spoke.

"I sat next to William Duncan Strong on the subway once this summer and asked him if he would serve as major adviser on such a project. Peruvian archeology is one of his specialties, you know. He agreed and he suggested that Sol Kimball, the anthropologist over at Teachers' College, might be willing to guide me on educational theory. I ran into Kimball in the cafeteria at TC yesterday and he said he'll do it. So my master's project is on the way."

"I thought you'd do a thesis on some aspect of the anthropology of early childhood. Something more related to your home situation, the third graders you're teaching out on the Island, and what you've been reading for my courses."

I felt like a three-year-old with wet pants. I shifted to the edge of the chair and agonized over how to say what I had to say in such a way so as not to antagonize her. "I'm more creative alone than together. I work better on a project like a thesis when I do it by myself. Strong and Kimball will give me free rein. The idea of going back full circle to write on Peru appeals to me too. Peruvian archeology has been my only brush with fieldwork so far. Archeology is, after all, just ethnology brought down to prehistoric brass tacks."

She shrugged her shoulders. "You'll do it your way no matter what I say, Pat." She glanced at her watch as she removed the staples from the shorter bib with a tine of her fork.

I said good-bye and got out of sight, 100 percent more deflated than my bloated boasts betrayed. Once you've worked for Margaret Mead, Sis, you can work for anybody. I patched a punctured ego as I talked to myself and kicked leaves away with each step between her apartment and the subway station on 14th Street.

So she pooh-poohed the slave labor I put into sorting out a lifetime's worth of her papers? Only a lunatic would have tackled the task to begin with. Maybe she doesn't want to feel that much obliged to anybody. Maybe she actually prefers to hunt and howl for missing pieces of paper every hour on the hour. Who am I to change somebody else's habits? Why can't anthropologists learn to keep their long noses out of other people's patterns?

Sharply contrasted in mood from the naïve Pollyanna who got off the downtown subway earlier, an older and wiser Pat Grinager immersed herself in an inner monologue amid a bustle of morning shoppers on an uptown train. Two headstrong women had just survived their roughest confrontation so far. Not many people can fight and stay friends. I was a graduate now in more ways than one. From this subway trip forward, I would blow the dust of a Museum volunteer off my hands and don robes more appropriate to academe. As her departmental assistant, I would concentrate on the classes she conducted at Columbia University. This new assignment would involve more people than papers. And that would certainly turn out to be another major project with another set of hell-zapoppin' pressures.

I was drained. Except for coffee, I hadn't the stomach to consume anything at Margaret's invitational breakfast. I stopped off at the employee's cafeteria in the Museum to dawdle over soup and a salad until it was time to pick up the revised bibliographies. I delivered them to the General Studies office on the way to Schermerhorn Hall. There, in a dimly lit room slightly below street level that Margaret shared with a handful of other professorial part-timers, a line of students awaited my arrival.

Any concentration of course-taking adults in a metropolis the size of New York City is bound to sweep in a preponderance of ambitious, ordinary people, as well as a smattering of both geniuses and jerks. Most professors have little or no say about who attends their classes. Margaret controlled the population of her courses by requiring that would-be students submit to an interview by her graduate assistant before being granted permission to register.

I conducted these interviews in her chair at her desk at Schermerhorn Hall in a corner by a window that looked up on the legs of an endless procession of passersby. So many of the candidates seemed to be so well prepared and so highly motivated that I fidgeted over the time interviewing consumed.

Three weeks into the new semester in the fall of 1957, the headline in a neighborhood newspaper proclaimed, "Margaret Mead Student Axes Mother." She thrust the tabloid in my face minutes before class convened one evening. The young man pictured on the front page had a distinctive appearance with a wavy jet of black hair adorning his head and upper lip.

"Nobody who looks like this guy ever came to talk to me," I insisted. "Unless he's using an alias and a falsified photograph, he hasn't even handed in a biography card."

"You must have signed for him," she snapped at me impatiently. "How else could he have gotten into the course?"

"Beats me. He either forged my signature or he sweet-talked somebody over in the Registration Office into signing a permission slip for him." Somebody had, but officers with flashing lights on the tops of their cars prevented him from attending class. And I became an instant convert to the wisdom of preregistration screening.

Once her course gained momentum, postregistration interviews with big-city loners seeking a free pair of ears for personal problems practically immobilized me. I asked Margaret's advice on what to do about curtailing these unforeseen time takers. "Keep all interviews in context," she advised. "It's appropriate that we help students with problems concerning their course work. It's not necessary to get involved any deeper, that is, unless you want to play clinical psychologist. But you have neither the time nor the credentials."

By far the most responsible part of my graduate student assistantship involved the classes themselves. I used to meet her just outside the lecture hall minutes before they began. I had already placed fresh chalk on the blackboard, a glass with a pitcher of ice water on the lectern, and whatever papers students were supposed to pick up on a table by the door. She usually handed me her cape and purse for safekeeping. I sat in a seat directly in front of the podium, ready to activate her requests and close enough to observe her in action.

Margaret Mead the college professor spoke with authority, fluency, and sudden flashes of humor. She knew, in a general way, what she was going to say and never referred to any notes. Instead, she watched the expressions of her students carefully, building her lectures around a major theme, always taking her cues from their responses. She, and they, were alert and relaxed. She wouldn't know from moment to moment what illustration she would pop up with next. Their indications of interest supplied her with stimuli as she proceeded. It was an intellectual duet. Five minutes short of the hour, she reviewed the main points and finished with a flourish "because so many of you have to take late trains home."

Each semester, guest lecturers took over a number of sessions for her. "I would rather you get firsthand information with the dew still on it than secondhand information," she briefed her students ahead of time.

I introduced the busy friends who came to cover for her in her absences. I remember meeting Lawrence K. Frank, a genial, older man, prior to class one evening. He called himself a philanthropoid. "A philanthropoid? What's that?" I asked as we approached the podium together.

"It's someone a philanthropy hires to spend its money," he replied with a twinkle. He sipped from his water glass, adjusted his green eyeshade, and smiled at two hundred faces.

"Mr. Frank says he's a philanthropoid." I described him to the class in his own terms. "That's someone whose job it is to spread money around. At that rate, there's probably not a person here who doesn't want to hear everything he wants to tell us."

Frank traced the emergence of the culture and personality field from a conference he had called at Dartmouth in the mid-1930s. He related it to a changing climate of opinion in which leaders in at least twenty highly guarded disciplines began to let down the boundaries separating their professions to formulate the interdisciplines that shared names with two of Margaret's courses, National Character and Culture and Personality.

"It takes a lot of specialists working together to study a culture; to deduce how an individual learns to become a member of a national society," Mr. Frank enlightened his audience. "We need materials from all kinds of specialists in order to understand culture and personality better."

Margaret forewarned the class that Frank had fathered two families, a generation apart, so his listeners knew he tempered knowledge with experience. "Each time a human being is born," he said, "it has the potential to become a member of any culture or of a particular culture. Each baby is at once a complicated idiosyncratic personality, as well as the innocent bearer of a specific culture."

Another evening Margaret's friend Martha Wolfenstein reviewed contrasting concepts of babyhood in our own country as evidenced by recommendations annually made to parents and distributed through the U.S. Printing Office. Had we not been confronted with the data she displayed in successively published copies of *Infant Care* from 1919 on, no one would have believed the same government printed the lot.

When initiating a discussion of the ways in which individuals within a given historical tradition acquire their national character, Margaret pretended to be an anthropologist from a governmental agency. She let the class listen in on an interview she conducted with Sula Benet on what being a Pole means to a Polish person. "It's hard being a Pole," Benet confided. "We get pushed around. We have extreme tolerance for total defeat. We stand up until the bitter end. We fight for a lot of lost causes."

A former Museum volunteer stood in the back of the room and chided herself as she heard Polish national character described. From what Benet said, I diagnosed the mixed Irish, French, Norwegian, and American Indian genealogy of the people who raised me as a case of mistaken identity. Might I have been a foundling? Sure, I had to be Polish.

At least once a month "we" spiced Margaret's classes with real slides or motion pictures: she provided the running commentary while I was supposed to obtain the film and the projector, thread one into the other, and guarantee proper functioning throughout. To better gird myself for faultless performances, I enrolled in a Teachers' College course on audiovisual aids.

"Totally ridiculous. You don't need it," she discouraged my efforts. "I don't know how to run a motion picture or slide projector and I get along fine."

"In order to maintain a temporary teaching certificate in the state of New York," I reminded her, "I must take at least one course at TC every semester. And this time it might as well be this one. I can't count on someone's jumping in and rescuing me every time the film jams. I'll find out how to run these A-V contraptions and then I'll show you."

"No, thanks. That's one thing I don't want to know. Sometimes it's smarter to be dumb. Once anybody knew I had such skills, I'd be expected to manipulate all kinds of projectors and lecture at the same time. That's plain stupid."

She customarily presented a verbal survey of an entire culture before she zoomed in on details provided through photography. She had helped shoot most of the films she chose to show in class. They depicted situations common to all human beings.

Wherever in the world babies live, for example, and no matter what the social status of their parents, every last one of them requires frequent ablutions from navel to knee. In her film *Bathing a Baby* mothers in New Guinea, Los Angeles, and Bali matter-of-factly wash their infants in a river, a kitchen sink, and a pail in a busy courtyard. Margaret pointed out how each mother ritualized the task according to different sets of beliefs and values.

"Attention to details is very necessary to anthropology," she coached her viewers. "Culture gets pinned down in the life of any one individual. Whatever is inside a person shows on the outside. After you've mastered the patterns of a culture, you can pick out any single segment of behavior like bathing a baby and follow through until you've grasped the whole culture."

Her method of using slides or film as teaching tools demanded total student involvement. Some teachers might sneak out for coffee or a smoke, leaving the assistant to run the projector. Not this one. She stood at the sidelines firing away remarks about frames that flickered by at the rate of sixteen per second. "Notice this next sequence of interactions," she periodically cautioned, "and interpret it in terms of what you now know about the culture."

Her film *Four Families* revealed inevitable differences in lifestyle among farm families in France, India, Japan, and Saskatchewan while illustrating how basically alike all families are in terms of having an infant join a household with two slightly older siblings.

Despite such opportunities to peer into other lifeways, those students, accustomed to blackboard, lecture, and text, sometimes facetiously referred to her course as "Tuesday night at the movies." Margaret shrugged off the implied criticism. As far as she was concerned, one picture was worth a thousand words. She knew she communicated more information faster with photography than without it. Film focused her teaching and facilitated our learning. No matter what the age or interest range of her students in any one class, a film always provided a common experience on which to base lively discussions.

The biographical cards that she had her students fill out enabled her to know more about her students as individuals than did most professors and she took a great many of us under her wing. Sometimes she stood up in front of her brood like a voluminous mother hen, ruffling her feathers and grousing over chicks too eager to fly the coop before familiarizing themselves with their home barnyards. She clucked at fledgling anthropologists to make sure they understood their own behavior before presuming to comprehend anybody else's.

"There are various ways to expose yourself to those parts of yourself usually inaccessible," she announced. "You can go into psychoanalysis, but be careful. You may not be able to put yourself together again.

"You can work with children and babies. The only way to get to know a baby is to hold one.

"You can have a psychosis and get over it.

"You can have a religious conversion and get over it.

"You can study a primitive people or you can marry a Russian. Russians think like psychoanalysts all the time. If you can't find a Russian, a Gypsy comes pretty close."

Her protective instincts extended to the friends and relatives of students who invited themselves to sit in on her classes. For years the university tried to plug this financial loophole by occasionally requesting that persons entering her lecture hall present their student identification cards. Margaret favored an open-door policy and battled these gatekeepers, or spies, as she called them. In terms of paid tuition, her large evening course brought in more revenue than most other classes on campus and she knew it. Whenever she heard that spot checkers prevented visitors from sitting in with her flock, she sent feathers and threats to quit teaching flying in all directions. The university invariably left her lectures unpoliced for a spell. But no one ever knew for sure when sentries stationed at the entranceways, come class time, would lead to another bristling skirmish.

Once in class, veterans took notes at sixty miles per hour. With the aid of God, Gregg, and Grinager, I improvised a shorthand that enabled me to capture nearly every word. Tape recorders weren't widely available yet and anthropological information is slippery. It's related to what is known already without ever having been noticed or labeled, and it slides away quickly. So when a chunky little woman with a Buster Brown haircut stood at a lectern chatting with a stream-of-consciousness ease while wiggling a glass of water as though it were her favorite scotch and soda, even a graduate assistant was prone to sit transfixed.

Yes, I know that. Yes, that's right. That's exactly how it is, I often thought as her words made a beeline in one ear and out the other. I dared not let her charm me out of taking notes too often, or I wouldn't be able to tell my seatmate on the train going home just what it was she did say. And it made so much sense at the time also.

When I think back to those midcentury evening classes, I see in retrospect that Margaret Mead didn't try to fill her students' minds as much as pry them open. She teased students with the names of books too new to be on the reading lists or not even published yet. She taunted them to surpass the minimum reading requirement of a paltry 1,200 pages. She tempted them to be ingenious in their choice of projects by describing imaginative research being conducted around the world by intellectual groundbreakers whom she knew on a first-name basis. They included Konrad Lorenz and his study of the ethology of instincts and species-specific behavior; Ray Birdwhistel's investigations in kinesics or the recording of molecular bits of movement; Harry Harlow's analyses of tactility; Gregory Bateson's observations on communication theory; Erik Hamburger Erikson's magnificent insights on the cross-cultural physiological development of infants in terms of zones and modes; J. M. Tanner and Barbara Inhelder's on the psychobiological development of the child; and Jean Piaget's on how children think. "You grow into this," she goaded us. "As educated people, you're going to live in the heights of your time, so you'd better be aware of the great idea makers of your time."

Who could foresee which of us might someday lead professional lives as full as her own? No matter, she encouraged balancing cerebral activities with more relaxed ones. Her all-night talkathons with fellow undergraduates at Barnard alerted her to the creative productivity that sometimes springs from lifelong college friendships. By holding open house the first Saturday evening of each month, she provided her students with regular chances to interact with each other, as well as herself, socially. Many anthropological participant–observers who made their way down to her apartment in the Greenwich Village brownstone that she shared with Rhoda Metraux watched her work even as she partied. Talk predominated at these get-togethers, and she saw to it that those with similar interests or projects found each other.

A direct correlation exists between long-windedness and keeping late hours. She wasn't always able to shoo everybody home early enough to get a good night's sleep. "In terms of fatigue, teaching is one of the most expensive and tiring things I do," she sputtered between clenched teeth as we hailed a cab in a downpour after class one evening.

"I don't know why I do it," she continued as one splashed to a halt in front of us. "Oh yes I do," she scrambled in and sat wiping raindrops from her spectacles. "It's the students. They're the only ones who'll ever see the future." As she dozed off, the assistant at her side reflected on some of the historical reasons for this particular professor's allegiance to students and to teaching.

Margaret Mead's love for learners and for learning had deep family roots. All her life, students and teachers made up her closest relationships. On her father's side, she identified herself as a teacher of the third generation; on her mother's, the second. Her paternal grandfather, Giles F. Meade, met elementary schoolteacher Mattie Ramsay when he came to her hometown in Winchester, Ohio, to be the school principal. Their only child, Edward (Margaret's father), completed the requirements for a Ph.D. in political economy in 1899 at the age of twenty-five. Before his diminutive firstborn reached her sixth birthday, he rose from instructor in commerce and industry at the all-male Wharton School of Finance of the University of Pennsylvania to full professor and chairman of the Wharton Evening Extension School.

Her maternal grandparents were well-traveled seed merchants and community do-gooders. Their oldest daughter, Emily Fogg, Margaret's mother, taught evening classes in Evanston, Illinois. She worked days for Henry Hoyt Hilton of Ginn and Company, publishers of schoolbooks. She completed requirements for a bachelor's degree at the University of Chicago in 1896.

Margaret and the three siblings who survived infancy grew up in a household that expected its members to earn a doctor's degree and teach in a university. Her father made it; her mother chipped away at it for years.

The breadwinners in the homes of most of their neighbors brought a Ph.D. back with them from Germany, the "in" place to go for a doctorate at the turn of the century. The Meads wintered in houses rented from faculty on sabbatical leave. Many of these homes were so close to campus that professors lived next door to them on both sides, across the street, and down the block. Whole families took turns entertaining each other for breakfast on Sundays. Weekdays, the

Mead youngsters played with neighborhood children, "faculty brats" all, on each other's look-alike front porches or in their postage-stamp backyards. The home life of most university faculty occurred inside an academic cocoon, inside a world far removed from the marketplace.

Under his sometimes socially polite exterior, Margaret's father disdained professors who lectured about the real world without entering it. He never forgot his boyhood and young manhood among Youngstown, Ohio, factory workers whose children his widowed mother taught at the Hill School. He never lost a missionary zeal for making it easier for working-class people to improve their status through attending evening classes.

E. S. Mead practiced what he preached. Despite the doubts of his peers about the schools that predated the present system of community colleges, he championed the establishment of the Wharton Evening Extension School of Accounts and Finance. It became a pioneer of its kind in this country; he, its first director.

For years, he lectured by day on the intricacies of corporation finance to students at the University of Pennsylvania in Philadelphia. At least twice a week, he then boarded a late afternoon train to teach evening students in branch classes in Scranton and Wilkes-Barre or Reading and Harrisburg by night. A rigorous taskmaster who insisted on standards of scholarship equivalent to those required of full-time students, he challenged weary adults who put in a full day's work before they trudged into class. He prodded them to think in terms of both theory and practice. He assigned them to analyze their job in relation to company policies and practices as their term project.

Over the years, he accumulated a wealth of student-contributed material that he utilized to make his own lectures more contemporary and his textbooks more compelling. After grading hundreds of these case studies, E. S. Mead knew more about the management of regional business houses than anyone else around. His recall for names of students allowed him to remark that he could walk into almost any bank on the East Coast and greet at least one former student working in it. And the same could be said of his office in Logan Hall. It was from the coed membership of his evening classes up and down eastern Pennsylvania that he recruited assistants and secretaries.

For her part, Margaret's mother, who would have been a university professor herself had she not raised so many children, aided in organizing a domestic science school in West Philadelphia. It trained immigrant women to qualify for employment as cooks, housekeepers, and nursemaids. Over summer sessions in which her family migrated to small towns, Emily Fogg Mead also served on committees to establish free public libraries so that any motivated citizens could obtain books and teach themselves.

In a home environment imbued with the importance of continuing education and social causes, each one of the four E. S. and E. F. Mead offspring who survived childhood earned at least a bachelor's degree; one of them, a master's, and the older two, their doctorates. Margaret, Richard, and Elizabeth all concerned themselves with learners both in and out of college. Priscilla, slowed down somewhat by more children than the rest of them, was working toward her master's at the time of her death.

The Meads' ambitions extended to the persons their daughter Margaret chose to live with during her adulthood. The four persons with whom Margaret Mead shared telephone bills and coat closets at one time or another taught university students. She was married and divorced three times: to Luther Shieleigh Cressman of Pughtown, Pennsylvania; to Reo Franklin Fortune from Paraparaumu, New Zealand; and to Gregory Bateson from Cambridge, England. She lived the last third of her life with Rhoda Epple Bubendey Metraux from New York City. All except Bateson received a Ph.D. from Margaret's own doctoral alma mater, Columbia University. Each of the three, in print, acknowledged Margaret's assistance in completing their dissertations. Luther, for aid in the revision and presentation of the text of his study, *The Social Composition of the Rural Population of the United States*, in 1925; Reo, for the final critique of his opus, *The Social Anthropology of the Dobu Islanders of the Western Pacific*, in 1931; and Rhoda, for providing a model for systematizing notes collected by a United Nations UNESCO team in her *Kith and Kin: A Study of the Creole Social Structures in Marbial Valley* (Haiti), in 1951.

Margaret and Rhoda combined households after each divorced for the last time. They raised Margaret's daughter and Rhoda's son. Both young people grew up to obtain a Ph.D. and go into higher education.

The teachers who first convinced Margaret Mead that the more education the better lived under her own roof. Her father, her mother, and her paternal grandmother felt that elementary schools wasted too much of a child's time. Grandmother Mattie supervised Margaret's learning the three Rs for an hour or so mornings; mother Emily, sciences in the afternoons. Her mother made occasional arrangements with neighbors to tutor Margaret in skills as varied as cooking, drawing, music, painting, and woodworking. Otherwise, similar to the Arapesh and Manus children she would eventually study, Margaret Mead, the child, was turned loose to run and play, finding "tongues in trees, books in running brooks, sermons in stone, and good in everything."

When she reached the equivalent of fourth grade, her parents sent her to public school in Swarthmore, Pennsylvania. An unexpected increase in enrolment taxed space, and the district rented a room for half days in the old town hall for Margaret's grade. The building ordinarily housed the office of the village policeman. It also sheltered the fire engine, a bright red horse-drawn affair with steam whistles and huge hoses. Under the tutelage of Lydia Rinehart, a "marvelous teacher" with whom Margaret corresponded until her death, fourth graders that year enjoyed the time of their lives.

Her second encounter with formal education was less successful. For eighth-grade courses in 1914–1915, the Meads sent Margaret to the Friends' School in Buckingham, a private institution run by Quakers. Until then, Margaret had received more positive than negative reinforcement for being precocious. From day one, however, her presence in Buckingham put her instructors in a bind. Margaret knew the answers before her teachers finished asking their questions. Still, they felt they had to call on her occasionally. Whenever they did, they wished they hadn't. Margaret, who wasn't at all used to having to give others a chance to recite, filibustered until the bell rang. The experience frustrated all concerned: fair-minded faculty, star pupil, and disgruntled classmates.

As a result, she stayed home and resumed study with her mother and grandmother during what would have been her freshman year in high school. She entered high school in Doylestown, Pennsylvania, as a sophomore. She boarded in town that year with a relative of A. F. Nightingale, who had been principal of Chicago's Lake View High School when her mother attended some thirty years before. At the beginning of her junior year, the Meads moved into town and rented a house on the block next to Carmon Ross, principal of Doylestown High, with whom her parents soon became fast friends.

Margaret's experience at Buckingham alerted her parents to the immense social difficulties confronting any child, particularly a bright teenager, who struggles with the transition from being taught privately at home to attending school.

Margaret's mother decided to upgrade her oldest daughter's popularity by opening their home to her high school acquaintances for dancing and snacks on the first Saturday evening of every month. She also began inviting the high school teachers over for dinner. George Cressman, who taught Margaret chemistry, demurred on receiving his invitation because Luther, one of his five younger brothers, was visiting him at the time. Mrs. Mead spontaneously included Luther, then a junior in military science at Penn State. During the evening, her daughter's social acceptance at school shot up at least ten points. Margaret and the young man who also came to dinner fell in love.

After Margaret graduated from college six years later, the sweethearts married. The young couple responded to Mead family expectations by studying for the Ph.D. degree that would lead them toward the goal of teaching in a university.

Four teachers most impressed Margaret Mead during her college years: two in English and two in anthropology. The English professors were Ralph Pence at De Pauw University in Greencastle, Indiana, and Louise Minor White Latham at Barnard College in New York City. Ralph Pence helped her polish her writing style; Minor Latham, by example, enriched her teaching style. Latham taught drama by conducting her classes as though they were scenes in a play. She paced back and forth, intoning theatrically with gestures and asides, suspense and surprise. Her histrionics inspired her students to love Shakespeare and the theater. They extended their affection to their teacher also.

As a graduate student at Columbia University, Margaret was attracted to Professors Franz Boas and Ruth Benedict. Boas, often referred to as "Papa Franz" by his disciples, resented what he called academic red tape, disliked formal texts, seldom sent anyone to his own writings, and gauged the quality of a student's thinking by the caliber of the questions she asked. He peppered his lectures with graphic examples gleaned from his own fieldwork, as he moved back and forth, now considering large general principles, now wondering aloud with the fresh curiosity of a child. Sometimes he sat back and let guest lecturers command his classes.

Boas was far more popular with his students than with his fellows. A German–Jewish intellectual with fervent convictions about the universality of human oneness, he insisted that all so-called differences among people in regard to food habits, language, philosophy, and ability to think scientifically were learned after birth. He believed that all beings, whether they were literate or not, belonged to the same species with the same range of capabilities. He saw all categories of races, as well as justifications for waging war, as senseless and beneath the dignity of the supposedly civilized. And he didn't hesitate to say so. Before and during World War I, very few of the supposedly civilized welcomed his ideas.

Even though, as a statesman–scientist, he mapped out the entire discipline of anthropology for most of the rest of the century, Franz Boas suffered ostracism and loss of prestige at the hands of his contemporaries. For this reason, he had the time to reach out to undergraduates and cross the street from his headquarters in Schermerhorn Hall at then male-dominated Columbia University to teach young women at Barnard College. His course surveyed archeology, art, ethnology, folklore, linguistics, and physical anthropology. He knew that the more highly motivated would become experts in their areas of special interest on their own in due time.

Ruth Benedict, his graduate assistant, shyly mediated between the patriarch and his students. She translated his densely packed lectures, which his German accent sometimes made incomprehensible. She identified the systematic study of child rearing as one of the most neglected and necessary aspects of fieldwork and one in which women should be particularly adept. She described cultures as personalities writ large, as vastly dissimilar one from another as are the personalities of individuals. She passed along Boas's concern for recording the "personalities" of disappearing tribes before they vanished forever.

Benedict's and Boas's messages inspirited Margaret Mead. Ruth's simple declaration, "Professor Boas and I have nothing to offer but an opportunity to do work that matters," clinched it for Margaret. She dropped her plans to do graduate study in either English or psychology and applied for acceptance as a graduate student in anthropology instead.

She finished the requirements for the bachelor's degree at Barnard in 1923 and joined a handful of graduates to study under Franz Boas. Ruth Benedict received her Ph.D. that same year. Despite the decade-plus discrepancy in their ages, Margaret Mead and Ruth Benedict became close personal friends. They mothered each other. When the necessity arose, either one of them filled in the other's appointments. They shared perplexities and poetry. They read each other's writings and listened to books in process. When Ruth's mentor, Franz Boas, died, Margaret wrote an obituary for him in the Barnard College Alumnae Monthly. When Margaret's mentor, Ruth Benedict, died, she took up Ruth's projects where she left off and became her biographer.

Margaret Mead didn't let go of Benedict and Boas easily. She glued a picture of each of these two anthropologist ancestors to the glass doors of the bookcase that stood across from her desk at the Museum, reminiscent of the heads of their ancestors that hang from the rafters in the huts of her New Guinea informants. For fifty-two years, she looked over whatever she wrote and beyond whomever she interviewed to their photographs just above eye level straight ahead of her.

In her own career as a teacher's teacher, she promoted Boas and Benedict's concern for doing anthropology that mattered, as well as her parents' faith in educating working-class adults ambitious to improve their status through university-guided readings and evening class attendance.

Her family's fervor infected some of her students as well. They too earned their doctorates and taught in universities. In fact, one of them blinks back at me every time I look into a mirror.

4

ON THE LECTURE TRAIL

W ho could he be? Early in Margaret's career, when groups began to invite her to recount her South Sea travails, a tall, spare-haired, older-looking Edwardian dandy often accompanied her. He made a point of sitting up front. He wore a cutaway frock coat, a vest trimmed with heavy white braid, a stand-up collar with a stick pin in his cravat, and pink coral studs in his hard-boiled shirt front. He wasn't a particularly jovial fellow and often glared at her over rimless spectacles.

Who was he? He was one of the few people in her life who could, and would, call her down. "You're too short. Speak up, but don't do it from behind a podium," he directed. "You talk too fast. Don't move your head back and forth and spout over the tops of folks like a lawn sprinkler. When I'm along, look at me. When I'm not, don't just gaze anywhere. Pick out one or two people who are sitting in a place that will make your voice right for that group. Talk to them."

As much as a parent's skill can be transmitted, Edward Sherwood Mead passed his eloquence on to his eldest daughter. As far back as his own student days, his magnificent memory and "natural windiness," as he put it, earned him a place on the debate team at Oberlin, De Pauw, and Chicago. He habitually carried a pocket notebook for saving colorful phrases that flew his way by thought or by ear. In the privacy of his study, he drank deep from his favorite source: a twelve-volume set, *The Works of Edmund Burke*.

Long before Margaret began to address the public, her father had survived years of reaching and keeping the toughest of audiences. If his lectures weren't "interesting and accurate in context," provocative and witty in delivery, drowsy extension students slumped down in their seats and dozed off. How he said what he said about such ordinarily dry subjects as the reorganization of railroads or the relative stability of gold and silver was crucial in seizing the attention of workers who put in a full day on the job before going to school at night.

Her father's delivery shaped Margaret Mead's style; her mother's speeches introduced her to more humanistic choices of subject matter. As a female role model, Emily Fogg Mead showed her daughter that economic topics by no means exhausted public speaking possibilities; that spreading the word from the female point of view was both necessary and important.

Emily talked to ladies' clubs about marriage and the family, education, world peace, and the women's suffrage movement. Her lack of a definite word-for-word structure and spontaneous delivery relaxed her audiences into remembering more of what she did say. "If you plan a speech too tightly," she advised her daughter, "your listeners feel the weight and structure from the start as they do a sermon."

Off and on, as she was growing up, Margaret sat in the academic or community audiences of one or the other of her oratorically talented parents. As far as any of us learn by imitation and example, she had triple opportunities to do so. The senior Meads weren't at all surprised at their firstborn's success in public speaking. All three of the teachers who raised her (I'm counting grandmother) expected it. Hadn't she always been the spokeswoman for neighborhood play groups? Hadn't she directed down-home dramas in the meadow or on the front porch at Holicong since she was twelve? Had she ever eaten more than she talked during mealtime arguments?

Her career as a formal speaker began almost as soon as she returned from Samoa. Along with churning out articles about her fieldwork for such periodicals as *The Delineator, Parents' Magazine, The Nation,* and *Natural History,* she addressed the membership of her mother's numerous ladies' clubs. She described the daily routines of South Sea Islanders whose existence barely resembled the everyday lives of urban or suburban Philadelphians. Her topics piqued their interest. Titles such as "South Sea Hints on Bringing Up Children," "Living with the Natives of Melanesia," "Water Babies of the South Seas," and "Going Native for Science" titillated the curious to invite her again.

As her writings became known, invitations to speak arrived from communities far beyond Philadelphia and New York City. Conference planners representing churches, clubs, various special interest organizations, universities, and professional societies requested her presence. She obliged as many of them as time permitted and pursued her lecture trail experiences with the energy of a political campaigner. She frequently declaimed before two or more entirely different interest groups between breakfast and bedtime. She became as familiar to college-town America as had nineteenth-century headliners for the Chautauqua in her grandmother's day.

Along with so many of the rest of us, she put on weight during her fifties. Her new physique surprised audience members who didn't expect to find a celebrity so refreshingly off the cuff as a speaker, so folksy in manner, or so fuddy-duddy in appearance. Her brusque, husky voice bounded off the back walls. Her tongue darted in and out of her cheek with reptilian rapidity. She shocked sophisticates, who expected to be at least half-bored, into staying awake to catch each poisoned barb or witty innuendo. She customarily invited feedback in her opening remarks in the form of questions put to her on the platform. She requested that these queries be written and signed. At the end of her speeches, she sorted through the slips of paper brought up to her, and she identified and read aloud those she chose to answer. Persons who submitted questions like, Why save the wilderness? or Would you let your daughter marry a black? were commanded to stand up and look her in the eyes as she responded.

She took these queries back to her typewriter and recycled them into ideas in her published material. Her books and articles generated more invitations to speak, which supplied her with even timelier audience concerns, which became the source of ever more up-to-date writings, which multiplied the number of her lecturing engagements, which supplied her with fresh, new questions, and so on. Death alone ended the spiral.

Most of her undergraduates, Museum volunteers, and departmental assistants were too occupied to be aware of her expeditions into the country's grass roots. Neither the university nor the Museum claimed any direct connections with this part of her career. She carried it out on the side. And she donated most of the larger lecture fees to the scientific and social causes in which she believed.

Once I earned my master's degree and left Columbia with more questions than answers about my own future, I became increasingly aware of the extent of her peripatetic lecturings. For the next twenty years, whenever circumstances permitted, one of my sons or I sat in the audience at one or another of her cross-country whistle stops. If we were living anywhere near her speaking engagement, we brought her home with us to stay the night.

It was the summer of 1957 and I was thirty-nine. Jobs were scarce in business and even more rare in a pursuit as esoteric as anthropology. Unemployed anthropologists, both seasoned and otherwise, were as numerous as books on the shelves of a well-stocked village library.

The weekend after I turned in a rented cap and gown for the second time at Columbia, my husband flew from Chicago to press for our locating in a house he had rented near Libertyville, Illinois. A large bottle of bourbon fortified his arguments. His dependence on alcohol forewarned me. Any financial benefits that might result from my rejoining him would soon be swamped by feelings of entrapment in a suburb whose name prophetically mocked my situation there.

"The moving van will arrive as early as possible on Wednesday, July 21." His ultimatum slapped a date on a decision whose time had come. "Either you and the kids follow that van back to Illinois, or you're on your own."

For the next five weeks I wandered around the house as preoccupied as a poet. To go or not to go, that was the question. A fork-in-the-road decision that would affect the life of an entire family loomed ahead. I stared off into space, grappling with the pros and cons and maybes of moving or staying. Had the long-awaited time to escape what I felt to be a buried-alive marriage arrived? Dared I chance making a break for it? If so, how find a nonanthropological job lucrative enough to support five people? Where? When? Doing what? Margaret pointed out that staying was not even an alternative. We were going to have to go somewhere on July 21, whether we went to Illinois or not.

Intense necessity sometimes opens our eyes to opportunities lying in wait under our very noses. A newspaper report informed me that 250 public schools in the state of New York lacked art teachers for fall. The fascination of my own quartet of native artists for the long ago and far away gave me an idea. Why not adapt my master's paper, written to foster attitudes for international understanding through a study of known culture change in ancient Peru, to teaching grade schoolers art? That's where the jobs were. Archeologists dig up more art than bones. The complex designs in Peruvian weavings and the vivid shapes of Peruvian pottery told volumes about the beliefs and everyday activities of those who fashioned them. Why not prepare syllabi for teaching art to preteens by exposing them to a culture as long ago and far away, as contemporary and close, as undeniably American, as pre-Columbian Peru?

Hazel Jones, the mother of a friend, owned a cabin up a rocky road in a grassy clearing by a stand of tall trees on a mountainside near her home in Saratoga Springs. It lacked both electricity and running water. It needed a thorough houscleaning and a replenished woodpile. It was completely furnished and the roof didn't leak. I phoned Hazel Jones. Yes, five human sardines could fit into it more or less comfortably. Yes, she was willing to rent it. If I took the cabin before the horse races started in August, I could have it for the preseason price of $25 per month.

"It's a deal," I told her. "We'll get up there before dark on Tuesday."

Next I called Margaret's office in the Museum. Nora Holland answered and I wondered if she would agree to forward my mail from Northport to the Museum and then on to Hazel Jones in Saratoga Springs. "How are the files holding up?" I asked before making a second request.

"Just yesterday, Margaret reached for the phone to call David Rapaport for one of his reprints," Nora recalled. "I pulled out the file drawer you labeled R, fingered for the R-A-Ps and up popped Rapaport's paper. She hung up the phone as I handed it over to her and exclaimed, 'Pat, forever.'"

"Good!" I rejoiced. "Then maybe she won't mind writing a recommendation for me. It's got to be general because I have no definite idea of a job except it will probably be teaching. But I do need a recommendation from her fast, like yesterday." Margaret's "To Whom It May Concern" arrived the next afternoon. It read:

> I have known Mrs. Patricia Grinager as a graduate student, as a volunteer assistant, and as my departmental assistant in Anthropology at Columbia University. She has immense energy and zeal, determination, and a capacity to conceive a plan and carry it through. She has proved herself highly intelligent in her course work and in the written projects which she has submitted. Her experience with teaching, journalism, organization of materials, combined with her graduate work in anthropology, should prepare her to tackle new problems with energy and enthusiasm. She has a genuine interest and concern for students, a sense that teaching should matter.

This ought to do the trick, I said to myself as I read through her recommendation. Into the glove compartment of the car it went for safekeeping and for quick access.

The morning before the moving van's due date, to escape the prying eyes of the Mrs. Antwerps in the neighborhood, I drove in behind the house and backed up to a bedroom window. The four boys and I lined the trunk of the car with newspapers. We stuffed all but the skeleton of our terminally ill old Ford with minimal necessaries for five. The boys squeezed into the backseat and sat atop their folded-up clothing, each balancing his own most treasured possession on his lap. The car's belly sagged like a pregnant dachshund in need of a spare roller skate beneath her middle. We pointed the car's nose northward and inched toward Hazel Jones's home in Saratoga Springs. We planned to headquarter with Hazel while we cleaned her cabin in Porters Corners prior to moving in.

On Friday, August 2, the day before Miles's birthday, I presented a proposal for introducing archeology through art to the superintendent in Saratoga Springs and to a couple other administrators in nearby school districts. Two of the three appeared intrigued with the notion, thought it over after I left, and called a message of good news to me care of Mrs. Jones.

I opened Hazel's kitchen door, weary from a day of job seeking, and caught her sticking candles in an applesauce spice cake: fourteen for the birthday boy and an extra one to celebrate his mother's rebirth into the world of salary checks. I returned the calls and accepted the offer from Saratoga Springs. It was closer to the cabin we'd soon be living in, as well as to the spacious home of my friend's mother. Hazel had adopted us, five strong. Nobody appreciates mothering like another mother.

Mrs. Jones watched the kids for me Monday morning when I drove over to the office of school superintendent Claude VanWie to sign a one-year contract for teaching art to children in grades 5–8. At his suggestion, I also paid out $1.50 to join the Saratoga Springs Teachers' Credit Union. Just in the nick of time, too. On the same day, without any warning, our old Ford emitted its dying gasp. Mrs. Jones loaned me her car to drive back to the credit union, where I applied for a $1,500 loan toward the purchase of its successor. This was to be the first new car I'd ever owned. The boys and I shopped for a vehicle rugged enough to commute to and from the cabin, as well as roomy enough to transport art supplies among the community's four elementary schools.

As a roving art teacher, I drove the VW microbus all over town every weekday. My schedule allotted me fifty minutes to distribute materials, inspire twenty-five or more pupils, retrieve their outpourings, and clean up. I soon learned that my popularity with teachers depended upon the tidiness of their homeroom when they returned from coffee and doughnuts in the faculty lounge. They favored media that entailed less mess: crayons, scissors, and colored construction paper. Not so, the diminutive artists. They reveled in smearing finger paint or paste, smudging watercolors, or squishing clay and papier maché. The messier the media, the better the youngsters liked them.

Should I teach the art of ancient Peru with dry materials in deference to the wishes of the adults, or wet to please the children? Clearly, the issue called for a compromise. By rotating messy with clean art on odd and even weeks of each month, I pleased somebody at least half the time.

On the first day of a dry week in October, the Russians shot their Sputnik into outer space. Within hours, Margaret Mead contacted my school system and had me paged. She asked me to send her as much evidence as possible showing how older grade school children pictured scientists. She wanted everything I could send her—fast, while the news about Sputnik was still hot off the griddle. And then, before she banged the receiver down, she inquired how we were getting along.

I told her about our doing homework and lesson plans by kerosene lamplight, pumping water, chopping firewood for heating a cabin recently commandeered from porcupines, and about investing $1.50 to borrow $1,500 to buy a VW microbus. "Write your own story some day," she quipped, "nobody'll believe it."

Klunk.

She cut herself off from further communicating. My name was only one on a list of many friends earmarked to receive a similar request on this day.

I collected 1,000 crayon and pencil drawings for her. The back of each sheet bore the name, grade, age, and sex of its artist. As the first space capsule zoomed away from planet Earth, fifth, sixth, seventh, and eighth graders in the public schools of Saratoga Springs, New York, depicted scientists as bald, bespectacled, and bony. They worked in laboratories cluttered with caged albino mice or test tubes. Most of them wore white lab coats. Some of them smoked pipes. Not one of the scientists in these sketches smiled or seemed to be the least bit concerned about other people. None was young and none was female.

Anthropological scientists can criticize Missy Makarit all they want, I thought as I fit the children's artwork into a former canned tomato packing box from the grocery store, but who beats her for keeping abreast of what's going on in, and now off, the world?

There was one aspect of my teaching art that seemed out of this world too. An astronaut unencumbered by stop-and-go traffic lights might have had a hand in setting up my schedule. Each Wednesday, for example, I raced green lights and ran yellow ones to reach three classes in just as many schools by noon. My arrival involved much more than simply getting there with lesson plans. I had to drag the art materials with me and keep them clean. Without four built-in assistants, a brook outside our cabin door, and a minibus, I wouldn't have lasted the year.

"You gotta have a car this big to carry all the art stuff around, don'tcha?" eager pupils remarked as they vied with each other for the honor of lugging trays of paint or paste jars from the bus to their classrooms and then back to the bus again forty-nine minutes later.

After school, weather permitting, the boys waded into the stream alongside our cabin and washed out paint jars until dark. Other evenings, by lamplight on the linoleum floor in the kitchen, they dunked the jars into pails filled with water pumped from the well.

It was rugged all right. But the job in Saratoga Springs served as our refuge between universities. We began to put down roots. I debated whether to give up the security of teaching in a friendly community for the insecurity of tackling the third and last degree in some place yet unknown. "You're not getting any younger," Margaret advised. "People stagnate in small towns. Get that doctorate before you or the kids become entrenched. You'll disintegrate if you don't. Move while you're movable." She liked the combination of twin majors I'd stumbled upon. "Visionary education," she called it.

I wrote to various universities about the possibility of a two-pronged doctorate in education and anthropology. The University of Oregon in Eugene, Emory in Atlanta, and Stanford near Palo Alto, California, responded positively. Which to choose? Kent was newly eight, and his brothers were approaching their eleventh, twelfth, and fifteenth birthdays. Would Eugene or Atlanta or Palo Alto provide the most enriching environment for the boys' remaining years of childhood? I purchased a three-month subscription to each of the local newspapers.

Even though Stanford's fellowship was not the most generous, it didn't take too many weeks of newspaper perusal to rate the town of Palo Alto highest as a youth-oriented community. It supported a children's zoo, a municipal swimming pool, annual campouts on the village green, and newly opened Foothill Junior College. Full-page advertisements for a cooperative grocery store appealed to me too. Potential six footers consume their weight in peanut butter, chicken, and creamed corn each week.

Professors George Spindler and Louise Spindler also attracted me to Palo Alto. They shared appointments there in the school of education and the department of anthropology. Perfect. I purposefully attended the 1957 American Anthropological Conference in order to meet them and have them meet me. "Most students interested in these two fields are education majors curious to learn more about anthropology," the Spindlers said. "An anthropologist who wants to specialize in education? That's a new twist! We'd like to see you come to California."

Notification of my having been awarded a graduate fellowship in the school of education at Stanford arrived around Easter. I wrote Margaret and she phoned to inform me that she'd been invited to be the commencement speaker at Skidmore College in Saratoga Springs on June 8. "I'll call President Wilson right away," I thought aloud. "You've got to be met and chauffeured here and there. He ought to be grateful to find someone here in town who knows you and who'll do it."

"I like having former students scattered around the country and meeting me at airports," she greeted me after her plane landed in Glens Falls. I suggested that she wait for her suitcase while I scurried through pelting rain to the parking lot for the bus. "Is this the car you bought after you paid some ridiculously small amount to join a teachers' credit union?" she asked as I hoisted her up into the front seat.

"Yes. It's been a boon for trucking art stuff around all year. In another six or seven weeks the five of us will camp in it on our way to California."

"A Volkswagen is an *ethnic* automobile." She made herself comfortable. "A wagon-for-the-folks. This is the first time I've been in one."

"There aren't too many of them around yet. We've gotten used to having station attendants ask where the gas tank is. And others who own one flash their lights in greeting when we pass one another on the road." We drove along, talking in synch with the swing of the windshield wipers. I brought her up-to-date on the current state of my marital situation. "Since you've got to prove adultery to get divorced in New York, a legal separation seems to be the most civilized way to go."

"Everybody should be married at least once if only for a day," she responded with sisterly frankness. "People need at least one experience in life when they give themselves to another. Once children come, the ideal is to stay married until they're grown."

"Ideals are a far cry from reality," I weighed my words. "And the stark reality is that the man and woman involved grow too, and at decidedly different rates. Ray was nearly a dozen years older than I. When we married I had a lot more growing to do and I've done it. I don't know which will come first, once we get to California, the divorce or the degree."

"Divorce isn't the end of the world. I'm still friends with each of my former husbands."

"That's good to know. We've got to get to California before anything else, though. My immediate concern then will be finding an affordable place to live. The boys and I will sleep in the bus on the way out and maybe even the first few nights in Palo Alto. House hunt during the day. The trouble is, I'm not sure what I should look for: a place to rent or a place to buy."

"Rent."

"One would have to rent in New York City where you live, yes, but I doubt that's the case in Palo Alto. The newspapers indicate the town's full of homeowners. I'm saving for a down payment just in case. If it turns out monthly mortgage obligations about equal rent, then I think it would be smarter to buy; accrue an equity in some property with the same dollars."

"Rent. I've never owned a house, nor a car either for that matter, and I get along fine."

"There are only two of you and you're both females. There are five of me. I wouldn't want to rent to anyone with four boys, so I can't expect somebody else to want to do it."

"Rent. A house is a burden you can get along without. A house never leaves an owner alone. Something's always got to be done to it or for it or in it or something. You'd have more time and money on your hands if you rented."

"Who says time and money are everything?" I balked. "I think the kids should be able to build tree houses and dig to China without having some blue-nosed landlord circling around saying, 'Don't.' I spent my childhood shoveling to China or tying rag rugs to the forks of trees. I can't deprive my own youngsters of doing the same thing. Renting is not fair to kids."

The wheels skidded as we entered Saratoga Springs. The slick streets gave me an uneasy feeling of driving on glass. Rather than alarm my precious cargo, I let her take over more and more of the conversation by default.

Pride in the accomplishments of her seventeen-year-old daughter emanated from Margaret's every pore. "Cathy's going to concentrate on Middle Eastern Studies," she boasted.

Damn smart, I mused, for a young lady with such individually prominent parents to zero in on an area in which neither of them is an expert.

"Only this morning," Margaret bragged on, "someone called Cathy on the phone and the two of them talked in Arabic the whole time."

My bulky bus slid to a stop at a red light atop a hill amid late afternoon traffic in the center of the rain-drenched village. "Arabic?" I grimaced as I simultaneously released the brake pedal and pushed down on the gas without backsliding into the bumper of the car behind us. "I've seen that alphabet. Dragged-out curlicues for letters without a recognizable squiggle anywhere. Do you mean to tell me that people actually talk that stuff?"

"Any language scriptable is speakable," she snapped.

"Oh, quit being such a proud mother. Do you think your kid is the only one who ever learned Arabic? I'll bet 10,000 Arabian two-year-olds talk it."

"So what's new with Kent, Laird, Miles, and Neal?" she shifted conversational gears.

"What a memory!" I exclaimed. "You got all their names right! I wouldn't be able to do that for yours if you happened to have that many."

"It's easy. All I have to do is remember the initials, K, L, M, and N and go from there. How are they doing?"

We turned into the spacious driveway of the Gideon-Putnam Hotel. I relaxed a white-knuckled grip on the steering wheel. "Why don't you ask them yourself? I'd like to hear what they tell you.

"We can't invite you out to the cabin. The accommodations are too primitive to allow you a decent sleep before your big speech. Besides, driving back and forth between Porters Corners and Saratoga in these spring rains takes too long."

We pulled up at the baronial headquarters in which Skidmore College reserved rooms for its visiting dignitaries. "So we're inviting you to breakfast in the morning, right here. Let's meet in the dining room at seven. We can finish in plenty of time to get you to Skidmore for all the graduation pomp and circumstance."

I turned off the ignition and hustled around to take her bags out of the back and then helped her down from the bus. We walked in together. I leaned on the counter while she registered.

"See you at seven in the morning then," I reminded her as she turned to follow a bellhop to the lobby elevator. "We'll all be in the dining room, looking as little like hayseed mountaineers as possible."

The boys hadn't been near a hotel as luxurious as the Gideon-Putnam for over a year. Nor had we spent a dime in a restaurant. I wanted breakfast this particular overcast Sunday to go down in their memories. Even though they had labored many hours in the Museum for her, none of the boys had yet met Margaret. They dressed for the occasion as though they were about to attend an inaugural ball.

"We've pinched pennies all year," I announced on the trek toward town. "And this morning we make up for it. The treat's on us and we're going to splurge. We can stretch nickels afterward."

We arrived a few minutes earlier than she. "This place sure has a lot of tables," Neal scanned the dining area. A hostess approached and led us to a table with seats for six. We sat down. I spied Margaret enter and stood up as she made her way toward us. Miles pulled her chair out for her.

"I'm as big as you are!" Eight-year-old Kent blurted out before any of his taller brothers could stop him.

"Then you're big enough to order double portions." She put the four of them at ease at once. Any adult who gives growing boys a green light in a restaurant, rates.

Someone came with a pitcher of water. "My glass has lipstick on it already." Sharp-eyed Laird held up the evidence for all to see.

"Somehow, lipstick's the last thing I'd expect to find on drinking glasses in a place as ritzy as this," I lamented. A busboy took away Laird's glass and replaced it with a cleaner looking one.

"A place can be as plush as this," Margaret's eyes darted around the restaurant, "but none of it is worth a hoot if the people who work here don't take pride in their job. I thought of it last night too after I took a bath. The maid forgot to leave clean towels." Her eyes returned to the table and focused on us. "My grandmother used to say, 'Good, better, best. Never let it rest until your good is better, your better, best.' I don't know whether she got it out of a McGuffey's Reader or not, but the little verse smacks of the spirit that built this country."

She shrugged her shoulders and shook her head from side to side. "Nobody wants to be dedicated anymore. An alarming many of us don't know what pride in a job well done is or don't care. It's too bad, too." A waitress brought us our menus. Each boy became as engrossed in his as though he hadn't eaten yesterday. And he ordered accordingly. Margaret, much more sparingly.

"Come on, you can eat more than that," I goaded her. "Go ahead and order more. Live it up. Bolster yourself for your big speech."

"Two waffles with sausage, juice, and a cup of coffee is plenty," she handed over her menu.

"I'm appalled at the amount of food that is wasted in the United States," she continued when the waitress disappeared. "Restaurants, for example, serve far too much. Customers try to eat it because they have to pay for it. When you consider that most people in the world don't even know what a full stomach feels like, it's obscene."

"Are you going to say something about that in your speech this morning?" I asked. "The paper reported that you've named it 'Discipline and Dedication.' That's a good title for spurring sweet girl graduates upward and onward and out." I raised my eyebrows and glanced from her to the boys. "The title 'Discipline and Dedication' makes a statement about you too. You discipline yourself when you beat the birds getting up in the morning to write before the phone starts ringing. You've dedicated yourself to the cause of humanizing everybody's worldview."

"Flattery will get you nowhere," she grinned amiably. "You know only too well how not perfect I am." Without looking for lipstick, she sipped from her water glass and glanced at us over her spectacles.

"It's fun to catch grown-ups not being perfect," Neal declared with mischief in his eyes. "Did Mom tell you what she did the other day? She found ants in the honey. So she took the jar to the sink and poured the honey through a strainer. All the honey went merrily down the drain and guess what was left in the strainer?"

"Ants!" Kent and Laird proclaimed in unison. We shared a laugh over the lost honey.

"Grown-ups definitely aren't perfect," Margaret said with a mission in mind, "but that makes me want to find out about each one of you all the more. And I know boys well enough to get at it before the food comes." She interviewed them without prodding. I leaned back in amazement. Just before delivering a keynote speech, I would not want to talk to God. Here she sat, bantering back and forth with four children as spontaneously as if she had the day off.

When the waitress brought our bill, she laid it upside-down on a saucer beside Margaret's plate. I considered it mine and reached over for it. My guest grabbed it away from me. "Come on! Give that back! I never would have let the kids order what they did had I thought you were going to pay!" I protested. "Can't you remember? I invited you to this breakfast."

"My pleasure," her square smile displayed every tooth. She tucked the bill into her big, black purse of many compartments and winked at four coconspirators.

We hurried to the rendezvous on Union Avenue where President Wilson, Dean MacRury, Chaplain Sather, and Skidmore's band of trustees were preparing to pose for pictures prior to lining up for the academic procession to the green between Griffith Hall and Newman House.

Partly because we didn't have much time to spare between the end of the ceremonies and her scheduled departure from the airport in Glens Falls, the boys and I stayed to listen. If it is the role of a commencement speaker to bear down hard on graduates and members of their support systems in an event charged with emotion, Margaret Mead was just the one to do it. She bore down hard on herself and a commencement address provided her with a chance to pontificate in public.

Though short, she stood tall on the platform, bespectacled and berobed in black, as full of "you shoulds" as a hellfire-and-damnation revivalist. She disdained canned joke beginnings. Instead, she described actual examples of slipshod performances by people who took no real pride in how they did what they did that confront us at every level every day.

I thought about the lipstick on Laird's glass and Margaret's towelless bath the night before, as she went on to say that motivation imposed from the outside through threat or through punishment is never effective for long. Motivation that springs from the mind of an individual doing the performing is. Demands of the task itself should dictate discipline. That's what spurs dedicated athletes, artists, and scientists to do what they do. She verbally goaded the graduates to generate their own inner motivation from this day forward.

She acknowledged the discipline and dedication of teachers and parents who had showered them with comforts and advantages of "the good life." But physical enjoyment should never be enough. As alumnae, they shouldn't allow themselves to grow soft. They should work toward sharing the basics of the good life with underfed and unsheltered people wherever in the world they might be.

After the graduates of 1958 received their diplomas, President Wilson presented an honorary doctorate of humane letters degree to the already much degreed Dr. Mead. He cited her as an anthropological trailblazer who, in a time of international ferment and explosive possibilities for space exploration, had dedicated herself to the cause of all humanity.

Everybody involved with the ceremony assembled in Fathers' Hall afterward for a buffet luncheon. Along with all the others we exchanged congratulations and gobbled celebratory snacks until the clock tolled time to head for the airport. "You really surprised me on that breakfast switch," I confided as I bid her adieu. "And that's something. Nobody succeeds in surprising adults very often." Each of the boys shook her hand and thanked her for spicing up their weekend. Miles gave her the carry-on shopping bag that he had brought in with her suitcase from the parking lot.

Obviously pleased with our attention, she turned to smile one more time before she disappeared into the hatch. Whether she saw us or not, we stood at the gate and waved good-bye to her. And to her plane. We watched until it became a gray pinprick in the white sky. The next time she visited us, we would be in California.

5

A PALO ALTO HOUSEGUEST

Have you ever driven down the main street of an about-to-be hometown and wondered what the next few years of your life there would be like? I did as we proceeded down University Avenue in Palo Alto. The kids and I gawked at mansion-sized homes. Who lived behind these carved front doors? Who moved their water sprinklers and looked back at us over flower hedges in the residential area? Might any of those shoppers strolling down the sidewalk in the business section become our acquaintances or friends?

We entered the campus at the end of the street and drove between stately palms leading to a cluster of Spanish-style stucco buildings shingled with curved red tiles. Stanford University. We parked and picked up some maps at an information window. They helped us find our way to the Housing Office in the Inner Quad. "Yes," the older female clerk assured me. "Stanford does indeed have married student housing. But only for males. There haven't been that many female heads of household going on for advanced degrees to merit any other policy," she continued. "If no one in the School of Education mentioned this, perhaps no one thought that you would bring your children with you."

She referred us to a file of assorted rental listings submitted by local residents. We copied down a few phone numbers and addresses. One listing, by G. Bateson, gave "?" as the rent. "?" rent caught my fancy. A male voice with a slight British accent answered my call. He said the rent was a question mark because he wanted his tenant to do some light housework on top of paying him $100 a month (which was over 50 percent less than the other rents on file). Too good to be true. Who knows? Maybe I might follow Margaret's advice for a change and rent after all? The man on the other end of the line made a date with me to come out and look his situation over anytime after 8:00 that evening.

"There's just one detail that should be mentioned before we meet," I cautioned. "I have four kids." News of this magnitude would have discouraged most potential landlords. But not G. Bateson.

"How close can you pack them?" he responded without a pause. The man's rapid rejoinder tickled me. Sight unseen, I liked G. Bateson and his wry humor.

With the evening set up, our next goal was the co-op grocery store whose advertisements we had drooled over for months. The boys wheeled a cart around while I signed up for membership. We picked out a whole ham, two gallons of milk, and their choice of fresh fruit. Then we made a second phone call, this time to another teacher from Saratoga Springs who had moved to Palo Alto earlier in the summer. She had offered us shelter while we house hunted. She had given us instructions for getting to her place from the co-op, and we made a beeline for it. After dinner, we took out the map again and traced the shortest route to the Bateson address.

A tall, slightly stooped middle-aged gentleman emerged from the house as I parked under a tall, slightly stooped palm tree in his driveway. He walked toward the bus to extend a western greeting. Eureka! Before he got close enough to introduce himself, I knew who he was. I had filed snapshots of this man in one of the three drawers reserved for each of her husbands when I cleaned out Margaret's office. G. Bateson was Gregory Bateson. In person! My gosh, why didn't I think of that this afternoon? I asked myself as I resolved not to mention Margaret's name unless he did so first.

The grounds around his home were as orderly as shedding eucalyptus trees permit. The inside looked like the aftermath of an earthquake. Were I in G. Bateson's slippers, I would have denied any connection with the place. "It belongs to a neighbor, a distant relative, somebody, anybody else. I just stopped by to help show it."

But the shambles didn't ruffle him a mite. He led me, matter-of-factly, from disarray to disarray, hurdling hastily piled-up carpets, casually sidestepping piles of undone laundry where a washing machine used to be, and ambling past rumpled beds as though we were tourists in Westminster Abbey.

For want of something polite to say, I mentioned noticing an empty fish tank in nearly every room. "Do you want to buy a fish tank? I latched onto a batch of them through an ad in the *Palo Alto Times*. Got more than I need, actually."

"No, thanks."

We stopped short at the kitchen doorway. My eyes were drawn to a column of ants marching in single file across the linoleum, up the door of the cupboard under the piled-high-with-many-dishes sink, to a puddle encircling an uncapped liqueur bottle. There, some of the ants dallied briefly, resumed formation, continued down the countertop, and out toward the doorway leading to the back porch.

I looked up at him wordlessly. Our eyes met. "This kitchen," he assured me with a gently furrowed smile, "is clean at bedrock."

"At bedrock?" I literally guffawed. In other words, a thousand or more miles beneath this kitchen, and all the other rooms in this disheveled house, all, all of it was crystal clean? At bedrock. The basic basalt. At the outer covering of the inner core of planet earth. What a guy! No wonder a gal like Margaret Mead fell for him. He must have charmed her with incorrigible whimsy.

A teakettle whistled on the stove. He selected a couple of cleanish mugs and stirred up some tea. We moved into the living room to negotiate. I told him that I held a bachelor's and a master's degree in anthropology from Columbia and that I planned to begin doctoral study in education at Stanford. He explained that his second marriage had just broken up and that his soon-to-be ex-spouse was in the hospital. Some of her friends had recently gained entry and carted off the missing furnishings. He wanted me to pick up the pieces, keep the house shipshape, shop, prepare all meals, chauffeur his eight-year-old son to and from the Peninsula School five days a week, and pay him $100 a month.

I hesitated.

"A penny for your thoughts," he urged.

"They cost more than that," I hedged as I weighed the time-consuming realities of fulfilling his assignments and those of my own four dependents, as well as upcoming responsibilities connected with graduate school.

"Are you thinking of what Mrs. Grundy might say?" he fished for comment or commitment.

"Partly," I bit my lip. "Whether there are children around or not, the imaginations of neighbors do burgeon when two unattached singles sleep under the same roof." To be frank, which I wasn't, the possible gossip didn't bother me as much as the prospect of taking on the care and feeding of a third pair of males. A certain fealty to Margaret, whose name was never mentioned, also slowed me down. Aloud, I opted for more time to consider the proposition and suggested that he leave his listing on file in the Housing Office.

Later that evening, I discussed my reservations about Gregory Bateson's offer with my Saratoga Springs friend. She responded by calling the real estate agent who had helped her locate a home earlier in the summer. Mr. Meagher agreed to show me some houses at 9:00 in the morning. The ages of Agnes's five children and my four overlapped. Were I to buy, it would be prudent to find a home in her neighborhood so that our nine transplanted New Yorkers might play together. She lived within walking distance of a library, a park, a shopping center, and elementary, junior high, and senior high schools.

Mr. Meagher, who had once majored in anthropology himself, showed me five houses. I got a hunch when he opened the gate to 871 Rorke Way that this was the one. A few hours later, a clerk in the title company informed me that mortgage payments every thirty days would amount to slightly less than $100. In other words, by buying rather than renting, the same monthly outlay of money granted the boys license to dig up their own backyard and their mother freedom from who knows how many hours of servitude in the Bateson menage.

Some time passed before Margaret heard about her third ex-husband's unintentional influence on my final decision not to take her advice about renting. And some time passed before I learned the story of her involvement in the unusual reception I received at Stanford as well.

In my first week of attendance, one after another, the professor in class after class stopped as he read my name off the roster, frowned, squinted over his glasses and made sure he knew exactly which of us was Patricia Grinager. The ritual embarrassed me. Months later, Dean Quillen's secretary let drop the news that Margaret Mead never wrote a recommendation for me when I asked her to send one to Stanford. She cabled it—from London—on purpose.

She followed a lecture trail to England almost as often as anywhere else. Anthropology is a vocation that mixes well with the avocations of its more footloose practitioners. Wherever she went, she visited far-flung relatives and friends.

The friendly, positive responses of ordinary people toward her and her works outnumbered instances of approval from her professional peers. She got her strokes from folks. I remember her saying, "I like to have my professional experiences buried deep in a personal context." Whenever she visited us, I watched her daily reinforce the statement.

The presence of her mother's nonagenarian sister, Fanny Fogg McMaster, and her only brother, Prof. Richard Ramsay Mead, in the Los Angeles area guaranteed that she would be lecturing in California as often as feasible. She was never long on advance warning. After not having heard from her for months, I'd pick up the receiver on the telephone late one night and break in on an announcement already under way. "Pat, I'm arriving on flight so and so tomorrow at such and such a time. Will you meet me?" And then would follow a simple-sounding but unbelievably time-consuming second request like, "And bring along Elizabeth Barrett Browning's *Sonnets from the Portuguese* and Sara Teasdale's poems too."

Klunk.

Klunk plummets a heretofore competent person into helplessness. Once she disconnected the line, I couldn't protest. I stood speechless. Immobilized. When I recovered enough to move at all, I tried locating Elizabeth Barrett Browning's and Sara Teasdale's long-out-of-print poetry books after the hour libraries and bookstores customarily close. Margaret Mead could have supplied people who dream up scavenger hunts with teasers like that one every hour, on the hour. They bubbled up out of her as does CO_2 in mineral springs. She never gave me time to answer back, so I scampered around filling her requests like a kid chasing the rainbow with a sky hook.

I usually met her at the airport in a tired state. Her eyes shifted anxiously from face to face as she disembarked. She smiled with relief when they landed on someone she knew. She usually carried her coat or cape ("it's easier"), as well as the inevitable shopping bag full of survival items should her luggage go astray. She almost always ducked into the first phone booth—whether in the middle of a sentence or not—to get a few quick calls out of the way while her plane unloaded. No use wasting perfectly good minutes standing around waiting at a baggage carousel.

Once we walked together through the gate at 871 Rorke Way in Palo Alto, Margaret was home again. Ours was one of her several homes. Like a participant–observer in the field, she dipped into the rhythm of our lives and blended in as an instant family member. She spoke to each boy relevantly and by name. She didn't take up a lot of space, make unfamiliar noises, or hog the bathroom. She ate whatever we ate and with gusto. She rarely refused seconds, either liquid or solid.

"I don't dare take seconds anymore," I kept saying. "I've simply got to lose some weight."

"Don't," she advised. "When you mature, your organs get used to being in a certain spot. I went on a fish and cucumber diet and lost twenty-eight pounds once and got a fallen womb out of it."

"I read that those guys who'll go into outer space won't have any weight when they're up there," Laird chimed in.

"Weightlessness wouldn't bother me," Margaret helped herself to more scalloped potatoes and ham.

She always brought along some current topic on which to expound at mealtimes, be it flying saucers or space travel. "We're getting ready to leave the planet in person, you know," she predicted in one of her earliest visits to us in California. "It took the past five hundred years for human beings to get around the world. We thought the world was big, but space travel will make it small. Before you boys are grandfathers, we'll be venturing to outposts in the universe just as Prince Henry the Navigator and his men once explored planet Earth."

She put down her salad fork. "Five thousand years ago, a few tribes learned to band together, live with the same rules, and eat the same kind of food. One hundred years more and space travel will be as commonplace as my flying out here from New York City."

She chewed pensively on a bit of buttered banana bread. "I hope space travel enables everybody everywhere to realize finally that we are not so much Americans or Arapesh, whites or nonwhites, as we are *Earthlings.* We breathe Earth's air. We eat Earth's food. We're held onto the same star by Earth's gravitational forces. We're Earth's people, every one."

With eyes as round as the yolks on sunnyside-up eggs, the boys watched her. They swallowed her every word, whole. "Would you go to the moon?" Neal asked.

"I wouldn't stop at the moon," she confessed. "I'm so curious, I'd go right on by to see whether Venus is really clothed in gasses."

"Margaret Mead comes to visit you? And your mother goes to Stanford?" a schoolmate with whom Kent shared accounts of these conversations asked. "You must be rich."

"You can be rich or poor and go to Stanford and have Margaret Mead come to visit," I told Kent as I scraped an exploded sweet potato from the oven just before dinner late one afternoon. "Three guesses. Which do you think we are?"

"What's rich?" Kent wondered aloud, as we worked in the kitchen. "What's poor?" It was his turn to set the table.

"I'd say you live quite comfortably on the jagged edges of an economic frontier," Margaret joked from her perch in the combination living and dining room.

Kent carried a tray full of dishes through the large archway separating the kitchen area from where Margaret relaxed with her girdle off and her feet up, awaiting dinner. She watched him equip six places with plates, napkins, and silverware.

"You've got it right," I cut the remaining potatoes in half because now we had less than one apiece. "We live from hand to mouth, from month to month, but we mostly manage."

"Luther and I lived like this in our own graduate student days in the early twenties."

"I almost forgot. That's right. You were a married student once yourself." I put some water on for tea. "An experience like graduate school shows us how little we can live on. Were I to have to choose between having all the c-e-n-t-s or s-e-n-s-e I needed in life, I'd choose s-e-n-s-e every time."

Margaret got up and walked back to my bedroom–study. She usually headquartered in my room during her visits. She appreciated the use of a typewriter and didn't mind sleeping on a cot that doubled as a davenport by day.

Many a morning I knocked on the study door to awaken her. Then I'd peek in to make sure she'd heard. I never caught her asleep. There she sat, propped up against pillows, with an old-fashioned duster cap over her curls, quietly correcting examination blue books, so as to allow everyone else in her instant household the last precious moment of undisturbed sleep.

"Breakfast will be ready in fourteen and a half minutes, and we've got to head for the campus in thirty-three. Can you make it?"

She put the exams aside. "Okay."

"My idea of heaven," she hinted, when she learned about the two fig trees in the front yard, "is figs and cream for breakfast." She liked to catch the morning news. The boys and I paid less attention to these broadcasts during her visits than to her. We shared amused glances with each other as we listened to her talk back to newscasters on one-way television.

"Why help India?" I remember she harrumphed when that subcontinent suffered a border dispute with China in 1959. "China's going to take over the leadership in Asia anyway."

Early in the summer quarter of 1960, the Ford Foundation Secondary Education Project staged an invitational conference at the School of Education at Stanford. It was billed as The High School and the American Public: A Search for Quality. Faculty invited a prominent social scientist, a professional educator, and a layman to share ideas with high school teachers on this topic. Each of three major addresses was to be interspersed with small discussion groups. The trio of speakers was to appear together in a panel presentation in a grand finale late in the afternoon of the second day. The planning committee asked Margaret Mead to lecture first and from a social scientist's point of view. She was scheduled to speak Tuesday evening, July 12, in Cubberly Hall on the Stanford campus just outside of Palo Alto.

Whenever possible, she liked to give at least two speeches with a similar theme. Her booking agent arranged for a luncheon talk on the same day at San Francisco State College. Her title was "American Education on the Changing World Scene."

She agreed to stay a day beyond the conference in order to sit before TV cameras at Station KPIX in San Francisco to tape a program for a Stanford-sponsored series called *Career*. She was to discuss the opportunities for a woman in society, marriage, and a career, and the importance of "the family," with four Stanford undergraduates. She planned to go to the airport directly from the studio for a flying visit to friends and relatives in central and southern California.

She informed me of my part in these activities in a two-page letter mailed twelve days before they were to begin. She enclosed copies of her correspondence to and from Stanford, San Francisco State College, the producer of the *Career* series, and Felix Keesing, a senior professor in the Department of Anthropology, who evidently invited her to stay with them. She replied:

> I have decided that the felicitous thing for me to do is to put the burden of my crippled state and all the errand running and toting involved therein, onto the shoulders of my former assistant, Patricia Grinager, and all her little boys. As I am coming out primarily as a guest of the Department of Education at Stanford, it will be convenient for Pat to engineer the technical details of my life. She will know what my compulsory schedule is and will be able to make such plans as you both would like, so that we have a real visit together while I am there.
>
> I know that you would both surround me with tender loving care, but I think that on the whole, it's wasteful to have things that can be done well by little boys, done by either of you!
>
> [In other words, her "former assistant" was to be not only the hostess and chauffeur for her San Francisco Bay area interlude but also coordinator of whatever transpired between her arrival and her departure. She expected me to set up a time and a place for separate and private two- to three-hour meetings with fellow professionals, Alex Bavelas, and the Felix Keesings. She asked me to "cope" with fitting these "intellectual exchanges" in between the time demands of the Cubberly Conference, at least one cocktail gathering, two dinners, and a reception.]
>
> And, also, I'd better tell you the state of my ankle. Though I am out of a cast, the bone is not yet healed and I get around in a wheelchair and on crutches. I'll bring my own wheelchair with me. I suppose you'll need the "minibus," so we will have room for my wheelchair. It folds up. In regard to my mobility, I do not want to walk on crutches down long halls or in airports and I need to sit in the wheelchair when lecturing or at formal dinners, if possible. I can go up and down short flights of stairs with relative ease now.

Her letter stopped me short. It arrived on the first day of the most concentrated session of the school year. I had accepted an acting instructorship for one course during summer school and had registered for two others. I knew that the cable she sent on my behalf two years previously made my current schedule possible. Now she was coming to the School of Education at Stanford. Margaret Mead: anthropologist–educator whose classroom was the world. She selected me to attend to the details of her highly visible four-day stay. On top of making all the connections, she would have to be wheeled everywhere—from airport, to car, to bed, to bath, to conference hall. No, I couldn't turn her down. Unexpected assignments like these test our mettle, even though we know full well that they're more laden with labor than laced with glory.

To perfect our taxi service while she would be with us, the boys removed the backseat from the microbus and replaced it with an upholstered chair from our living room. Laird cleared off space above the motor to accommodate her wheelchair and the crutches. Neal made sure there were small pillows within arm's reach to help make her back more comfortable. Miles thought about a footstool for resting her legs in transit and diminishing the number of times she might bump her head getting into or out of the bus. "If I didn't know when you bought this car," she gloated, as she sat resplendent on a cushioned throne in her mobile sitting room, "I'd swear you got it just for this visit."

A World War II roommate whom Margaret called GiGi met her at the airport late Monday, July 11, and took her to the luncheon at San Francisco State College by noon the next day. Margaret had requested that both GiGi and P.G. be invited to that luncheon. GiGi was to get her there, eat, and listen. I was to eat, listen, and take her back to Stanford. If all went according to plan, she and I would be on the highway by 3:25 at the latest and heading for a 4:30 cocktail party twenty-nine miles down the road. It was the first of a flurry of evening events. Dinner, her speech, and a reception at the dean's home would follow before I pushed her wheelchair through the home gate around 12:00 a.m.

My own midmorning class prevented my leaving Stanford in time to eat or to listen to more than the last half of her San Francisco State College speech. I remember frowning over the approach to the city from the south. Nothing looked familiar. All the old signs were down. Buildings I used as landmarks had been razed or removed. What was once a street was in the throes of becoming a superhighway.

When I tackled the route again with her in tow three hours later, early commuters clogged the one available lane, bumper to bumper. In no time at all, I didn't know where we were. There was no room to turn off, no place to ask, no time to lose. Margaret watched me search for clues to the right, to the left, and back to the right again. She read my worried expression in the rearview mirror and commented about it.

"I don't want to alarm you," I apologized, "but we could be lost. We're traveling at a snail's pace, as you know, and I have no idea if it's even in the right direction. If we are still heading south after that last detour, okay. But if we are going north, there's no way in hell we'll make any cocktail party by 4:30."

"You're doing the best you can," she calmed me. "Relax and don't worry another minute. Nobody will be able to do a thing until we get there. They'll just have to wait for us." A smile formed despite my despair.

In the next half hour, I crashed into the discovery that Margaret Mead didn't drive. Her arms were too short. Her lack of experience at the controls of a car left her absolutely useless for judging distances in traffic. Once we squeezed through the San Francisco bottleneck, she wasn't able to tell me when or whether I could change lanes.

As a result, I made all the driving decisions, solo, while she described her daughter's wedding five weeks before on June 4, 1960. Weddings are reunions in more ways than one. Lifetime friends came, including a carload from Doylestown, Pennsylvania, where she graduated from high school forty-two years ago. Cathy married Barkev Kassarjian, an Armenian whom she met at Harvard while both of them studied toward their doctorates. She designed her own high-necked, long-sleeved wedding gown. Godmother Marie Eichelberger helped whipstitch parting seams back together hours before the ceremony. Cathy's father, Gregory Bateson, flew from California to give the bride away. He brought his son, Cathy's half-brother, John, who sat beside Margaret during the ceremony. Cathy walked into the church with a dove on her wrist. The wedding couple cut the four-tiered cake with a sword.

All of this gushed out as she glowingly explained the context of each of at least twenty-five wedding pictures which she handed over my shoulder, one by one. "I hope they have enough sense not to have any children right away," she remarked as she stuffed the last photo into an envelope. "I want Cathy to concentrate on her career first." She snapped the envelope shut with a rubber band.

"Not every bride has someone like you in the background watching out for her career," I put my thoughts into words.

"Which reminds me," she interrupted, "is there anyone to whom you'd like me to put in a good word for you while I'm out here?"

"Not really. Do what comes naturally as occasion presents. I'm old enough to be the twin sister of half this faculty out here and I think they're on my side already."

When we got as far as Palo Alto, we stopped off at 871 to freshen up and unload her bags. She would be much too taken up with "education's show" this trip, but she did think it wise to make at least a roundabout attempt to contact Gregory Bateson. This soon after the wedding, she didn't want to talk to him particularly, nor did she want him to feel slighted. She figured it was late enough for him to have left his office for the day. So, at her request, I phoned a number she provided to relay a dutiful greeting to him through his secretary.

We made a belated appearance for predinner cocktails. I suffered a coordinator's qualms over her reason for being at Stanford when I watched her down the third glassful. But I needn't have. After dinner and after Dean Quillan introduced her, she sat in her wheelchair and addressed the assembled multitude with absolute fluidity.

Her opening sent a mild shock wave down the rows. "Why should our high schools be terminal?" she asked, as she proceeded to say that our society provides no place for nonacademically inclined teenagers to go after high school unless they get into trouble. Somehow, we must erase that period of nondirection "between high school and age twenty-one." She talked to conferees as casually as if she were sitting across a table from each one.

"Whatever we decide to do will affect young people everywhere. Whether we bargain for it or not, our system of education is on display to the world. Other educators may not copy what they see us try, but they watch us. We don't want them to look at us and laugh.

"Our most stupid one-hundred-year-old mistake," this elder stateswoman scolded, "is the way we give numbers precedence over people. Year after year, we automatically bunch students together who have nothing else in common except that they happen to be the same age; the same number. All twelve-year-olds in one classroom; all thirteen-year-olds in another, and so on."

"Whether we like it or not, we'd better pay attention to her. She's not always easy to take, but her thinking is at least fifty years ahead of the rest of us," I overhead a contributor to an earlier Cubberly Conference tell the foreign student who sat between us.

"In the last century, we've learned about individual differences, but we've ignored them," she declared. "Bunching children together who do not like school and who have no desire to learn is not providing for individual differences. Nor is separating the gifted and treating them as though they're different from everybody else. And our calling a six- or sixteen-year-old chronologically 'ready' for something or other assumes no individual differences. Like it or not, we're still stuck with the same numerical categories that we were using before anybody ever heard of individual differences.

"In this numbering system, the law forces nonachievers to stay in school marking time. Consciously or unconsciously, they brand themselves as inferior and drop out the minute they turn sixteen. Another number. Everybody knows that the long-term results are negative for them; disastrous and expensive for society. We have no solution for what to do about our dropouts and nonachievers, and we don't seem to be doing much to find one.

"If high schools are what society does for adolescents, why don't we turn high schools into places where adolescents learn to make useful contributions to society?" She bared her teeth and glared at her audience. It was a warm evening. She reached for a glass of water with one hand and brushed back moist scraggles of hair with the other. The student next to me put down his pen and stretched the fingers of his writing hand. "She talks like she writes," he said, "witty, at times caustic and, in all, profound."

"If we really believe in individual differences," she continued, "we should put our money where our mouth is and transform high schools into community educational centers. Open the doors democratically wide and let anybody develop what talents they have for the purpose of using them. It would be a real continuum of education with no final ends, no artificial divisions. The choice of subjects would develop individual differences and foster an appreciation of them. By reorganizing high schools according to interests and talents, anyone with the basic three Rs, from puberty through adulthood to old age, would be welcome to drop in or drop by at any time, and for any length of time, to learn something. How about that? Education for development rather than ageism? Dropins rather than dropouts. Wouldn't both the long- and the short-term results of community educational centers affect society positively?

"Think the situation over," she challenged those who claimed to be concerned about improving the quality of American public education. "Inside, high schools are filled with teenagers who don't want to be there. Outside, they're surrounded by potential students of more mature years who'd give their eyeteeth to be there. How much peripheral vision does it take to see that our finest educational structures need be no more terminal than we, the so-called educators, blindly keep them?"

"The idea of making schools a type of community center impresses me most of all," the student at my elbow said as the audience began to disperse. "I'm going to take her idea back home to Nigeria. I hope it finds fertile soil to grow there as my people create an educational system."

I reported this comment to her and, if anything, it whetted her appetite for more. A reception, two speeches, two interviews, a panel presentation, and a dinner with Stanford's anthropologists later, she asked if she might accompany me to my comparative education class at 10:00 a.m. on her last morning.

"I promise not to disrupt it," she volunteered.

We made plans to leave for the taping of the *Career* program and thence to the airport immediately after. In the interests of time, I packed a lunch to eat in the car en route.

A rustle of excitement greeted us as I wheeled her into class ahead of me. The students were all West Coast high school teachers attending summer school to obtain their master's degree. Before beginning the lecture scheduled for that day, I invited them to share what they probably said or thought on their way home from her speech on the first night of the conference.

Although it was not completely in character, Margaret sat quietly on the speakers platform while the teacher–students fired remarks her way. Nobody stopped their flow.

"Your views surprised me, but that made them all the more worthwhile."

"Obviously, you don't regard the search for excellence as purely academic and intellectual. I liked the fact that you're not as hung up on producing more and better nuclear physicists and rocket designers as you are in discovering and encouraging the full spectrum of talents and abilities in everybody—whether they're thirteen or 103."

"I don't know. I think your idea is too revolutionary. It sounds good, theoretically, but I doubt if it would work in practice."

"It's idealistic. Something to strive for."

"I found the concept of the high school as a major social institution repulsive. It reminded me of Soviet state-run nurseries. It would just give the government more power, another chance to step in and take over."

"Your speech shook me up. I had a real twinge of conscience when you called the school a place where the ignorant teach the ignorant; a place where the ignorant come to be taught what they already know."

"We need shaking up. You gave me an impression of being an independent thinker. You poked fun at us without being irritating. It was all constructive criticism."

"You found humor in the faults of our school system which, in turn, should motivate us to think constructively about the future."

"Who copied from whom? Your style is the same as Pat's."

"You did a nice job of being provocative. I kept asking myself why you don't develop your comments into a nightclub monologue. You'd reach a whole new audience and get thousands of dollars per week. Some comics need replacing."

"Your loaded remarks came so fast they lost their punch after a while."

"Your just sitting there and being yourself did not fit my preconception of what you'd be like at all. Thank goodness. For my money, you can stand beside Mark Twain as one of the best humorists of our time."

"The impact of your lecture was due, in part, to your age, sex, and reputation. I kept wondering where your sources came from. Whether your remarks were opinions or facts."

"The opinions of independent thinkers are facts, distilled."

"I think an anthropologist has to be very broad-minded. They must have a difficult time trying to impress the values of democracy on all the people all at once."

"Your timing, your inflections, and your total lack of reference to any notes, sold me. I'd come to see and hear you again. Anytime."

"Let's quit while I'm ahead," she signaled me to take over even as she relished every bit of audience feedback. I delivered a hurried lecture on leisure during the last of the fifty-minute class hour. Then we departed posthaste for a broadcasting studio in San Francisco.

At KPIX, she talked with Stanford students before TV cameras for almost two hours. They discussed contemporary career opportunities for women. She feared for the younger members of her sex who either dropped out of college or delayed registering in order to help their males through, be they sweethearts, husbands, or brothers.

On our dash to the airport, she reported warning young women listeners that, for all their well-intentioned optimism, statistics nevertheless revealed that most marriages in which the wife supports her husband through college end up in divorce. The husband pockets the income potential of a degree. The wife, in contrast, is left with lost years, shattered hopes, a few kids, and no chances for the position she might have merited had she put some of her efforts toward a degree with her own name on it.

"The further along in graduate school I get, the more often I'm the only woman in the class. Mostly, women drop out so that their husbands can stay in," I said. "I've also noticed how few blacks are in graduate school at Stanford, compared to the numbers at Columbia. I've asked about it and have been told that they don't apply."

"They don't apply because they know they're going to be turned down. The very fact we're talking about it indicates that this too will change." She leaned back and shut her eyes.

All that remained of her stay was the airport send-off. In four days, we had logged almost three hundred miles in short trips and had talked to at least that many people. Drained of my usual zip, I welcomed having a legitimate excuse to park in a spot close to the terminal reserved for handicapped. It meant a shorter distance to push the wheelchair.

She had her ticket. We checked her bag. She wanted to pick up some paperback whodunits, so we stopped at a newspaper and magazine stand. "I can't believe you read these things," I doubted aloud, as we browsed through shelves of brightly titled murder mysteries. "I consider my eyesight too precious to spend on so-called light reading. I guess I automatically assumed it was the same with you, too."

"My mother's reading choices were as goal oriented as yours, Pat, but my father liked whodunits. I can't remember if they were called that then, but his enjoyment of them infected me. I've been more or less addicted to them since childhood. I buy them by the handful and can race through one in an hour."

"At that rate," I caught myself mothering her, "you'll have enough to read, but I don't feel at all good about your being up there in a plane and not able to ambulate on your own."

She pulled some money out of her purse and reached up to pay for five paperbacks. "Don't worry, Pat. I'll sit beside someone who has waited all his life to talk to me. I'll be well taken care of. The time will go fast."

I shoved her purchases into her now bulging shopping bag and glanced up in time to catch the clerk's eyes glaze over with the look of a cocker spaniel in love. She recognized her customer as someone she had seen on TV. Too enterprising a businessperson to let an opportunity go by, she handed Margaret a copy of the latest *New Yorker* magazine and asked her to autograph it for her daughter, Alfereda. "She's sixteen today," the woman said. "won't you write your name on this cover? My daughter won't believe I had you for a customer—someone on TV!"

"What's Alfereda's last name?" Margaret removed the cap from the clerk's ballpoint pen.

"Foote, with an e," the girl's mother replied.

As Margaret scribbled something on the *New Yorker* cover, the woman acknowledged her customer's condition. "I hope your injury is not serious," she empathized. "How are you feeling?"

"Terrrrrrrible," Margaret muttered, as she returned pen and magazine and then zoomed down the corridor. As I took off after my wheelchaired whirlwind, I heard the mother moan, "Oh, no! She didn't give me her autograph! She didn't write her name down! She wrote Alfereda's!"

In no time at all, Margaret rose from the wheelchair to a walking stick. A taxi delivered her to the sidewalk at the edge of our front yard on April 4, 1963. The gate banged shut and the clip, clip, clip of wood on concrete broke the late morning stillness. I looked out to see Margaret stomping up our inner walkway, bareheaded, with cape and curls flying. She held on to a forked stick that reached to her eyebrows. It could have been a branch someone sawed off an old tree. The bark was still on it. She stalked in through the open door and down the hall for the bathroom, visually checking out each bedroom as she passed. "Looks awfully clean for this early in the day."

"I did dust again, which I wouldn't have done if you weren't coming," I admitted.

We chatted over a brunch of fruit salad, sandwiches, and herb tea. The sun shone. The birds warbled. The flowers in the patio bobbed obligingly in a slight breeze. All was indeed right with our little world. It didn't surprise me that she preferred staying with friends or relatives to bunking alone in a motel or hotel whenever she hit the lecture trail. "How long have you been using a cane?" I asked.

"It's not a cane," she corrected me, "I wouldn't have one of the things. A cane forces you to lean and look down. I prefer to stand straight and look ahead. What I've got is a shepherd's crook."

"A shepherd's crook?" I repeated. "Where on earth did you get a hold of something like that?"

"I bought it in a shop in London."

"Hmmm," I wondered as I passed her a plate of home-cured bacon. "London? How could a store in one of the largest cities in the world stay in business selling shepherd's crooks, for gosh sakes?" I frowned as though the solution to my next query couldn't possibly exist. "Who would ever buy one of the things?"

"Shepherds," she barked.

I shrugged my shoulders. "Well, I never thought of it before, but I suppose even shepherds manage to straggle into town every now and then."

She outlined her schedule for the next two days. An informal talk to the Associated Women Students at Stanford at 2:15. Return to 871 before dinner for a short nap and a chance to rest her leg. A speech, "Creative Intelligence in Women," for the Institute of Personality Assessment at the Unitarian Church in San Francisco at 8:00 p.m. Talk and lunch with Gregory Bateson at the Veterans' Hospital in Menlo Park at 10:00 the next morning; a visit to Erik Erikson in nearby Los Altos at 2:00. And last, a late afternoon flight to the Monterey Peninsula where friend Barbara Heath would be waiting.

This was a typical stop. Her highly packed public appearances and private appointments necessitated the bing! bing! bing! synchronization of community fireworks at dusk on the Fourth of July.

During dinner, she challenged the brothers to put their heads together and devise a way to suspend the blankets over her feet. She wanted the warmth, but her toes were uncomfortably sensitive to the weight of coverlets lately.

It was immediately apparent that the tweedy director of the Institute for Personality Assessment had not paid enough attention to the information blurb sent out from her office. As academicians are likely to do in such circumstances, he created much palaver to cover up the oversight.

"Who's come here to give the speech anyway?" Margaret stage whispered. "I hate long-winded introductions."

As with her phone conversations, she jumped into her topic as soon as he gave her a chance. "Men have had the world to be creative in," she declared. "All women have ever had has been their own bodies. Women go to medical doctors for help on taking care of their bodies most of their lives. Once the pediatrician finishes with them as toddlers, most men don't go to the doctor again until they see a urologist, and then it's too late."

I squirmed in my seat. She was talking directly to me.

"Women don't try to change the world but rather to watch and to look and to listen and to wait and to observe it. That's why they make such good anthropologists."

She denied that the United States is a matriarchal society. "Women take their husband's names. They live in husband-chosen places. They work as hard at the same job for half the pay. I don't call that matriarchal at all.

"Too many women buy the phony bargain of being a satellite to their men. Lots of men don't want satellites; they're boring.

"One of women's biggest problems comes from the fact that they don't know how to cooperate with other women. That's why they get married so early. They could be a lot more productive in their careers if they learned to cooperate with each other as women."

She paused to sip from her water glass long enough to let the impact of her message seep in. "Women helping women, that's the way to step up women's creativity! I ought to know. Other women have worked with me all of my life."

At the end of her speech, she stood beside a podium almost as tall as she and gripped her shepherd's crook. Her eyes glistened as she beamed her big, square smile out over the mostly female members of her audience. Their applause reverberated to the rafters. After a while, she walked toward the end of the stage. I ran toward her with cape and purse.

Women who came to hear about their creative potential surged behind me. They encircled us. Awakening consciousness of their developing identities as persons stirred questions and comments beyond counting. I stood at her elbow, watching and listening as she held court.

An hour after the time for which she had been hired to talk, the janitor approached me to say that he wanted to go home. As soon as I could insert his message between fast-flying questions and answers, I did so, but she brushed me aside. "When I'm ready to go, tell him I'll let him know."

A half hour passed and the caretaker sidled up to me again. He couldn't close the place until she left. I relayed his message. She shrugged and said nothing.

I looked down at her. In my mind's eye, I saw the same diminutive and doughty fieldworker who labored with comparable disdain of packaged time among eight different groups of Pacific Islanders. She watched the janitor approach me for the third time. She scowled at him and growled impatiently, "Pat, tell that man I'm going on until the questions exhaust themselves. I can't stand men who want to turn off the lights and go home."

No matter how tired she got or how long it took, Missy Makarit stayed with a job to the finish. She expected janitors and people like me to follow suit. Janitors and friends sometimes criticized her, yes, but never for apathy. Or laziness.

When we finally departed shortly before midnight, a forty-five minute drive lay between us and 871 Rorke Way.

Light-sleeping, pajama-clad Laird jumped from the davenport in the living room to open the front door. He led us into his bedroom where he demonstrated a Rube Goldberg contraption he'd rigged up over the foot of his cot. Margaret slept in Laird's room that night where a pulley, some rope, and a couple of four-inch heavy-gauge safety pins kept the weight of his blankets off her toes.

"No wonder I like visiting here," she complimented us over figs and cream in the morning. "Where else could I find four young men so eager to wait on me?" The boys disappeared to school.

She went into the study to fast peck a letter on my typewriter and close her suitcase. I cleared the breakfast table and turned on the faucet so that the dishes would soak while I took her to Menlo Park for her appointment with ex-husband Gregory Bateson. When she joined me at the sink, she removed her spectacles and sloshed them around in the hot, soapy dishwater.

"I don't have to be young," she took down a tea towel that hung on a rack above eye level, "and I don't have to be beautiful." She held her glasses up to the light and squinted through them for a final check, "but Gregory does like my glasses cleaned off."

We left the house in time to arrive at the Veterans Hospital at 10:00 a.m. sharp. While she visited with Gregory, I planned to set up a card table in the back of the bus. Then when she met with her friend Erik Erikson between the end of her lunch with Gregory and our 5:00 p.m. dash to the airport in San Francisco, the card table would make a sturdy surface on which to do my income taxes.

Gregory Bateson and Margaret Mead were sitting together on a bench on the grounds of the Veterans Hospital where he researched schizophrenia when I returned shortly before 2:00 p.m. They walked over to the driver's window. She reminded him that I was one of those with whom he'd considered sharing his house five years earlier. He smiled without opening his mouth. They walked around to the passenger side. He opened the door. A microbus rides high, and she bumped her head as she boarded. It stung and she rubbed the swelling sheepishly.

A kiss would ease the ouch, I thought, but none was forthcoming, for either the bump or the good-bye. He handed her some of his most recent reprints, smiled again, and walked away. We watched him trudge along toward the hospital buildings and then I turned on the ignition. "Gregory is much more cooperative now that he has remarried. His third wife is good for him," Margaret commented as she leafed through the reprints he'd given her. "I only lost my temper once," she reviewed the high points of their morning together, "and that was when he didn't know the anthropological work that's been carried on in Bali since we were there."

I sideswiped one of those big trees that stick out into so many streets in conservation-minded hamlets like Palo Alto. "I like the way you drive, but I don't feel safe at all when Gregory's at the wheel. I went with him when we drove over to El Camino to buy the fish we had for lunch. He's never had an accident, but he takes everybody's life in his hands when he drives. You and he both go lickety-split, but you take fewer chances."

As we approached Los Altos, she brought me up-to-date on the daughter she and Gregory parented. "Cathy's the apple of her adviser's eye," she boasted. "She got her dissertation in two days early. She already has a job for next year writing a basic text on Arabic. Her husband's been teaching part-time, so he's not got his doctorate yet. Cathy and Barkev like Boston and I think they'll stay there."

She opened her purse to rummage around for the directions to Erik Erikson's house. "Erik's been writing another book during his stay at the Ford Behavioral Center this year," she looked over at me as she unfolded a hand-drawn map. "When they leave here, he and Jean plan to go to India."

I volunteered some local lore that she might not have otherwise heard. "People around here refer to the Ford Center as the think tank," I said. "They say it's full of scholars enjoying 'the leisure of the theory class.'"

"I've been invited to come to the center myself," she confided, "but I'm not going to accept. It's too near Gregory. When we were married, he objected to being referred to as 'Mr. Margaret Mead.' I'm sure he and his new wife would appreciate his being called the 'ex-Mr. Margaret Mead' even less."

We were closing in on the general area of the house we sought. I asked her to read her directions aloud slowly as we came to and passed each landmark in Erik Erikson's instructions. "These directions aren't complete enough," she complained. "I can't understand it. Before he was a psychoanalyst, Erik was a Raphael in Vienna. His strong visual acuity should have given him a better sense of direction than this." She frowned at her watch. "We don't have time to drive around in circles."

"It's easy to get lost in Los Altos." I remembered every time I'd been there before. "The roads confuse. They curl around, up hill and down dale with little offshoots that aren't even labeled sometimes. All we can do is have faith and keep on keepin' on."

She must have told him she'd arrive in a microbus. After a series of left turns, right turns, and windings around, we spotted him. He waved to us from beside the road. As soon as I braked to a halt, Margaret hopped out and hurried toward his front door—clip, clip, clip.

He hesitated long enough to invite me to come in, too.

"No, thanks," I declined. "Go ahead and enjoy your visit. I've got to stay here in the bus and struggle with taxes."

He walked toward the house. Minutes later, I looked up and into the kindly eyes of Erik Erikson shining out from under his halo of frizzy white hair. "Come and work inside," he said. "I've cleared off my desk for you. It has more space than your card table. You won't bother anybody. We're on the patio."

I packed the papers into a briefcase and followed him. He brought me a glass of cranberry juice and gently shut the door of his study so that I might be able to work free from distraction. His thoughtfulness softened me so much I lost the mood for tackling a tax report. I walked along the shelves of books in his study instead. I picked out his own *Childhood and Society* and was deeply engrossed in it when Margaret opened the door at 4:45. We bid him a hasty good-bye. "That man's got one of the most outstanding minds of anyone in the twentieth century," she praised Erik Erikson as we drove away.

"Did you know he acknowledged your helpfulness in the preface to *Child and Society*? He said something like, 'It would be impossible to itemize my overall indebtedness to Margaret Mead.'"

"He should have," she pawed through her purse for a handkerchief. "I helped translate at least twenty versions of it. He has such a strong background in Latin and Greek that he made up words that weren't in the dictionary. Perfectly fascinating."

We talked about how important it is to encourage children to gain experience in writing; in feeling at ease with putting one word after another on pieces of paper. As a child, she had written plays under her mother's watchful eye. As soon as her own daughter could wield a pencil, Margaret encouraged Cathy's making up stories and writing down dreams.

"Yes. I remember filing some of Cathy's accounts of dreams and family happenings when I cleaned out your office," I replied.

"Rhoda and I have got her son, Daniel, involved in quite a writing project too," she disclosed. She went on to explain that Daniel was solving the very normal difficulty of corresponding with his absentee father, Alfred Metraux of UNESCO's Department of Social Science in Paris, by putting out a monthly newsletter. Daniel named his paper 'The Waverly Times' and filled it with a boy's reports of personal, local, national, and even international news. He duplicated it in her office at the Museum. He was succeeding so well that relatives and friends on both sides of the Atlantic regularly received copies.

"How much does he charge for a subscription?"

"A dollar for ten issues per year and that's very reasonable when you consider that it includes postage."

When she walked down the ramp to her plane, Margaret carried a check made out to Master Daniel Metraux to pay for my first subscription to "The Waverly Times." I wonder if Daniel realizes what a crackerjack saleslady he's got in her, I thought as I subtracted a buck from the balance in my checkbook.

Some months later, at the end of the first week in December 1963, I answered the phone and recognized Margaret's voice. "Pat, I'm in Davis. Can you come and get me? I'll be through here at 2:00. I'm in an apartment building next to the campus sculpture garden."

I wished I hadn't heard the phone. Midmorning and minutes before the ring, I had spread the notes for the rest of the first chapter of the dissertation across my desk. I thoroughly intended to spend the entire afternoon and the next day finishing it. The last thing I wanted to do was to slide those papers under cover, prepare the house for company, and drive God knows how far, round-trip, to pick up an unexpected house guest.

I remember asking the walls if she thought I existed for her convenience; if she assumed I had nothing else to do but stand at attention and wait for her summonses. Most women spend their lives putting their wishes second to those of another person, whether husband, lover, parent, or child. What was unique about this situation was that one woman, myself, kept putting my own wishes second to those of an unrelated other woman, Margaret Mead. When I wasn't too busy otherwise, I didn't mind. My resentfulness toward visits related to work. The more some big project like a dissertation absorbed me, the less I welcomed interruptions from anybody else, mortal or spiritual.

But how about Margaret Mead? She was . . . Margaret Mead. Mortal and spiritual? She had grown used to my instantaneous availability and acted as though she expected it. Probably even took it for granted. Where did all this put the real me? My prior plans didn't have a chance in such a scheme of things. How many other persons in Margaret's life found themselves similarly afflicted? Could this condition have anything to do with her third husband's being an author of a theory about the double binds people get into when they're faced with conflicting alternatives?

I did and didn't want to spend the weekend away from the dissertation-to-be. But what could I do now? She hadn't given me a phone number. I couldn't call her back. Would it be humane to leave a woman of her age and stature stranded near a sculpture garden? If she hadn't helped me along the way, would I even have a dissertation to do?

I'd compromise. Leave the chapters spread out in my study and assign her to Laird's room, where she slept last time. Maybe her toes still hurt and she'd like that better anyway. I stripped his bed, dressed it in clean sheets, and piled his blankets near the door to put them on a rush order at the neighborhood cleaners. I could pick them up when I returned with Margaret.

I pulled a pot roast out of the freezer, stuck the frozen hulk in a Dutch oven, doused it with vinegar and spices, and turned the heat on low. I left a note to the kids to put carrots, rutabagas, and onions into the simmering stew at staggered intervals after school. They knew they could nibble at it if we were late and hunger overtook them. Hopefully, they'd leave enough so that we had something hot on our arrival.

I asked Laird to please keep his dog off the clean sheets on his cot and to gird himself for sleeping on the davenport in the living room.

I didn't take any time out to eat a late breakfast or look at a map. I'd never been to Davis, but I vaguely remembered seeing signs for it on the way to Sacramento. And I knew the way to Sacramento.

Thirty miles from my starting point, and at least ten miles further than I thought I would have to go in the first place, I leaned out of the microbus and hollered to a toll booth attendant, "How much further up this road is Davis?"

"About thirty miles," he called back.

Thirty miles further on, now 100 percent doubtful that I'd ever seen a sign that read Davis and in tones that sounded like I'd personally lost it, I asked another toll booth stalwart, "Say, where in the world is a sign that says Davis?"

"About twenty miles straight up," he replied.

One could get across the United States with this kind of treatment, I thought, as I debated whether to turn around and go home.

Nearly half an hour later and a total of eighty-two miles from my front door, I stopped by the sculpture garden in Davis. With bladder nearly bursting, stomach screaming "empty!" and eyes at half-mast, I literally bolted through the open door to her apartment. She sat by the telephone, paging through an open directory that lay on her lap. She nodded a greeting as I headed for the room where two pairs of nylon stockings hung drying from the shower curtain rod above the tub.

Next I made my way to the kitchen to forage in her refrigerator and cupboard. Bare. Not an edible crumb. Nada. I lay down to stare at the ceiling while she systematically resisted accepting what appeared to be an established fact: every last soul who worked on the switchboard at the University of California in Davis had taken off for the weekend with no intention of servicing anybody until Monday. "This is fantastic!" I listened to her protests with a tired smile. "I've never been in such a barbarous place! I can't believe that in the 1960s there's actually somewhere in the United States where a person can be out of reach for forty-eight hours!"

Reach or no reach, with no reason to linger, I grabbed her suitcases and literally bustled her out of the deserted place. No wonder she called to have me rescue her from what would otherwise have been a lost weekend.

Once aboard and en route, she projected her disappointment with the telephone system on me. "Pat, why haven't you finished your dissertation yet? Cathy's half your age and she finished hers months ago." I was too polite or too timid to confess that a legion of friends, any one of whom could and did call on me for all kinds of time-consuming favors, threw almost as many roadblocks in my way as did a divorce, teaching three courses in just as many colleges, and running a five-part household.

She must have read my mind. "And don't say it's because you've got too much to do. You and Dorothy Lee are just alike. You're anthropologists and single mothers with lots of kids. The more you have to do, the more you do and you do it better. Both of you work best under pressure."

I drove along in a starving semistupor. Her words sounded good, but I couldn't eat them. Colorful billboards periodically announced our approach to an elaborate roadside eating place. "I think about you and Dorothy Lee when I mention women as models in my lectures."

"Takes one to recognize one." My stomach rumbled louder than my words.

"That's true. Cathy is a fourth-generation professional woman."

I slowed down at the advertised turnoff. "We're going to stop here long enough for me to grab a bite," I announced. "If you're not hungry, there's a country store attached to this restaurant that sells just about everything. You might be able to find something to give away for Christmas."

"That's a good idea. I won't be home until the sixteenth and I hate shopping at Christmastime."

Twenty minutes later, I found her wandering impatiently around the shop. She hadn't bought a thing. "Just junk," she snorted. "I can't believe people spend time thinking up and manufacturing expensive junk."

Back on the road, I nearly drove off it when she startled me with a question best asked when none of the boys might overhear us. "And how about your abortion?"

"My abortion? What abortion? When would I ever find any time to dream up a reason for having an abortion?"

She goaded my memory by mentioning a long-distance call I'd made to her some months before. Then I remembered. An older neighbor approached me for information about where his daughter, who had become pregnant in Atlanta, might go to get an abortion. Abortions were not yet legal in the United States, so anybody who wanted one got the necessary information surreptitiously. I told him that I knew of a woman who had gone through the ordeal, and I would try to locate her within a week.

She had worked with me in Margaret's office at the Museum years before. Women change their names throughout life, so they're never easy to locate after years of little or no contact. After two days of futility, I gave up and called Margaret.

As abruptly as was her style, I dove into my mission. "Margaret, I need to know where to get an abortion. You may not have known it at the time, but Dorcas Lamb got one when she worked in your office. She flew to the Caribbean somewhere. Can you find out where she went and who the doctor was?"

"Give me a week," Margaret swung into action.

"Can't spare a week. How about five days?"

"I'll try."

Four days passed. At 6:00 a.m. on the morning of the fifth, the phone jarred me awake. It was three hours later in New York City and she probably forgot about the time difference.

"Pat, do you have a pencil?" I groped for some kind of a writing tool and copied down the name and address of a doctor outside the country. As soon as I could contact him, I passed the information on to the father of the young woman in trouble and put the matter out of mind as something best forgot.

So! After all these many months, Missy Makarit assumed the abortion I inquired about was mine! I smiled in spite of my stupor. "Fine anthropologist you are," I chided her. "You should have been able to tell by my voice that I wasn't personally involved."

"Don't kid yourself," she retorted. "Remember, you did begin the telephone conversation by saying, '*I* need to know where to get an abortion.'" The conversation stopped. We absorbed ourselves in our own thoughts—she, perhaps with some regret that Pat had no juicy secrets to share about having sinned; I, with the sequel to the story.

The voice of my elder passenger broke the silence. "And don't put that in your book!" she commanded.

"Why not?" I teased. "It tells a lot about your loyalty—your willingness to come to the aid of a friend. You got right to work and met my deadline with the follow-through. Considering how busy you always are, I think that's positively marvelous."

She chose not to respond.

"There's an interesting epilogue to that story," I said. "When Nell's father approached me, I cautioned him about being absolutely certain that his daughter wanted the abortion as much as he.

"'Make sure, because if she doesn't,' I warned him, 'the loss of that fetus could haunt her for the rest of her life.'

"He was too anxious to avoid scandal to listen to me. Or to Nell either, for that matter. Can you guess how she communicated her feelings to her father? She waited until her parents' anniversary and simply swallowed one too many sleeping pills."

We discussed another suicide, of the new widow of an anthropologist whose children found her hanging from a tree in her orchard when they returned from looking for a nursing home for her. "I've been grazed by suicides many times in my life," she confided. "They've come too close, too often. As a Christian, I accept the tenet that God alone has the right to give or to take life. Yet, as a rational human being, I recognize that suicide can be an ethical and responsible way to deal with an impasse. The line between suicide and homicide is a very narrow one."

The recent assassination of President Kennedy had catapulted the nation into a state of shock. "I think one of the biggest problems with any kind of death is the guilt that haunts the survivors," I said. "I've been amazed by my students' hypersensitivity toward death since Kennedy's assassination."

"We're all survivors of that assassination," she declared. "But strange as it may sound, we should be more upset about the shooting of Oswald than of

Kennedy. In our culture, presidents expect to expose themselves to danger of the kind that mowed down Kennedy, but Oswald was a manacled man."

We stopped at the neighborhood cleaners. I had a lot of things on my mind when I hurried in to get Laird's blankets. I hoped the dinner hadn't burned; that the dog had not spent the day on Margaret's clean sheets; that the house looked okay; that Betty and Russ Risser would let me bring her along to the party they were having that evening; that I had something ready to wear.

I tossed the oversized cleaning bundle toward the back of the bus and climbed up into the driver's seat. "Did you see that Indian come out just as you went in?" she chuckled with high humor. "He carried an armload of *Indian* blankets."

"No, I didn't. Another time I might have, but I'm thinking of a lot of other things right now." I turned on the ignition and stepped on the starter. Catastrophe incarnate. The motor didn't even whimper. I dashed back into the cleaners and phoned the kids. Margaret and I hiked three blocks home, lugging the blankets sans the easy swinging gait that would have been possible were we equipped with backpacks. We passed Miles and Laird on their way to rescue the car.

We were eating leftovers alone when the boys returned with their verdict: a frozen motor. There was nothing that could be done about it late on a Saturday afternoon. I had a weekend with Margaret Mead on my hands with no car. Unless she volunteered to rent one, we would have to hitchhike to the party that evening and to San Francisco by noon on Sunday. Adventures lay ahead.

I phoned the Rissers to explain my predicament and to ask if it would be okay to bring Margaret along to their party. "Guests from the city arrived a few minutes ago," Betty said. "Russ will come and get the two of you as soon as he can. It won't be long."

Before Russ arrived, I told Margaret that the six couples invited to the party were upper-middle-class business executives and their wives: manufacturers, distributors of products, an insurance broker, and the like. She decided that she would like to go as incognito as possible and be introduced simply as "Miss Mead."

The Rissers obliged. One of their female guests recognized Margaret as we entered and jumped to her feet. Another thought "Miss Mead" might be *the* Margaret Mead but didn't dare believe it. Three of them, along with all the husbands, suspected nothing. In fact, the sixth wife regaled us later with a mental note she made when we arrived. "Those Rissers are such nuts on being democratic. They've even invited the woman they've hired to do the dishes to have drinks with us."

Margaret and I didn't circulate immediately. When we took our coats and purses to the back bedroom, she played a game with herself. She tried to match the cars out in front—which included a Porsche, a Mercedes, a Cadillac, and various luxury Fords—with the owners of the mink, chinchilla, and seal coats, as well as a trio of cloth ones like hers and mine. In some instances, she even attempted to match cars and coats with the companies that employed the respective husbands.

By the time we made our appearance in the California combination living–dining area, everybody knew that the stranger was no ordinary guest. One woman named Zelda, several drinks ahead of everybody else, didn't care one way or the other. Zelda, who insisted on criticizing her absent son, instinctively perceived the newcomer as competition. Margaret, on the other hand, aimed to get the reactions of the business community to the assassination. Guests wandered from Margaret's talkathon to Zelda's or retreated to the patio. The lifestyle of Zelda's son didn't concern them, nor did they itch to discuss a subject as heavy as Margaret's. When Margaret and Zelda met head-on and talked at each other, Zelda usually had the advantage.

After Russ brought us home about 11:00 p.m., a friend of Laird's agreed to transport us to the farmhouse of an elderly immigrant couple. I had not seen them since the assassination, and I thought Margaret might be interested in their comments on it. I knew that they would be awake because they stayed up to catch the eleven o'clock news. Leo, who came from Yugoslavia, had never learned to read. Anna, who hailed from Sweden, deciphered parts of the newspaper to him at mealtimes. Otherwise television and radio provided Leo with information from the outside world. He talked back to commentators all the way through their broadcasts and daily practiced telling the president how to run the country.

Anna took it all in with wifely patience as the chief executive in faraway Washington, D.C., bungled along without Leo's input. Neither Leo nor Anna had ever been within hog-calling distance of a famous person. They greeted us in the same well-washed and weather-worn clothes they had perspired in all day. We sat in their spacious kitchen. Anna served gingerbread topped with applesauce and a homemade cookie as big as a saucer, which, in deference to calories we consumed at the Rissers', Margaret and I halved.

They addressed Margaret respectfully as "Mrs. Doctor" and talked to me mainly about how the assassination affected them. Margaret chose to sit and listen. "I felt worse when they shot Kennedy than I did when our baby died," Leo unabashedly brushed a tear away with a big, thick, callused finger.

"He was so young, so smart, so handsome," Anna lamented.

"He was our handsomes' Pres'dent," Leo corrected her.

"I try to get all the clippings," Anna reported, "but I can't get any. I t'ink it must be hard for anybody to get clippings. Everyone is snatching them up and hoarding them."

"The You-nited States is the greates' country in the whole wide worl'." Leo sang his adopted country's praises every chance he got. "I want my citizenship papers be bury with me. Until they shoot Kennedy, I give my share of our money to the government in Washington, but now I t'ink I will give it to the Boy Scouts." At midnight all four tired adults welcomed the return of Laird and his obliging classmate with a car.

Before anyone awoke Sunday morning, I sat at the phone trying to find someone who would accept my offer of a free breakfast in return for helping me deliver Margaret to her friend GiGi's apartment in San Francisco at noon.

Calamities come in clusters. I called Brenda, a peer who taught anthropology in Foothill Junior College in town. While she was agreeing to my proposition, she saw her car back down her driveway and crash into a tree across the road. Whether she could bring that one or borrow another car from a neighbor, Brenda promised to be at my house in two hours.

She arrived in a neighbor's. The car had no hub caps and a banged-up door on the passenger side that wouldn't open. Margaret squeezed past the steering wheel to the front seat. I got in behind her. "Everybody who drives should ride in the backseat at least once a week," Margaret announced as she lit a cigarette and settled down.

"Could I please have one of your cigarettes?" Brenda asked. "I left so fast this morning that I forgot to put mine in my purse." Smoke from two human chimneys drifted through the car.

"I'm disappointed that neither one of you has been able to kick the habit," I coughed from the backseat.

"One conclusion that came out of some recently published data on cigarette smoking," Margaret retorted, "is that if you started early enough, you died of an unrecorded cause." The two sinners made no effort to conceal their delight.

Some minutes passed before I spoke up again, and this time it was about my surroundings. "Cars can be wastebaskets on wheels," I said, "and I think I know something about who owns this one."

"Try me," Brenda caught my eye in the rearview mirror.

"Do they have three kids? Two older boys and a younger girl?"

"How did you figure that out?"

"Well, I'm sitting in a nest of Dick Tracy and Batman comic books. There's also one Raggedy Ann doll and a baby pillow. The kids must eat constantly. Pop-corn, Hershey bars, Planter's peanuts, and pretzel wrappers abound. The children like orange pop and root beer. Chewing gum. At least one of the parents smokes and the preferred brand is Chesterfields."

"Isn't anthropology fun?" Brenda's reflection grinned back at me. "Once you learn to look and to listen and to watch for patterns, you do it automatically."

"Anthropologists are people watchers," Margaret chimed in, "and women make good ones."

Brenda asked Margaret what to do about night school students who come in for advice and wind up asking for a date. "Keep your sessions professional," Margaret advised, "unless you want to get personally involved. And professionals shouldn't."

We delivered her to the stairs leading to GiGi's apartment on the stroke of noon. Margaret fumbled for whatever kind of a lever opened the door. "There should be a law to standardize how car doors open," she muttered. "I can never find the handles."

"Oops," Brenda opened her door and jumped out. "Your door doesn't open, remember? You've got to squeeze past the steering wheel one more time. Sorry about that."

Margaret placed what was left of her package of Lucky Strikes on the dashboard and wriggled out. She was halfway up the steps before Brenda spied them. She reached over to roll down the window and called out, "You forgot your cigarettes."

Margaret turned and smiled. "They're yours," she said, "you'll need them on the way home."

As we drove back to Palo Alto, I told Brenda about my initial negative reactions when Margaret interrupted my weekend plans to work on my dissertation. "If whatever advantage someone takes over another in a relationship is measured in terms of inconvenience or excitement," I reviewed the weekend in flashback, "Margaret's visits rate about even." And I did finish the dissertation eventually.

6

MARGARET MEAD, EMPLOYMENT AGENT

Not many people ever realized that Margaret Mead ran her own employment agency. She had never been trained and she never had a license. She never rented office space nor did she advertise. Recipients never paid her for her services. She just mixed and matched hundreds of jobs she heard about to people she considered could do them.

Her daily mail brought inquiries from directors of small college departments in the social sciences who appealed to her to suggest stand-ins to replace staff members taking off on short-term research grants. Anthropologists, whose positions disappeared out from under them, could always look up her number in the New York City telephone directory and ask her please to keep their availability in mind. Acquaintances at social gatherings beseeched her for information about jobs for bright sons or daughters. Whether they asked her for them or not, she sometimes boosted and often pushed closest relatives and old school friends into meeting deadlines for her. Hungry admirers dogged her heels at conferences. And then there were those special adoptees, her students.

In 1952, when I returned to college to prepare for gainful employment, my four sons then ranged in age from two to eight years of age. At that time, I was immensely curious about how babies turn into toddlers and toddlers into children. I yearned to learn everything about the possible universality of preschool and early childhood development. Outside of Margaret's course, the Study of Cultural Character, academic offerings in the department of anthropology at Columbia University skipped over the culture of childhood. Such courses were about as common as those on computer-based research: they didn't exist.

Three of my sons were teenagers and I was forty-six twelve years later when I finally walked across the stage of an amphitheater to receive a doctorate at Stanford. My oldest son was twenty. My interests grew with the children. As a Ph.D., I now burned to put anthropology in the postschool education of adults who knew enough to know that they did not know everything and desired to continue taking courses. My dissertation, "Extension Education by Land Grant Colleges and Universities through Television," explored opportunities for making formal education readily available to such lifelong learners. I had roughed out chapters for a book to accompany a program for broadcasting that I dubbed "Instant Anthropology." Whatever position I accepted would have to allow for fanning the flames of these smoldering fires.

In her mother-hen way, Margaret watched for what she perceived to be the perfect appointment for me. Oblivious to my more recent preoccupation with extension education for already educated adults through television, she categorized me as an anthropologist–mother who should be working in family and early childhood education.

She goaded me to apply for a three-pronged opening in a women's college in Connecticut. I would direct the Department of Early Childhood Education, be professor on the family, and oversee a conjoint nursery school. 'It's made for you, Pat,' she insisted in a long-distance call.

"You keep sticking me back into kindergarten," I restlessly switched the phone receiver from one ear to the other. "Haven't you read my dissertation?"

"No. I didn't get in on it as you wrote it and you know very well I'm more interested in process than product."

"It probably looked too ponderous, too. I remember your dissertation, 'The Question of Cultural Stability in Polynesia,' was a thin eighty-five pages. Mine's 401, counting the index.

"You did more work than necessary. How many times have you heard me tell students that a hundred pages is sufficient for a doctoral study? A dissertation is just an exercise to prove you can organize information and do research." Her speech bristled with impatience over how much shorter I should have made my doctoral paper and how much longer I should consider taking the position she'd found for me.

To oblige her, I sent a letter to Connecticut in which I halfheartedly applied for a job I didn't want. In the meantime, the Placement Center at Stanford assisted me in finding an associate professorship in the Department of Anthropology and the School of Education at the University of Delaware. Under its extension department, the faculty conducted classes off campus in surrounding communities and some of these courses were being scheduled for imminent broadcast.

When I arrived in Newark, I heard insiders jokingly refer to Delaware as the "state of DuPont." I soon began to think that the same might be said of the university. The breeze of academic freedom barely rippled the ivy that clung to the buildings, inside which management regulated students and faculty with the efficiency of a factory. Students chafed under rules forbidding them to dress casually in class, to drink beer on campus, or to use their automobiles. A young man signed his date out of her dormitory "like a book." If she did not return by curfew, a university official notified both her parents and the state troopers after fifteen minutes.

Comparable restrictions curtailed the faculty. President Perkins personally checked posted office hours. I caught myself teaching with an uneasy feeling that the narrowed eyes of an all-seeing Big Brother judged my every move. I thought I saw the eyebrows of tenured teachers shoot up and their lips crinkle in when word got around that I conducted exams by asking students to critique copies of the morning newspaper or selected movies in light of what they'd learned about their own culture. Nobody directly confronted me with my unorthodox examination procedures, but I sensed that I might undergo a third degree any day.

I liked the students, whom I knew by name, and enjoyed the pleasure of watching them think through the social environment of the mid-1960s more as born-again anthropologists than as members of the state's educated and white elite.

I liked the campus, which resembled a small-scale Harvard. I didn't like the impression I was receiving that the administration seemed to look upon professors as irresponsible hirelings not to be trusted. I felt wing-clipped and stifled. Every possible weekend, I escaped from the Newark campus for breaths of fresher air somewhere else.

Partly because of my dissertation, I had been asked to chair the mass media section of the Adult Education Association for 1965–1966. It was in this capacity that I addressed that organization's national conference in New York City late in November. Conferees stood elbow to elbow after the speech in a smoke-filled hotel cash bar. Eugene Johnson, former Stanfordite and executive director of the Adult Education Association, introduced me to Basil Karp, an assistant to the new dean of faculty for the School of General Studies at Columbia. Looking like a bespectacled, conservatively dressed, rather gaunt panda, Karp didn't look at all like Cupid, nor did I guess that I was being courted.

"It was a pleasure to learn that you are a graduate of the School of General Studies," he purred. "Would you by any chance be interested in coming back to G.S.?" He lined the fingers of his right hand against his lower lip in a gesture that I was to see many times. "The dean is looking for someone like you for an administrative post."

"You flatter me," I replied. "A chance to return to the college that opened its doors when I wanted to take a night school course with Margaret Mead is absolutely marvelous." I promised to have the placement office at Stanford send my papers to General Studies.

When I entered his office for the first time early in January 1966, Dean Clarence Walton stood up. He was a slight man with a small, pinched face and beady eyes. His large desk dwarfed him. "I've looked forward to meeting you, Pat," he glimmered with sweetness and light. "I have gone over your record here at General Studies and it's something to be proud of."

"Thank you." Miss Innocence looked demurely downward. "My going back to school as a thirty-four-year-old housewife–mother becomes less believable the further removed in time I am from it. It always seems that the person I used to be was somebody else."

"I'm also very much impressed by your papers from Stanford, Pat." His words flowed sweet as maple syrup.

"I had to earn scholarships to be able to stay in school, so maintaining good grades was a necessary part of life."

"We're considering combining the current Office of Admissions with that of the Dean of Students plus the Office of Scholarships and Financial Aid," he said. "My degree is in business and I'm convinced that three offices are not as efficient as one. It's our idea, Pat," and he shot a sidewise glance at his assistant who beamed in agreement, "that you might be just the person to put in charge of this consolidation." His wizened face broke into an unctuous smile.

"The trustees and the faculty would be happy to hear that one of our alumni has returned to the fold." Walton's Alter Ego adeptly pushed the right button.

"I think we have here an excellent opportunity for you as a woman too, Pat," the dean said as he flipped through the pages in front of him once more. He paused, squinted his eyes and popped the big question. "How committed are you to the University of Delaware?"

"I like my courses and the students. The salary's okay." I hesitated, not wanting to play too hard to get. "Since I was a student here myself, I've liked the idea of a liberal arts college for mature adults. To me, a school like General Studies in a polyglot city like New York demonstrates American democracy in action. It took a country like the U.S. to make a school like G.S. possible."

We agreed to meet again in another month. Dean Walton requested that I be discreet about informing anyone of our conversation. "Dr. Hall recruited me for Delaware," I said. "I'll have to tell him so he has time to find a replacement."

As soon as I returned to Newark, I told Dean Hall, head of the School of Education at the University of Delaware, about Walton's proposal. He suggested that we walk over to the president's office immediately. "You want to be a dean of students?" President Perkins leaned across his desk, "I'll make you a dean of students."

"That's not it," I answered. "If I stay here, I'd prefer to teach." The bid from Columbia had turned my head just enough to prevent my catching the unconscious truth embedded in that response. I identified with teaching, not administration.

"Please stay," coaxed Dean Hall. "We need you here."

"Stay," ordered President Perkins. "You could be another Margaret Mead."

Unless I were willing to let Margaret make a decision for me, she was the last person in the world to approach in a time of indecision, but I needed to talk to someone whom I trusted and who had my interests at heart. I phoned her at the Museum and we arranged a Saturday rendezvous in the Greenwich Village many-storied brownstone that she shared with Rhoda Metraux.

We sat together in Margaret's dimly lit ground floor living room. She shut her eyes and rested her head in the palm of her right hand. I poured out my dissatisfactions with administration at Delaware and gushed with expectations for working in administration at the School of General Studies.

She saw the situation whole and without my blinders. "Don't take it," she snapped. "You can't whip three offices into one and still conduct business as usual when you've got a population of 5,000 students to deal with at the same time. Do you need me to tell you that? You'll have to wear three different hats. You'll be an ex-officio member of every single committee on campus. You don't like academic committee meetings any more than I do. Committees will take so much of your time you won't be able to get anything else done. I can't believe that you'd be so stupid as to even consider such a preposterous assignment. Besides," she rubbed her eyes wearily and shook her head, "good teachers are too rare to sacrifice a one of them to administration."

I bit my lip. If good teachers were too rare to sacrifice to administration, then how come she kept steering me into administrative posts in early childhood and family education? "I might still find time to teach." I made some kind of excuse to appease her.

"No, you won't. And it's a shame. I can name one anthropology professor after another who teaches so badly that students change their major. They're the ones who should be going into administration, not you. You're a natural teacher. I've lost track of all the times former students of yours have come up to me to praise a course they've taken from you."

"Really? First I've heard of that. I wonder who they were?"

"Albany State Teachers College is looking for an anthropologist. But I'm not so sure you'd want to go there after the University of Delaware."

"Depends upon what Albany is doing in educational television. I wouldn't even apply until I knew."

"Television's taking off with lightning speed, and educational television's not far behind. Now that you hold down the chairmanship of the mass media section of the Adult Education Association, start writing about that! Get in print! Be their spokesman!"

"Frankly, my writing is another reason why I'm attracted to this offer from General Studies. I don't want to write articles; I want to write books. It would be a lot easier getting my work marketed had I the visibility of a deanship in the middle of the publishing capital of the world!"

Then my voice softened and slowed down. "An appointment in New York City would be like coming home again too. Three of my sons were born in this vicinity, you know."

Her face reflected disgruntlement. "You're not listening and you're wasting my time. I can tell by your voice that your mind's made up in favor of General Studies no matter what I say."

She rose to show me to the door. "Go ahead. I see you'll have to find out the hard way that administration's not your cup of tea. Just remember, I warned you."

She gave me a bum's rush good-bye.

I walked along a snow-lined sidewalk with my head down and my hands in my pockets. Was I the only ingrate who'd made such a pilgrimage to the "oracle of anthropological employment" and then refused to follow her advice? Only she knew how many irreverent beneficiaries provided her the periodic pleasure of banging on the nearest flat surface and booming out, "I told you so!"

"This letter acknowledges my acceptance," I wrote sentimentally and foolishly to the secretary of Columbia University soon after Valentine's Day. Sentimentally, because the school was my alma mater. Foolishly, because only someone as idealistic as I would have pledged her troth to begin with.

Marry in haste, repent at leisure, the old saying goes. I resisted seeing it at the time, but my chances for success in making Dean Walton's merger work were as rosy as those of any one of the first five wives of Henry VIII. They too entered their mergers full of love and expectations far removed from the grim certainty of their master's chopping block.

Once he snared me, the dean fired the head of Scholarships and Financial Aid, the director of Admissions, and the dean of students. The dedicated effort of those three men was broken off in minutes. Between March 1 and my arrival shortly before fall registration five months later, the secretaries, receptionists, file clerks, and advisers for the three former offices requested transfer to other departments within the university.

Three truckloads of cardboard boxes, stuffed with some 15,000 file folders and stacked on the floor along empty walls, crowded our rooms. The labor of integrating this paper avalanche into one workable set of 5,000 combined files would take a trained staff months to complete. Yet the task had to be done, abracadabra-style, amid a daily barrage of inquiries from registrants and applicants by a crew of underpaid neophytes and an administrator who should have stayed in teaching.

Blinded by loyalty to G.S. and still deaf to Margaret's wisdom, I rolled up my sleeves and doggedly determined to "keep on keepin' on." Giving up would be sissy. I owed it to my sex to prove that a woman needn't quaver; that she could tackle the impossible and win. I tricked myself into believing the assignment to be the same kind of challenge I'd undertaken at the Museum the summer Margaret left me in charge of her office. Similar to it, yes, and multiplied 5,000 times.

Office hours, which now stretched from 8:00 a.m. to 9:00 p.m., forced me to rely on relays of part-time assistants and counselors. For a while, each arriving registrant (or phoning registrant) set off a tizzy in which all hands fanned out to locate at least one of that particular student's three folders. Emergency followed emergency thirteen hours a day, five days a week, and slightly more than half of every Saturday.

In desperation, I sought out each of my three predecessors for counsel. "We didn't know who the newcomer would be when we all left the ship," confided the ex-head of Scholarships and Financial Aid. "We figured it would be just our luck to get another cold fish like Karp."

"When Walton asks you to do something, you'd better do it," cautioned the ex-director of Admissions.

"Duck," warned the ex-dean of students.

"Podden my frankness, Dr. Grinagah," my London-born secretary said as she brought in some draft board appeals to be signed one afternoon. "There is so much work to do around here that it is embarrassing. We shall get it done and then we shall be replaced. I've seen it happen before. There will be a lot of new faces around here in a few more months. New people will be brought in to reap the benefits of our hard work. Wait and see."

I don't know as much about what dreams foretell, but I do remember a particular dream that recurred during my entire stay at General Studies that year. I was clinging to the bottom of the wing of an airplane that was being piloted by

Dean Walton. It was being bombed. The sky lit up every time a bomb exploded. Flash! Flash! Boom! Boom! The shots were aimed at him, not me. I swayed between one close call after another; winced and wished I'd left G.S. before the war started. No time for afterthoughts now. The air pressed sharp and cold against my chest. My heart beat like a primitive drum. I breathed with difficulty. My mouth dried out. I wondered how long I could hang on as the pilot looped the loop and wove figure eights through the clouds in his efforts to evade fire. The horizon teeter-tottered. I flopped back and forth in front of it like a beanbag. After a while, my grip loosened and I floated, visibly and vulnerably, off into nowhere.

The more unrelenting the calls on my time and attention became, the more determined I became to maintain equilibrium by pursuing some outside relaxation. Margaret still taught a class one night a week. For old times' sake, I decided to reserve Tuesday evenings to listen in on her lectures once again. "But you've heard me so many times before," she protested when she learned of my intentions. "Are you sure you won't be bored?"

"Heavens no! They're never exactly the same and there's always something to learn from them. In fact, would it be all right with you if I taped them this time around?"

"Why? What on earth would you do with them?"

"Just keep them for my collection of memorabilia." Such interest flattered her. Before she uttered a word in any one of her lectures that fall, she ceremoniously waited for my signal that the equipment was ready.

"Her lectures are better than usual," Nora Holland, still around after a decade, remarked a few minutes before Margaret strode into class one night. "I'll bet it's because she knows you're taping them."

"Dr. Mead's lectures are too rambly for me." An older drop-in student who sat between Nora and me broke into our conversation. "I think someone who was new to the study of anthropology would find them a bit too disorganized for an initial presentation." I never expected to defend her, but I sat there and heard the concentrated impressions of a dozen years well up and spill over.

"There are those who learn and teach by systematically accumulating organized bits of information, step by step by step," I said. "You're probably one of them. As teachers, these people feel safest when they have an outline to lecture from; as students, they're most secure when they can regurgitate lectures into outlines on contact. But Margaret's not that kind of teacher, nor is she best for that kind of student. She wants you to absorb anthropology sensually, the way she learned the Manus culture in New Guinea.

"The Manus lived on water. She's told about going there, dipping into the water with them, swimming around, looking and listening; playing and entering into their activities. Unobtrusively. A part and apart. When she came out of the water, she made notes and then thought through what her notes meant in terms of their culture, as well as her own education in anthropology. She read ethnographies and travelers' reports. She interacted with the Manus people on a day-to-day basis for months on end. She ate their food, held their babies, helped at childbirth, doled out aspirin and Band-Aids, and took pictures.

"She lived in a see-through house in the middle of the village. It had no walls. She could observe the villagers from anywhere inside her house and they could look in on her from anywhere outside. After a while, she began to understand Manus culture from the same two perspectives provided by that air-conditioned house: from the inside looking out and from the outside looking in.

"I think she teaches anthropology as though her students were coming to live in a Manus village. Just like that. She first immerses us in its all-at-onceness. Impressionistically. Finally, she gives us a chance to organize the bits into 1, 2, 3, and A, B, C, which you seem to feel safer with, when we construct outlines upon which to write the essays she asks for in exams." Margaret strode in. We ceased talking and faced the front to listen to her.

Before many another evening class, Margaret took a taxi after work from the Museum on 79th and Central Park West to my apartment on 100th. There we'd share a meal and then proceed another twenty-five blocks to the lecture hall at Columbia.

My oven once went on the blink the night before her fall semester opener. I buzzed the office of the apartment house manager at 8:00 a.m. "Dr. Margaret Mead is coming for dinner tonight," I wailed. "How soon can you get somebody up here to fix my oven?"

"Listen, lady, I'll put your name down, see? There's a couple big repair jobs ahead of you, see? I can't promise anything before the end of the week. That's the best I can do, see?" Dr. Margaret Mead was not one of his tenants, nor did he know me. I covered the intended casserole with aluminum foil and stuck it in the freezer.

"What would you serve Margaret Mead if all you had to cook on was the top of the stove?" I asked a portly office gourmet of Austrian descent. "Beef stroganoff," his facial flesh wobbled and he salivated as he intoned the name. "It's easier to fix than it sounds. I'll give you the recipe."

My bell rang at 5:00 p.m. sharp. "Come in," I called out, "the door's unbolted."

"Pat, you shouldn't leave your door unlocked. It's dangerous." Margaret shut the door, loudly bolted it, and took two steps into the kitchen.

"Oh, you little worrywart." We hugged in greeting. "It had to be you. You're always on time. But dinner's not."

"That's all right. I'm allergic to food these days," she sniffled and fished a Kleenex from her pocket. "Have I got time to make a couple of phone calls? Would you mind? One's to California, so I'll use my credit card."

She sat, half-lying down, on the sofa. She rested her little-girl shoes on that morning's copy of the *New York Times*. I brought her a vodka and bitter lemon and retreated to the kitchen which, in the manner of many a big-city apartment, was no more than an area marked off by open archways in a corner of the living room by the front door.

In the first call she made, she spoke affectionately to someone. Then she made another in which she said that her brother Dick was not as sick as a morning telegram indicated and that she was eating at my place.

Oh dear, I thought for the first time. Should I have invited Rhoda? I turned the stroganoff down low, laid out a salad, and put fresh broccoli in the steamer. It's too late to invite Rhoda now. I know Margaret doesn't like to eat alone, but Rhoda probably appreciates some solitude.

I'd set up a card table on the terrace where we might savor the beauty of city lights and watch helicopters land and take off from atop the Pan Am building at the end of Central Park. "Is the job going any better?" Margaret finished phoning and stood in the kitchen archway with her glass in hand.

"No. It's absolutely the worst mess I've ever tackled, bar none. Only a damn fool or a woman would be dumb enough to stick to it."

"If you find you're not going anywhere, you don't have to stay, you know. Merrill Palmer would like to have you in Detroit. I've told you that before, but you've never been as interested in them as they've been in you."

"Thanks, but I hate to quit now I'm here. I'll stick it out." I turned off the burners and lined the serving dishes on the sideboard next to the stove. "There's no room on the table for serving dishes and the beef will keep warmer if it sits on the pilot light. Here," I handed her a place. "Help yourself, smorgasbord style."

I lit the candles and filled the wine glasses.

"I'm not hungry," she began to ladle skimpy portions onto her plate.

"Me either," I agreed with her for a change. "It's anybody's guess how this stroganoff tastes anyway. Somebody in the office told me to make it because it is a top-of-the-stove dish and my oven's not working. The tuna casserole we were going to have can wait until you come again."

"My brother Dick's in the hospital," she announced, as soon as we both sat down. "He's bleeding and he's probably got an ulcer. He's communicating well, though, so he's not at death's door."

"If he's in the hospital, a call from you must have really lifted his spirits. I'm glad you made it."

She asked about each of my boys; I, about her daughter, Cathy, and son-in-law, Barkev Kassarjian.

"Barkev's doing some research at a university in the Philippines and Cathy's with him. She's teaching anthropology and other things in a Jesuit school there. I'll visit them in the spring on the way to New Guinea. Rhoda may come along." Her voice trailed off as she returned to the kitchen for a larger helping of the stroganoff.

"I took three couples from Columbia on my last field trip to New Guinea. I suspected one of the young women got married just so she could go. I got NIAH and other money for them. All three wives came back pregnant and never finished their research. Women ought to get out of the scene if they're not going to follow through."

Now it was the cook's turn for seconds. The stroganoff tasted pretty good after all. I left a spoonful in the pan. "My assistant has a baby boy," she lamented the vicissitudes of being an employer. "She's trying to be my assistant, a wife, a mother, and a student all at once, and she's flunking her courses."

"Babies have their own ways of usurping careers," I had to chuckle. Margaret's account of the perils of pregnancy reminded me of a soap opera. "Babies are so dependent and so cute they automatically charm caretakers away from career activities."

"Babies and careers don't mix. My mother found that out and she had live-in help. I'm glad that Cathy has followed *her* mother's advice and is still childless."

"I bet you won't escape grandmotherhood. Cathy's only twenty-six. She won't do what you advise forever. If she waits as long as you did to have her, she'll make a grandmother out of you on or before her thirty-eighth birthday."

Margaret changed the subject. "Unfortunately, over six hundred students have signed up for my course at Yale this semester. I've scheduled an exam in two weeks and I'm looking for readers. Will you help? I'll pay you $5 an hour. That's more than most of the others will get, but you're better prepared."

"My first reaction is, no, I'm too swamped," I said. "Outside of taping your Tuesday night class, I've been pouring absolutely all my efforts into those damn files at General Studies. But it's not wise to marry a job. Reading exams written for you by non-anthropology majors at Yale could be interesting. And fun."

"Would you do one hundred of them for me?"

"I would if I could, but I can't. I don't have time for one hundred. How about no more than fifty?" "Everything helps. I'll have Karen Graff bring Lloyd Warner's *Black Civilization* and Reo Fortune's *Sorcerers of Dobu* to you early tomorrow. The exam essays you'll be reading will be based on those two books and my lectures."

"I'll send the money to Neal," I cut the last of my broccoli into bite-sized pieces. "He's got a wrestling scholarship that covers his tuition at San Francisco State. He writes that he's living on "quite nothing." Isn't that a poignant way to say that he's starving? I worry about him."

"He'll get along," she called from the kitchen where she cleaned up the stroganoff and set the pan in the sink. "Your sons are so self-sufficient.

"Rhoda and I are going to move on October 14." Margaret returned to the table with the last of the stroganoff. "She's sold the house in the village. The buyers are ready to move in as soon as we get out. Money's tight on mortgages right now, but you can't miss on an apartment in the city. She's bought one on the sixteenth floor of the Beresford. It's across the street from the Museum, so I'll be able to walk to work."

"That'll save on taxi fares."

"I don't mind taxi fares. I don't own a car, so I can afford to take taxis."

"Do you ever go anywhere by bus?"

"Only when there's a taxi strike. We're ready to move into the new apartment but we need approval first. The review board met this morning. Rhoda just said she's heard nothing on the outcome yet. She dismantled her upstairs quarters in July, but I don't want to move until the last minute. Will you help me move?"

Once again, a smile condensed my thoughts. I recognized in Margaret my mother's genius for cajoling friends and relatives to pitch in and help her out. Even though I knew the pattern full well, I let her coax me and I, in turn, corralled three of my assistants to invest a Sunday, our cars, and our gas to deshelve, box, transport, and reshelve her entire home library.

"We're going to have a housecooling party for the brownstone sometime in the next few weeks. You're invited if you've got the time."

"Thanks. I'll try to come, but I can't promise any social activity this early in the semester."

Lights flicked on in the mammoth apartment building in front of us. We watched for movement and compared notes on what might be going on in all those stacked-up human pigeonholes. "I've heard of housewarming parties when you move into a place, but never a housecooling party when you move out of one. It's a clever switch and it makes sense. Where'd you get the idea?"

"When I was a child, we moved twice a year. Having some kind of party was a perfect way to say good-bye to our many neighborhoods. My mother thought of it."

After the meal, we stuck our dishes in the sink. Margaret covered them with water while I brought the card table inside and locked the door to the terrace. By 7:30 we were on our way to her lecture hall in Harkness Theatre at Columbia.

She stood guard over my cumbersome tape recorder on the corner while I ran out into the street to hail the first cab that approached from either 100th or Central Park West. "It's very difficult to get research organizations to grant money for movies. They don't think film is research. Perfectly ridiculous."

"I don't go along with their views, but I can understand them," I said. "The people in those research outfits think of movies as entertainment. Movies entertain, yes, but they can also teach. Look what your *Four Families* teaches about daily life in France, Japan, India, and Canada."

"That's right. Each one of the families in that film had two older children and a baby. At first, we were going to focus the movie around the vacations that families take. Then we realized that not every family takes vacations. They all have babies, though, which they hold and bathe and feed, so that's what we settled on doing."

"If I'd read about those families in a book, I think I'd have forgotten the details long ago. I forget some movies too, but I still remember *Four Families* vividly."

"That's because the theme is universal. The film only cost $60,000 and it's one of the best I've done."

Except for my weekly attendance at Margaret's classes that fall, I spent almost every waking minute in the Sisyphus assignment at General Studies. It seemed that the more I did, in any one of my three official capacities, the more there was to do. Trying to do the work was like having three headaches at once. Common sense required that I do something different, if only for a week, and examine the situation from a distance.

As Christmas approached, I made plans to join the family and our grandmotherly Mormon housekeeper for eight days. The draft board had called Neal and Laird up for service in Vietnam. Miles was preparing to leave for Peace Corps duty in Honduras. Kent expected to join the navy when he graduated from high school in June. War games are played with real bullets and losers pay with lost lives. Who knew? This could be the last holiday we might ever be together. I flew home in time to stuff their stockings and the turkey.

When my transcontinental airliner from San Francisco landed at LaGuardia airport the day after New Year's 1967, I awakened from another replay of the now familiar dream of my hanging from the underbelly of an embattled Piper Cub piloted by Dean Walton. The silver superliner back-motored as it sped down the runway. When it nosed to its portal, I stood in the aisle belly to butt with fellow passengers and waited for the doors to spread open. A spark of intuition forewarned me that this was my first and last round-trip to California.

The news arrived a month later in a hand-delivered envelope as I was meeting with the Faculty Committee on Admissions. I held it for a moment. The negative vibes that emanated from that piece of paper chilled me. I opened the envelope, scanned its contents, and passed this year's version of the dean's annual Dear John letter around to the rest of the committee.

The missive in which the dean jilted his unholy trinity—the Head of Scholarships and Financial Aid, the director of Admissions, plus the dean of students—arrived a year after he'd proposed my coming to Columbia, almost to the day. My secretary's prophecy and the premonition embedded in my recurring nightmare had come to pass.

Walton gave me the choice of resigning or being fired. Either way, I was out. "Administrators are expendable, Pat," Dean Walton explained the last time I stood in his office. "I'm not sure I've made the right decision, but I've made it." His mask wore a smile that insulted the sender as well as the receiver.

The faculty, the advisers, and the secretaries staged separate and hurried farewells. There was something funereal about being the guest of honor at them. When the wine and the munchies disappeared, the party givers had their work to go back to; I, only an apartment that had to be dismantled and sublet.

I wanted to tell Margaret about my dethronement before she read about it in the papers. A few days after Walton's letter arrived, I phoned the Museum to ask if we might have lunch together at 11:30. A meal that early should allow plenty of time for me to make a standing 4:00 Friday afternoon appointment at a beauty parlor near 125th Street and Amsterdam Avenue.

"I'm leaving for the Pacific in a week. I've turned down at least twenty people to keep this date with you," Margaret growled belligerently as I stepped into her office fifteen minutes early. Her antagonism stabbed me. I was too vulnerable to brush it aside.

We walked down the steps through the cavernous hall to the elevator and out into the fresh air to a nearby restaurant. As soon as we sat down, and before the waitress brought us the menu, I let her read Walton's letter of dismissal. "I told you not to take that job," she spit the words out as she banged the table. "You've failed! You haven't failed very often in your life, have you?"

"You're only looking at half the truth."

"That's an excuse and you know it," she scoffed. "You've failed all right! I've never failed! I've never been fired! I've never been asked to resign! I've nev-" and so on and on.

We ordered the same diet lunch. She's the big white goddess of anthropology, I thought as I gazed back at her and sopped up derogatory morsels without a burp. She doesn't know what the real situation is at G.S. She's talking from the top. Life's different up there. My appetite simmered to nothing. "You've failed. I saw it in your walk when you entered the office. I see it in your shoulders. You carry yourself like a broken spring." I straightened up. My shoulders realigned themselves ninety degrees to my neck.

"I'll tell you why you failed," her lambasting continued. "You tried to do too much too soon. You worked too hard. When are you going to get it into your head that working hard is not pertinent?

"No matter how much extra time you put in on election day and weekends, you should never have gone out to the West Coast for Christmas. I hate women who put their families first and everything else second. And they do it all the time! They get married! They have babies! They do not finish their dissertations! They do not publish! I've never been that stupid."

The waitress placed our lunches before us. Waitresses must hear some memorable snatches of talk. I bet this one knows who Margaret is. "I told you administration was not your cup of tea. You were a very bad judge of human nature when you bit Walton's bait in the first place. You used bad judgment every time you communicated with the faculty without checking with him first."

"I trusted the faculty and I didn't trust him," I chewed on a bite of hamburger, not caring whether I ever swallowed it or not. It tasted like cheesecloth.

"Well, you bit off more than you could chew this time around," she speared a cherry tomato. "I hope you realize you're not in much of a position to get any sort of a decent job. Thank God you've got a Ph.D. What do you think you're going to do now?"

I put down my knife and fork. Why pretend anything was right? The food was no more appetizing than a plate of plumber's tools. "Return to California and write a book on making anthropology quickly understandable. We have instant antiques and instant houses and instant replays in football games these days. Why not instant anthropology?" The analogy sprung a smile. "My kids have grown and gone. I'll be able to stake out time to write without being interrupted every other second."

"You write well, but you're not a writer. You work too hard at it. Your dissertation was too long and I don't like your idea for a book on anthropology made easy either. It won't sell. You can't talk down to readers. My books have been popular because I explain difficult concepts simply in easy-to-understand terms."

"You're partly right, but you're not completely right." When is my mother's daughter going to stop talking back to authority? "If I plan my life exclusively around the writing, the book's bound to flow. Sounds crazy, but I've even considered asking you to write the introduction for it."

"I'd have to see it first. I'd never make a commitment on the basis of an outline and sample chapters. Get it all done and send it to me. Then I'll know whether I'll write an introduction or not. Remember, keep it short, under two hundred pages."

"Okay." I surreptitiously deposited an inedible hamburger curd in a paper napkin. "Now, another thing, you had no business telling Yale you spent fifty-one hours on those term papers." She scowled.

"I read thirty-four papers. They averaged ten pages each and took at least ninety minutes to go through because I made many marginal notes along the way. One and a half times thirty-four is fifty-one. It took me another ten hours to read *Sorcerers of Dobu* and *Black Civilization* and I didn't even mention that in my letter to Yale."

"Nobody else took more than nine hours, total. You're getting a check for $50 in the mail, tax deductible. That's all I want to hear about that."

"Well, it's $205 less than what I thought I could send Neal, but I got two new books out of the job," I shrugged my shoulders, "and I've learned a thing or two." We sat in silence a few seconds and then I made conversation. "I suppose you know about the *New York Times* article reporting that course of yours was one of the most popular undergraduate ones at Yale and that you upset administration by giving out all As and Bs."

"That's the way grades should be. If students got more positive reinforcement, they'd learn easier." She stared across the table at me in her bossy, eagle-eyed way and then dove into my entrails again. "You look terrible. You can't trade on the fact that you're middle-aged and still pretty forever, you know. Your face is pasty. Your muscles have no tone. You're a person who needs a lot of outdoor activity. Get away from papers and books. Take the weekend off. Go outside. Play some tennis. Get back some color."

I swallowed her comment and hunched down. I would have preferred to drop through a trap door in the floor. Then without any warning, her wind changed direction. "I talked to Polly Knapp at Merrill Palmer Institute the other day. She needs an anthropologist on her staff. She's been interested in you ever since I told her about your teaching nursery and primary school at the same time you attended Columbia." Even though she's stereotyped me in cast iron, Margaret behaves just like a mother, I mused voicelessly.

"Go to Detroit. Talk to Polly. Don't volunteer anything about the fiasco at General Studies. Your shoulders will tell her all she needs to know about that. Just say you're taking the rest of the year off to write a book.

"Merrill Palmer believes in home economics for women. It serves a third generation of clients. There's a nursery school attached. A primary school. Play groups. A child development and mental health clinic. There're a lot of committee meetings; a lot of pressure to do research and to get it written up.

"I'm not so sure you could afford the job. Merrill Palmer will offer you less than you could get at a better-paying college or university. But don't forget, there's no one of real stature in family life education these days, Pat. You could go places in it. You could make your mark."

I didn't answer.

"Polly's name is Pauline Wilson Knapp. She's a Southern lady in every sense of the word. Even though I call her Polly, don't you make the mistake of calling her that.

"One more thing," Margaret wiped her mouth with a napkin. "Know that she has no patience with women who let their private lives wreck their work. She's got something in her memory about her mother's carrying on, no matter what. She chooses women to work at Merrill Palmer who remind her of her mother."

Since my time dangled loosely while I waited for someone to sublease the apartment, I agreed to fly to Detroit for an interview and to let Margaret know how it resulted. She picked up the tab as we left the table. Even though I'd invited her, I didn't argue. She owed me punching bag services anyway, and I could spend the money on my hair appointment. If I ran-walked from the Museum to the beauty parlor, I might make it by 4:00 p.m.

And the exercise would be just what the doctor ordered.

As I covered the three and a half miles to the hairdresser's, I remembered only two other times in my life when I had felt so desolate and so alone. Take growing up. My mother was the oldest child of an Irish couple who ran a hotel for a while and then farmed. My father, the oldest child of a Norwegian immigrant who struck it rich in woolens. He was the worker; she, the talker in that match. I was their firstborn. When I was a little girl, they ran the Sunshine Grocery Store in Bemidji, Minnesota. Paul Bunyan country. In the early 1920s, he hatched an idea for what we now know as self-service supermarkets. No one alive knows why his idea died stillborn.

My guess is that my parents married with misaligned expectations. She thought she'd hooked a millionaire's son; he, a young woman with wit, brains, and beauty. She lived to learn that a rich man's son is never as well-to-do as poppa. He, that wit can cut the guts out of a man, that beauties fatten, and that brains befuddled by babies and the housework that goes with them can breed frustration and fury.

No one cause brings on any breakup. Business reverses undoubtedly contributed to my parents' mounting disillusionment with each other. I sided with my father in most of their arguments. When my mother could not do battle with my father directly, I became her target. Without understanding why I had to fight at all, I endured the years of middle childhood fighting back. I struggled to be allowed to be me—neither her nor his crumbly cookie-cutter copy.

There was something in the ethos of the early twentieth century that guaranteed a happy life to anyone who worked hard enough. I remember a framed poem by Berton Braley, "Keep on Keepin' On," which hung on the wall in a bedroom I shared with a sibling or two. When I was ten, I ran away for a day. The morning after the evening I graduated from high school, I escaped for good.

I remember the end of my marriage too. Almost any marriage must be easier than being the second wife of an alcoholic. I met Ray's obediently Catholic mother shortly before her death. She was bent over double from having given birth every other year for twenty years. His father, a pious Irish teetotaler, impressed me as a man who solved his problems by "having faith." Whenever there was a full moon, an Irish holiday, or a payday, Ray's parents' third son handled his problems by helping close the local bars. When he finally staggered home, his wife provided a convenient punching bag on which to displace his life frustrations. "I can't understand you," he used to say. "The harder I throw you, the higher you bounce."

The summer I graduated from Columbia for the second time, Margaret and one of her secretaries helped me bounce for good. And now I realized that my brief stint as an administrator also belonged to my life list of disasters. It had taken me fifteen years to claw from the bottom to the top in academia; fifteen minutes to topple to rock bottom again. I wondered if there was any bounce left. The full impact of Walton's letter and Margaret's attack shattered me. I stumbled to my destination red-eyed and beaten.

My hairdresser, a stocky Greek with graying temples and a triple double chin, diagnosed my condition at a glance. "The Jews have a saying that I've always found helpful," he comforted me. "They say whatever happens is for the best." The kinder Aristides was to me, the more doubtful my holding back the floodgates became. I sat under the dryer and thought about beauticians. Their hands touch us, fuss over us, relax us. Their ears hear our happiest stories, our most secret wishes, our deepest disappointments.

In more jovial visits, Aristides and I joked about how few beauties go to beauty parlors. We'd decided that the name probably comes from what happens to the spirits of ordinary uglies who frequent them. They step into beauty parlors feeling "down" and come out feeling "up." Not so, this time, for me. I leaked tears and was temporarily, at least, un-come-uppable.

I trudged home with frizzled hair and watered eyes, unlocked the door, and made a beeline for the comfort of bed. Through a long and painful night, convulsive sobs welled up and spurted out in gasps of unadulterated despair. I'd been put upon before but the combination of the forced resignation from General Studies and the censure from Margaret was the worst, the nadir. Day finally dawned. Tears ran dry. I dozed off.

I awakened around noon and set the scene for a rejuvenating bath: balanced Louis Untermeyer's paperback anthology *Great Poems* on the metal soap dish, tossed a couple of breakfast oranges and a dollop of liquid soap into the water, and slid in after them to soak and to rehash the lunchtime encounter with Margaret.

She bawled me out for wanting more than fifty measly dollars for correcting the Yale term papers. How cheap. Stingy, too. I scrubbed my face and neck without getting any hair wet. She scolded me for going home for Christmas. How cold. No matter what she says, I'm glad I saw the kids. I'll bet she's jealous of my relationship with them. She's only got one child and that one keeps her distance, I notice. I turned the faucet on so as to assure a steady trickle of hot water and submerged all but my head in the suds. Except for her housecooling, she has not invited me to her apartment once. Still, she invites herself to mine nearly every time her class meets.

I sat up to put *Great Poems* on the toilet seat. For once I was too preoccupied to read poetry aloud while bathing. I bit a hole into one of the oranges and leaned back to squeeze it into my mouth and slurp up the juice.

To hear Margaret blow, you'd think she was the greatest writer this side of hell. I bet plenty of people aren't as impressed with her books as she is. She's getting too famous. No matter how carelessly she throws her stuff together, somebody will print it, somebody will buy it. She probably banks on that in more ways than one. I reached for the second orange and let the peel from the first ride the suds.

She imposes on people whenever it's convenient for her. I'm going to hang up the next time she calls to ask me for a favor. I won't be so available for ten years. She'll be over seventy then and sorry for herself. She's too cocky and hard-hearted now. Look at the way she branded me a failure. I threw the last orange peel to the ceiling and waited for the rebounding splat.

I'm not going to let her in on what I write, either. I'll write what I write without her. I splashed a tidal wave on the tiled floor, orange peels and all. There was something cathartic in surviving Margaret's tongue-lashing without giving her the satisfaction of a whimper. A warm bath gave me a chance to talk back to her, to recover.

Could she have predicted that I would rise to fight back again? Is that why she tore into me instead of comforting me?

I cleaned up the bathroom in preparation for a dinner guest from Idaho.

"I've been fired two times in my life," Jane Plane confided over a quickly defrosted casserole. Jane had called me from a downtown hotel where she was attending a science educators' conference. One consequence of living in New York City is that every professional person you ever knew eventually travels there for a conference. In this case, Jane and I resumed our friendly Stanford ease of interchange as though the six years since our last conversation were six days.

"The first time I got fired," Jane did her best to console me, "I discovered that the faculty most concerned about the injustice being done to me actually did nothing about it. Even I did not fight. Stanford was too male oriented then, and the battle called for more sustained effort than I could give. The second time I got fired, I fought back. I went straight to the president and won. Winning was worth the effort."

"I don't think I'd get anywhere confronting Walton," I shrugged my shoulders and looked out the window. "He's got the chef's tall hat on now, but he'll cook his own goose someday."

"When Thoreau said most of us lead lives of quiet desperation, he must have referred to how misfitted most of us are to what we do for a living," Jane continued. "I hope computers will be able to match more people to the most suitable jobs possible someday. So far, too many of us land them by hit or miss. There's got to be a perfect job for each of us somewhere. Wouldn't it be Utopian if computers connected us to them?"

"There are probably as few people happily working in the perfect job as there are couples happily living in perfectly matched marriages," I thought aloud. "In the meantime, I'd give a dollar to be able to talk to myself a year from now. I've seen nothing but uncertainties ahead each year for the last fifteen years. Every thirty-first of December, I look back on one year and ahead to the next and wonder how I'm ever going to swing it. This year, I'm more mystified than ever."

"Join the club," Jane joked. "Lots of people feel the same way. Jack and I solved the problem by buying ourselves each a horse. The most sure and certain certainty in our lives these days is manure. We hustle home from teaching all day and shovel the stuff. Very basic. Absolutely dependable." She treated me to a big grin.

I returned her grin. "This meal and the lunch with Margaret yesterday afternoon are as different in mood as a volcanic eruption in Hawaii and a morning mist in Maine." I doused two pieces of fruitcake with rum and placed one in front of Jane.

"Remember the Cubberly Conference in California when you and I rounded up a half dozen anthropologists and cohosted a dinner party for her?" asked Jane. "She was so pleased and pleasant that night. She couldn't have been nicer. Even though she was in a wheelchair, she offered to dry the dishes."

"She's like the little girl in the nursery rhyme with a curl in the middle of her forehead." The meal and Jane's companionship had mellowed me. "'When she's good, she's very, very good and when she's bad, she's horrid.' Plenty of us love her, temper tantrums and all. She knows that I'm one of them."

The telephone's impertinent bellow startled me awake. I emerged from a cocoon of blankets and yanked the receiver toward me. William McKee from Merrill Palmer Institute introduced himself long distance from Detroit. "I've heard from an indirect source that you may be available." He laughed when I guessed the identity of his indirect source. "We need an anthropologist for the three-generational kind of family setting that we have here," he said. "We want people with your broad background."

I told him to go ahead and set up an interview for me with his director, Mrs. Knapp, for a week from that day for all day. "I'm still wanted," I sang as I scurried to the bathroom for the morning's ablutions. Nothing like a good-news telephone call to patch up a punctured ego.

At breakfast a half hour later, doubts began to infiltrate my inner monologue. I'm not so sure I want to go to Detroit with all of its racial tension. I'm even less sure I want to work for anyone anywhere except all by myself on a book. But how do I exist in the meantime? People as educated as I am must support themselves. Those at the other end of the educational scale have their living handed to them. Darn it all anyway.

A few days later, I phoned Margaret to tell her about the call. Her apartment mate answered. "Margaret flew to Manila this morning," Rhoda reported. "She's gone to see her daughter and son-in-law. Then she's flying to New Guinea. She won't be back in town for several months."

Since I would have returned to California long before then, I asked Rhoda to tell Margaret about William McKee's call. While I had Rhoda on the line, I also inquired as to whether or not she knew his boss, Mrs. Knapp. "Polly Knapp built the Merrill Palmer Institute," Rhoda responded with emphasis. "She's very elegant and loves elegance. Be hair-curled and shoe-shined when you go to meet her, if you know what I mean."

"Has Mrs. Knapp ever had any children?"

"Not that I know of, but she's very much married to her job. She's got a good mind and a strong character. She's decisive. She likes to run the show. I admire her."

I thanked Rhoda and hung up. As I replaced the receiver, I realized how much easier it was to talk to Rhoda than to Margaret. Rhoda's description of Mrs. Knapp also gave me some insight into Rhoda's attraction to Margaret, and vice versa. All three of them were get-things-done women.

Michigan smelled refreshingly springlike after a long, cold winter in Concrete City. Birds warbled from flowering trees as I taxied from the airport to the Merrill Palmer Institute. Mr. McKee greeted me, put my coat and suitcase away, and notified Mrs. Knapp of my arrival.

I bought the teeth that fit into my lower jaw. They sit on a removable bridge that I take out whenever I'm tired. Before I napped on the plane that morning, I had slipped that dental bridge into my coat pocket.

As I was ushered into her ladyship's presence, this grande doyenne, this living epitome of feminine elegance, the memory of my teeth in the coat that Mr. McKee had closeted streaked across my mind. Oh dear, I thought, Rhoda cautioned me to have my hair curled and my shoes shined, but she forgot to remind me to keep my teeth in.

Mrs. Knapp sat behind a highly polished desk. She was dressed in a shade of silver blue that blended with her neatly coiffured gray hair. All I could offer her in greeting was a closed-lip smirk. I prayed that she would not notice the gap in my mouth during our interview. It would take a minor miracle, but a prayer was all I could muster.

Mrs. Knapp led me to a table by a window in her office. Someone placed a silver tea tray between us. She poured tea into thin china cups and reminisced about Lizzie Merrill Palmer who had founded the institute for which Mrs. Knapp had left her Kentucky home forty-four years before. She said a good administrator attracted good people and then brought out the best in them. She indicated that she thought I was the kind of person she would like to work with. She would be retiring at the end of the summer and wanted to leave a dedicated staff to carry on.

Mr. McKee appeared to show me around the Merrill Palmer Institute and introduce me to a number of her staff as we encountered them during our tour. Each of them smiled wider than I dared. At the end of a graciously pleasant day, Mr. McKee brought me my suitcase and coat. He arranged for a car to take me to the airport. I promised to write him later as to whether or not I'd accept the position of staff anthropologist at Merrill Palmer.

I resisted being buried alive again in another job that wouldn't give me time to write and yet demanded that I publish. I could have told him that on the spot, but it seemed more respectful to wait a few days before passing the position by. Like a pigeon, I wanted only to fly home to roost and rest awhile. I also planned to peck away at an idea for writing an instantly understandable book about anthropology.

Over the next two years, Margaret sent me Christmas photographs and inscribed copies of her most recent publications. I sent her Valentine letters and birthday cards. She appeared increasingly often on national television. I used to look for her name on the TV schedules published in the daily newspaper and tuned in to programs on which she was to be one of the guests. At other times, some unfathomable ESP directed me to turn on the tube when she wasn't scheduled but did appear.

In many parts of the world, older women carry the culture. They live longer than men. They remember the past and they're able to relate it to the present. I would think about that when I watched her dart her tongue in and out or wag her finger at talk show hosts and newscasters; scientists and senators. She was witty in a distinctly no-nonsense way and she knew it. She liked it when people on both sides of the tube laughed at or with her. Anthropologically speaking, she was probably one of television's first talking chiefs.

Meanwhile, in my own life, my father and his sister succumbed to lingering illnesses at opposite ends of the month of January in 1968. These deaths catapulted me into the position of the oldest direct descendant of an eighteen-year-old Norwegian who immigrated to the United States in the 1880s. Like Margaret, I was now the family matriarch. Next in line for ancestorhood. She who keeps track of everybody. The strong one to come to in time of need.

Only I didn't behave like the family matriarch at all. An attraction between my aunt's widower and me blossomed into love. Because Margaret delighted in romances, either hers or somebody else's, I knew this tidbit would tickle and surprise her. Her 1969 birthday card from me announced my remarriage at fifty-one years of age.

Eddie was a conservative, outgoing, roly-poly Milwaukee German. So that my friends might meet him, we planned an East and a West Coast reception for April–May 1970. Stanfordites J. B. and Earline Hefferlin offered us their New York City apartment.

Margaret's name topped the list for the East Coast event. Because she'd testified at a Senate committee hearing to urge decriminalizing marijuana smoking, Eddie vehemently objected to her being invited. "Marijuana's no worse than alcohol or cigarettes," the papers quoted Margaret.

Eddie blew bubbles from a predinner double martini up his nose. Her stand upset him so much that he refused to be in the same room with her. What should I do? Please him and not invite her? Or invite her and displease him? I took a chance. She was too much a part of my life to be slighted. She'd catch him off guard when she arrived at the party, yes, but he'd be too much of a gentleman to make a scene.

Surely, whatever gods may be lined up on my side when Missy Makarit failed to appear at the Hefferlin apartment on the afternoon of our reception, neither she, nor he, ever learned how relieved I was when old friend and new husband managed not to meet.

Our East and West Coast receptions were but incidents in a long line of others like it in the happiest of prolonged honeymoons. On Easter evening, a year after Margaret missed our party, Eddie sat in his upholstered chair in the den looking at the Sunday papers and listening to *Bonanza* on TV. I reclined in a loveseat nearby, reading *Future Shock*.

I think I sensed the presence of death. "Can't understand it," I shivered suddenly, "but I feel strangely squeamish."

"Why don't you go to bed?" he glanced over at me with amused eyes.

"No, I'll wait," I paged ahead to see how much remained in the chapter. "Haven't you learned yet that I won't go until you go? I don't want to miss anything." He didn't answer. I peeked up from *Future Shock* to relish his reaction to my wifely quip. His head arched back and the paper slid from his hands. I banged the book shut and leaped to his side. There would be no answer. Our marriage had brought the storm-tossed ship of my life into safe harbor. Eddie's death thrust it out to sea again.

On Good Friday a letter had arrived from Leila Lee, whom I'd worked with in Margaret's office in the Museum in the 1950s. Her husband had died, and she wanted to get away and planned to embark on a cruise around the world in the fall. Over hot cross buns and coffee on Holy Saturday, Eddie and I discussed Leila's letter. "Wouldn't it be fun to join her? Let's do it!" I enthused.

"No," he hedged. "A ship's too slow. The sky's the way to go."

Nearly a month dragged by before I could string together enough words in a telephone conversation to make myself understood. In that interval, the president of the company Eddie worked for all of his life presented me with a $5,000 death benefit. Leila's letter still lay atop the TV in the room in which Eddie died. I phoned her to talk over our mutual widowhood and to ask for more details about her upcoming excursion.

She planned to leave in mid-November on a freighter, the *Esmeralda*, of the Oriental Overseas Line. It was owned by C. Y. Tung, the "Onassis of the Orient." "A ship called the *Esmeralda!* The name alone would sell me a ticket." Later, Leila's travel agent called to inform me that I'd lucked into a cancellation; the *Esmeralda* had room for one more voyager. I cashed the five grand on a trip around the world with Leila Lee.

Except for my sons and a handful of old friends, including MM, nobody knew where I went. Except for Leila Lee, nobody on shipboard knew who I was or what I suffered. For five precious months, the vastness of the eternal sea solaced me by day and rocked me to sleep at night. I didn't hear a telephone nor a word of advice from one do-gooder. Widowhood forces difficult decisions. A traveler's anonymity ensured that mine would be my own.

When I waved hello to my sons and their mates on the wharf in San Francisco from the deck of the *Esmeralda*, I had decided to return to the home Eddie and I had shared. I hoped to locate a teaching position within commuting distance.

The clothes basket of accumulated mail waiting for me in Wisconsin contained a hand-addressed pale yellow envelope from 211 Central Park West in New York City. Inside was an original scissors cutting, or Scherenschnitte, of a thistle by a European-born American artist.

I deciphered the handwritten letter. It read:

Dear Pat,

I am so very, very sorry and sad that I missed meeting him in New York. I tried to. Turned the world upside down to get there and then the number I had was wrong. There was no way to find out.

I wish I did need an older former student to go to New Guinea, but I'm staying with other fieldworkers everywhere, not setting up a camp of my own.

Do keep in touch. It is just tragic for you.

Affectionately,

Tears shimmered the words. Here was a letter, written from a distance, on a Sunday afternoon, by the busiest of persons, in a loving attempt to assuage the grief of a newly widowed friend. It came from a tender little toughie who, if I didn't watch out, would "keep in touch" by finding me another job with a nursery school attached.

7

SHE BELONGS TO EVERYBODY

I entered the Algonquin Room on the mezzanine of the Royal York Hotel in Toronto, Canada, and chose a seat to the left of center and near the front. It was 7:30 a.m. Between then and 7:59, as anthropologists finished breakfast in the hotel coffee shop or dashed in from the parking lot, the room filled to capacity. Seven of the last to straggle in took places along the far side of a table equipped with water glasses, note pads, and a microphone. Except for the lone woman among them, the speakers looked as though they'd just stepped out of the Old Testament with full intentions to return to the safety of its chapters and verses once the meeting adjourned.

The one woman on the panel rubbed sleepy eyes and skimmed the paper she was scheduled to present. The six men drowsily twisted the ends of their hairy fringes or enjoyed the tactile pleasure of stroking bearded faces in full yawn. Their rings and watchbands, heavy with oversize chunks of turquoise, communicated visually that southwestern Indian jewelry was anthropologically "in."

This symposium, The Ethnographies of Visual Communication, was one of several that opened the seventy-first annual conference of the American Anthropological Association on the long weekend after Thanksgiving 1972. At 8:00 sharp, a firm-chinned Dr. Mead stalked into the Algonquin Room. A red cape flapped behind her and her shepherd's crook stomped one step ahead. She swished past without seeing me and plunked herself down in the middle of the first row. An entourage of sweet young things trailed and scurried for seats somewhere else.

The room woke up. People sat straighter. Idle chatter ceased. It was as though the shepherd with the crook were studded with neon lights. The few who didn't understand the stir felt her energy and wondered, "Who's that?"

Sol Worth, the chairman of the sessions, formally acknowledged her presence in his introduction and, for the next two hours, Margaret let no one forget it. When she disagreed with a remark made from either the panel or the floor, she resorted to one of two procedures: without waiting for a nod from the chair, she stood by her seat, turned to face the audience in a room suddenly silenced and pounded her criticisms home with forked stick and tongue. For statements she considered beneath extended comment, she remained seated and grumbled "rubbish" in mounting crescendo, while the source of her disdain visibly cowered.

During this session, I addressed a question or two to the panel. Margaret didn't indicate that she recognized my voice. After all, she had not heard it in five years. After the program, I walked over and stood a few feet away from her. It was the first time we'd been in each other's presence since our lunch together when I left General Studies. She looked up, smiled broadly, and signaled me to wait. As soon as the usual cluster of questioners disappeared, she grabbed my arm.

"Pat, do you know where there's a toilet?"

"I think I saw one near the elevators." I reached for the shopping bag at her feet.

"Still up to your old tricks," she admonished playfully.

"I'm younger and stronger and I don't mind carrying," I said, as I slung her bag over my shoulder. We picked up the threads of our friendship as though we had talked to each other yesterday.

"This is the first time I've ever seen you in slacks. When did you start wearing them?" I asked on our way to the ladies' room.

"In 1968 when I was sixty-seven, and I had no trouble getting used to them, either," she boasted.

"It took me longer. I wear practically nothing else now. Slacks are less bothersome than dresses and all the underpadding that goes with them."

"Right," she agreed almost in the same breath as she asked about each of my sons by name. We continued our catching up over the partition between our stalls. "Do you have any grandchildren yet?"

"Yes," I called out, "they're all black and have four feet and tails."

"That figures," she flushed the commode and opened her door.

"And yours?"

"Cathy's little girl, Vonnie, is three already. Later, I'll show you some pictures I brought along." I joined her at the sinks. "And how do you like teaching at the University of Wisconsin in Milwaukee?" We talked into the mirrors in front of us as we washed our hands.

"Rough. I haven't taught since the University of Delaware six years ago, you know, and the Columbia experience shot my confidence more than I realized. Getting three courses off the ground at once is a real pain, and I'm rusty as hell."

"You may be rusty, but you're a natural. Stay in teaching, because you're good at it." We held our hands under the same dryer. With eyes that rarely missed much, she measured me up, down, and sidewise. "I can remember when you were thin," she said. "You've gained some weight."

"Thirty pounds to be exact." No use fudging with this critic. "I felt so sorry for myself after Eddie died that I'd go into the kitchen and say, "What can I eat that I shouldn't?"

"I know the feeling," she said, "even though Tulia keeps us out of her kitchen these days."

"We're both beginning to look more and more like the Venus of Willendorf," I said as we started out the door. Two strangers who entered the ladies' room as we left overheard my remark, recognized Margaret, and smiled.

"Where's the closest place we can grab some lunch on the wing? I haven't eaten yet and the service will be faster if we go before twelve."

"The closest is the coffee shop right here in this hotel," I said.

We took the escalator to the ground floor and then the elevator down to the coffee shop. On the way, she inquired about my faculty status at the University of Wisconsin in Milwaukee. "The department has hired a hairy-faced white male and a svelte black female besides me," I said, "and has given us each a one-year appointment. I'm the only one of the three with a doctorate; the other two are working on theirs. I'm the oldest; the other two can't be much out of their twenties, if that. There's talk of budget cuts and falling enrollments. One of the trio will be asked to stay. Which do you guess it will be?"

"The black female, but she won't stay long."

"Why do you say that?"

"Because there aren't enough educated black males in Milwaukee. She'll have to go to a city like Chicago to have a decent social life. It won't take her long to figure that out."

A student interrupted us to introduce himself as we stepped off the escalator. "I've read your books," he breathed deeply, "and now it's such an honor to be in your presence."

"That's why we come to these meetings," she shunted him off and motioned me to keep up with her. We balanced on stools at the lunch counter. I put our bags and her cape on the empty one beside me. The waitress handed us a menu. Margaret ordered broiled cod and mashed potatoes; I, a house salad.

She asked for her bag, dug down deep, and brought up an envelope with a rubber band around it. It was stuffed with snapshots of her granddaughter, Sevanne Margaret Kassarjian. "Where did her name come from? I've never heard of it before, and I used to write a radio show on the meaning of names."

"Sevanne's the name of a town in Armenia, so not many people in this country are likely to have heard of it. Her father, Barkev Kassarjian, is from Armenia. We call her Vonnie for short." Margaret's just like any other grandmother, I thought as I walked my fingers through her cache of pictures. There must be forty snapshots here and one would be plenty. Margaret looked across my arm and remembered a story to tell about each time-lapsed glimpse of her daughter Cathy's daughter. "She's got the same rectangular smile you have," I observed as I began to pull out examples to prove my point.

"Yes, and her father's dark eyes."

I lined the four pictures up on the counter between our plates. "If you had these blown up and mounted them alongside similar views of yourself, anyone could see at a glance how markedly alike your smiles are. If you did it right away, they'd make unique and not too expensive presents for Christmas."

"That's a good idea." She penciled an *x* on the backs of the most likely candidates for enlargement. Now it was my turn to look over her shoulder. "I take it you don't like being a grandmother," I teased.

"I've written a piece on grandmothers for *Redbook*," she said, as she dropped the envelope into her purse. "As a child, I was very close to my father's mother, you know. All my life I've been attracted to people who were close to their grandparents."

"That could be another reason why we've survived as friends," I said. "My father's mother died when I was only eight, but my mother's mother and I were great friends. I used to visit Grandma Cavanaugh on the farm on school vacations. We laughed together every day and I smile when I think of her."

Margaret bent over to retrieve a napkin and I noticed she was wearing a lapis lazuli necklace that was new to me. "Whatever happened to that big crystal pendant you used to wear all the time?"

"Somebody unzipped my bag at Kennedy Airport last summer and took out all the jewelry," she answered. "Sickened me too because the sentimental value was far more than what anyone could have possibly got for it. Friends have been giving me jewelry ever since. A former assistant brought this piece from Chile." She inspected me for signs of jewelry. "I see you're still wearing a wedding band."

"Yes," I admitted. "It's special. Eddie gave this ring to me on the day we were married. Each of the four stones in it also reminds me of my four sons."

"I canceled everything to get to your reception that afternoon," she said. "Hired a taxi and drove all over the place. I had the wrong address and no phone number, so we had to give up. Eddie's death so soon after your marriage saddened me."

"Yes." We narrowed in on feelings. "He's been gone a year and a half. He'll appear in a dream occasionally. Believe it or not, I know it's only a dream, but he seems so real I don't want to wake up. When the wind blows a branch on the roof, I hope he's driven into the garage again and I catch my breath to listen better for his footsteps."

"Oh, Pat, it just doesn't seem fair, does it?"

"I don't talk about heartache much, but tears lurk just below the surface. I'm still in love, I guess."

"It's nice to be in love with someone," she whispered wistfully. "Are you lonely? How do you deal with loneliness?"

"The same way you do, by keeping busy. It's strange, but I now feel that if he had to die, and everybody does, Eddie died when I was young enough to be able to pick up the pieces of my life and get on with it. After we married, we moved my books from the West Coast. That library and my job anchor me in Wisconsin these days."

"You seem to land on both feet no matter what happens." Her eyes glistened approval. "I'll visit you next time I'm in Milwaukee."

"I dare you to. The house is so big you can choose what color bedroom you want." The coffee shop began to fill up. Some of the people I knew by name. Others looked familiar. "We haven't mentioned Cathy or Rhoda or Tulia yet. How are they?"

"Cathy's thirty-three now. She's in Israel with her husband. We're going to cochair an invitational conference just outside of Vienna in August. It'll help her meet the right people."

"And vice versa. I wonder if Cathy realizes how fortunate she is to have you for a mother. How many other young women would be so lucky as to be handed an opportunity like that?"

"She does and she doesn't. You know how children are." She surveyed the coffee shop, now crowded with anthropologists. "I've seen some of these same faces at conferences for the past forty-eight years. More of us older anthropologists should encourage younger people to participate much more actively at these meetings than we do. The younger ones aren't going to get visibility or conference expertise otherwise."

"And Rhoda?"

"She's in New Guinea. Her son, Daniel, is working on his doctorate at Columbia. He's very happily married into an Old World–style Italian family. He's even got grandmothers-in-law."

Next I asked about Tulia, the sweet-faced, soft-spoken Haitian housekeeper. "Tulia's sixty-two and still with us. Rhoda and I told her she could have her husband stay with her in our apartment when we went on our last field trip. She gave both of us a big laugh when she stiffened and said, 'I don't want a man on my job!' After all, he was her husband! And we'd be away."

"Aren't you gong to be seventy-one in a few days? How about you? Are you slowing down any?"

"No, I won't stop. Have you read about the research on the aged Russians? The ones who lived to be over a hundred? They lived longer because they had work to do and everybody expected them to do it. So they kept going and stayed alive. It's the same with me. I'm working as hard as ever. Before I came to the symposium this morning, for instance, I did a telephone interview for a television show out in Hamilton. It didn't take much time and the money will finance this trip."

When we paid for our lunches, Dutch treat, she asked to exchange some of her worn U.S. dollars for my new Canadian ones. We both intended to pay bills with Canadian money and to tip with U.S. dollars.

On the way to the elevator, I mentioned that Marshall McLuhan had invited me to have lunch with him at St. Michael's College at Toronto University the next day. "We were on Doxiadis's ship in the Aegean together last summer."

She perked up at the mention of McLuhan's name. "I'd like to talk with him. That man's got one of the greatest minds of the twentieth century. Greet him for me, please."

"I'll tell him you said hello." The car stopped on the sixth floor. I handed over her bag and cape.

"We've got twenty-nine minutes before the business meeting at 1:30," she looked at her timepiece. "I think I'll grab a nap." The doors opened. "See you at the meeting," she called as she walked out.

The doors closed behind her. I backed into a corner to count lighted numbers flicking on and off as the elevator zipped to the tenth floor. A spare-haired man no older than Margaret braced himself against the other corner. His bony hands trembled as they grasped the cane that kept him from lurching forward at each stop and start. "She's got enough energy to run this elevator," he joked in a voice that lost its timbre years ago.

"Don't forget the elevator alongside, too," I quipped.

Once inside Room 1001, I kicked off my shoes, propped one pillow in front of the other, and lay down on a twin bed. I opened a file folder of papers on or by Marshall McLuhan that I had brought to Toronto to read prior to our lunch together. His expansively positive interpretations of the influence of electronic media on our lives excited me so I skipped the rest of the sessions that day.

I read the papers far into the night. Until the invention of print, he seemed to say, all humankind lived in a "global village" and communicated person to person by ear and eye. Or sight and sound. When print came along, literacy diametrically separated those who could read from those who couldn't.

To an extent, radio began to bridge this gap by sending messages to literate and nonliterate alike, through the ear and the imagination. Pictures, particularly moving ones, added eye communication. But television leapfrogs over the limits set by literacy, nationality, language differences, and time. Television is both "the medium and the message." It has the potential to enable all humankind to live and communicate as "global villagers" once again. I dozed off with the light on and papers by or about Marshall McLuhan spread all around me.

A phone call from McLuhan's secretary at the Center for Culture and Technology at Toronto University startled me awake. "He doesn't have classes on Fridays," said Margaret Stewart, who identified herself as his secretary, "so he won't be in before 10:00. He wanted me to tell you to arrive sometime soon after 11:30."

I liked Marshall McLuhan before I met him. My first sight of him doubled the pleasure. He resembled a skinny, shaggy, older edition of my son Neal. His rust-colored corduroys and pullover sweater perfectly matched his freckles and his eyes and his reddish-gray hair.

As we walked over to the Faculty Club dining facility, he told me that he'd taught briefly at the University of Wisconsin in Madison after he completed graduate school. Sometime during the sherry that preceded lunch, I mentioned Margaret's being in Toronto. "I wish she'd let me know she was coming," he lamented. "I haven't seen her since last summer. Now that she's in town, I'd like to have her meet some of our faculty and students."

"We lunched together yesterday. She asked me to say hello and said she'd like to talk with you."

"Oh, she did?" He put down his sherry. "Will you excuse me for a moment? I'm going to call Corinne. If our Sunday's free, we could arrange a quick get-together at the house."

While he phoned his wife, I inserted new batteries in my tape recorder. If he didn't mind, I'd promised my Visual Anthropology seminar students that I'd tape our meeting so that they might hear this twentieth-century philosopher's voice and eavesdrop on our conversation as best they could between the clinks and clatters of dining room noises.

"It's all set," he smiled, as he rejoined me. "We're going to give a party Sunday afternoon. Margaret's to be the guest of honor. You're invited too. Mrs.

McLuhan will scoot over after lunch and take us to the Royal York so that I may invite Margaret personally."

I didn't have much to say in the car when Mrs. McLuhan taxied her husband and me to the hotel. The logistics of getting Marshall and Margaret together in a place swarming with anthropologists stymied me. Where to locate her? Where to keep him while I searched her out?

The coffee shop!

I took him there. We found a table. "Please have some tea and stay right here!" I told him. "Don't move! It won't make any sense to find her and lose you. I'll bring her back as soon as humanly possible. She wants to talk with you."

No use waiting for an elevator, I told myself. They never hurry when you want them. I took the stairs two at a time. A couple of students in tennis shoes sat to the side of the top step and pored over the list of afternoon sessions in the rust-colored program.

"Can I see that please?' I gasped breathlessly. "I need to find Margaret Mead, PDQ."

"We were just looking at her session," one of them remarked. "She's a discussant in L'Homme Nu: Methodological and Ethnographic Issues in Room A on the convention floor. It started at 2:00 and it'll last til 5:00."

"Thanks."

Within seconds, I opened the door to Room A. It was stuffed to overflowing. People sat rump to rump on the floor in the aisle. They stood elbow to elbow against the walls, along the sides of the room, and in the back. I groped through the semidarkness to the front row. There sat Margaret, her left arm curled around her thumb stick. She was taking notes with the speed of a stenotype machine.

I leaned across her neighbors and stage whispered. "McLuhan wants to see you."

"What?" she rasped.

"Marshall McLuhan wants to see you," I repeated much more slowly and in a slightly louder voice. "He's waiting for you in the coffee shop right now."

"Go away. Get out of here!"

Annoyed bysitters frowned at me. I turned and fumbled toward the door, shut it quietly, set my elbows on a high, narrow table just outside, and buried my head in my hands.

What in the world would I tell Marshall McLuhan? Certainly not that Margaret had rebuffed me. And what about his party?

A middle-aged man moved away from the table when I paused at it. He held a copy of *Blackberry Winter* under one arm.

"What are you waiting for?" I asked him.

"I'm going to see if Dr. Mead will autograph this book." He touched its cover with his free hand as he spoke.

"If I were you, I'd stay away from her today." I shook my head disconsolately. "She's not in the best of humors. Why don't you wait and try again tomorrow?"

The doors to Room A flung open. Margaret burst out like a race horse released from the starting gate, wide-nosed nostrils flaring and eyes narrowed for a strong wind. "Pat, what in hell do you want?" she snarled so furiously her head waggled.

"Remember I was going to have lunch with Marshall McLuhan? Well, he got his wife, Corinne, to bring him back with me. He's waiting in the coffee shop. He wants to invite you to a special party in your honor at his house on Sunday."

"I'm flying home tonight! I won't be here on Sunday! And there's no way in hell I can go down to the coffee shop now! I'm one of two discussants in this symposium. I've got to pay attention so that I can make intelligent comments afterward."

"Okay. I'll make some excuse to cover for you," I sighed. "Marshall McLuhan will be disappointed. He really wants you to join him in the coffee shop."

"He's not God!" She stomped her stick, turned 180 degrees, and flounced back into the bowels of Room A. Nor are you, I muttered under my breath as the man holding *Blackberry Winter* skittered away.

Of all the anthropologists at this conference, I told myself as I throttled down, at least 999 of them would stop everything this afternoon to chat informally across a table with a man like Marshall McLuhan. But how to find a one of them at a moment's notice?

Four graduate students from my own Department of Anthropology in Milwaukee crossed my path. I buttonholed them and talked them into coming down to the coffee shop to drink tea and listen to McLuhan.

Back at the table, I fabricated something about Margaret's regretting not being able to see him because she had to fly to New York minutes after the symposium ended because she had to be the speaker at another meeting at 8:00 in the morning. Whether he believed me or not, he took the news in stride and graciously regaled the five of us until his wife returned to take him home.

Filled with more tea than I've ever imbibed at one sitting, I made my way back to the room that I shared with Dana Raphael. Dana and I had known each other since we were students together under Mead in the early 1950s. "She can be difficult, but then she's always helping us in one way or the other," Dana responded to my tale of the afternoon clash with Margaret outside Room A. "I saw her around lunch today myself. She hardly let me open my mouth. Said she didn't have any time for me in Toronto. She could always see me in New York."

"She belongs to everybody and everybody makes incredible demands on her. We can't forget that." My heart pounded faster than usual and I felt drained.

"Being a friend is never easy. Imagine how much more difficult it is to keep your friendships when you become famous," Dana complained. "Margaret's time is so damned asked-for always."

"Yes, I know. Whatever she does for any of us takes a lot out of her. She showed me umpteen pictures of her granddaughter yesterday. That part of her doesn't surface very often."

"Have you ever tried to give her anything? I sent her a handmade table-cloth shawl once. She never wore it and she never thanked me for it. God only knows what happened to it. When I heard she broke her ankle at the Birdwhistels, I sent her flowers! Know what she did with them? She gave them to Ray and Marion Birdwhistel! She told me later that it was nice to have something to give to her hosts."

"If you really want to get her goat, give her something with her initials on it. Then she can't even give it away. Wait a minute. I just thought of something. If a present had only a capital 'M' engraved on it, she could give it to her apartment mate, Rhoda Metraux! If there were two Ms? Marshall McLuhan! She could send her overflow to Marshall McLuhan! After this afternoon's fiasco, she owes him some little courtesy."

Blackberry Winter lay on my bedside stand. It had just been published and I'd brought it along for between-times reading. "Listen to this," I said. "She says this book will go through 1940. Here's a picture of her granddaughter, Vonnie, who wasn't even born until 1969. Twenty-nine years later. Some editor should have caught that discrepancy."

"I wonder why she called it *Blackberry Winter*? I don't get the connection between blackberries and winter and Margaret Mead until 1940."

"She was a girl in Hammonton, New Jersey, you know." I flipped pages slowly enough to take in the gist of each. "Hammonton's on the edge of the Jersey Pine Barrens. It's been quite a market garden spot for ages. Supplies fresh fruit to cities like New York and Philly and Washington."

"How do you know that?"

"I've driven through there, stopped at some of the fruit and vegetable stands, talked to the locals. A lot of Sicilian-Italian farmers immigrated to the area around the turn of the century. In fact, Emily Fogg Mead, Margaret's mother, did one of the first community studies in this country, and it was on those very immigrants."

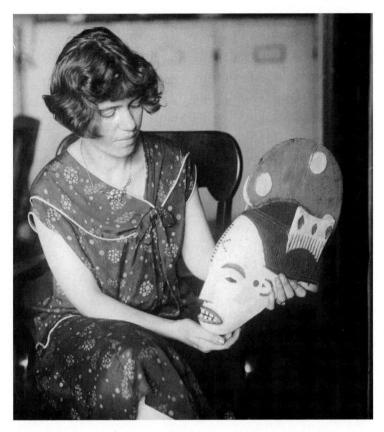

A young Margaret Mead studies a mask from the South Pacific. Analyses of such artifacts were relevant to her dissertation, "The Question of Cultural Stability in Polynesia," and to her book *Coming of Age in Samoa. CORBIS/Bettman.*

At the age of twenty-four, Margaret Mead was responsible for South Pacific displays and artifacts at the American Museum of Natural History in New York City. *CORBIS/Bettman.*

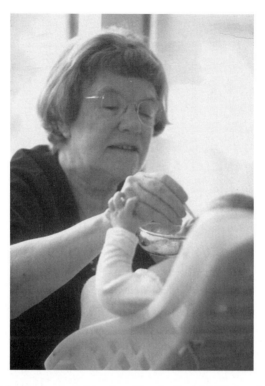

Margaret Mead feeding her granddaughter, Vonnie. Grandchild–grandparent relationships were intensely interesting to Margaret. She had been close to her paternal grandmother who stirred her imagination as a child and was involved in her early education. © *Robert J. Levin/Black Star/PNI.*

Margaret Mead in a discussion with Dr. Benjamin Spock, in whom Margaret found a colleague interested in natural childbirth. He assisted Margaret in the birth of her daughter, Catherine. © *Robert J. Levin/Black Star/PNI.*

The author in 1957 with her four sons, (left to right) Kent, Neal, Laird, and Miles on Long Island, New York, shortly before she journeyed to California to begin her Ph.D. in Anthropology and Education at Stanford University. *Photo courtesy of Pat Grinager.*

A wooden replica of Margaret Mead carved by Bricy Muir, husband of Margaret's niece. *Photo courtesy of Pat Grinager.*

Margaret Mead poses with her thumbstick, an accoutrement she was seldom without in later life and which became her trademark and, some would say, a hallmark of her authority. *UPI/CORBIS/Bettman.*

"They reclaimed some of the Pine Barrens and grew berries just as they had in the Old Country. Evidently, they believed that they got a richer blackberry crop in the fall when and if snow nipped the blossoms in the spring."

"I still don't get the connection."

"It's just an idea, but I'll bet you a dollar to a dime that Margaret perceived some symbolism between that saying and her own life. Hammontonian gardeners grow more strawberries and raspberries now, but blackberries were the thing when she was a girl. If blackberry bushes that had been endangered in some way during the period of early growth produced a "richer crop" than those that had not, my hunch is that something frightened or threatened Margaret in some way during her early development and she went on to produce a "richer crop" of books, or whatever, than her playmates who had a smoother time of it."

"Nobody's childhood is perfect," Dana said as she brushed back her long hair. "I thought she had a pretty good one."

"She had an outstanding mother, I'm convinced of that. She mentions her mother to me all the time, even though she's written that her father's mother influenced her the most."

I propped *Blackberry Winter* on my belly and picked out snatches of it to read to Dana about Margaret's own motherhood when she gave birth to Mary Catherine Bateson. "My young women students in Milwaukee tell me that they like the part about her having a baby the best." I looked up and talked to Dana's attractive reflection in the long mirror that hung above two adjacent hip-high chests of drawers.

"Margaret was critical of the way babies were delivered in hospitals at the time so she set up what would have been considered a very primitive situation for herself with a doctor who would go along with her. He was Benjamin Spock, by the way. She had no anesthesia, she wanted to nurse her baby, and the whole event was photographed."

"Interesting." Dana opened her eyes wide and rubbed her little finger around the edges of them. "In other words, she determined how that birth would go and found a doctor who'd go along with her. How typical. So many hospital deliveries are still at the convenience of the physician with little or no respect for the mother, the baby, or the family."

"I've always puzzled over how she was able to spend as much time with Cathy as she claimed and still gallivant around the world while that kid was growing up," I said. "We've got children too. We know the conflict that paralyzes a mother when she has to leave her brood even temporarily, let alone as much as was the case when Margaret made weekly trips to Washington, D.C., and Cathy was no more than a preschooler."

"She presents a carefully constructed image of her own maternity to the public. It's common knowledge among anthropologists that she farmed that kid out to everybody."

"Talking about the image Margaret might want to project," I continued as Dana put the finishing touches on her eyes, "have you noticed how much she darts her tongue in and out of late? She does it face to face and on television. I doubt if she realizes what it looks like. If she did, she'd quit."

"Yes, I've noticed it for quite some time. It's a sign of aging, poor dear. She probably has dry lips, too. I'm bothered by dry lips in this warm hotel myself. It's terrible."

"You give me an idea," I brushed my shorter hair with two swipes and kissed on some lipstick. "Let's mosey down and see who's at the bar on the first floor before you're off on your dinner date."

I followed the path of the indicator lights as we waited for the elevator. "You know, Dana, she sets her alarm for 4:00 a.m. The rest of us sleep at least three hours longer and then fill our days with piddling tasks that chimpanzees could be trained to do. Margaret's of another ilk. She pushes herself. Relentlessly. You'd think she were trying to live the nine lives of one of Rhoda's cats."

"Think thin," Dana joked when a nearly full elevator opened its doors to us.

"Ah ha," I pulled in my stomach. "I've gained too much to dance anymore."

"You'd lose it if you did," Dana whispered as we walked in, turned around to face the big brown doors, and stopped talking, like everybody else.

Three months later, on Valentine's Day 1973, Margaret flew from Denver to Milwaukee. She arrived late in the middle of a snowstorm at 4:00 p.m. She was to deliver a speech at the local branch of the University of Wisconsin three hours and fifty-five minutes later. I had planned to get her back to the house by 4:00, which would have allowed her an hour and a half to freshen up and take a nap, two hours for a leisurely dinner, and thirty minutes to get to the lecture hall. There wouldn't be a moment to spare.

The storm changed all that. The storm and the media people. She made a smiling beeline for me as she debarked. She apologized for having kept me waiting for an extra half hour. "You don't have to apologize," I said. "It's not a passenger's fault when the plane's late." She was handing me her shopping bag carry-on when an airline official waylaid us.

"Some television people and journalism students want to interview you for the evening news," he said. "They're waiting in an area that is equipped for airport interviews."

I followed them to the door and cornered him when she stepped into a room busy with television cameras and recording equipment. "Listen, Mister," I declared authoritatively, "you must impress upon those newsmen that they've got to finish with her in thirty minutes. No more. They'll put her life in my hands if they keep her so much as one minute later. You know yourself how bad the roads are. She's absolutely got to leave here by 4:30." He looked at me as though I were the Maharani of Swat. I can get tough on occasion, and it feels so good.

"What's so magic about 4:30?" she asked when we finally took the escalator down to the baggage carousel.

"Nothing, really, except that those newsmen needed a definite time limit or you'd never be able to take a nap before dinner. You're not getting any younger, you know."

"Do you mother everybody the way you mother me?" She liked my idea of a nap for her.

Her plaid zippered suitcases were the only pieces remaining on the carousel when we went to pick them up. "These are my favorite bags for traveling," she explained as we pulled them off the moving strip. "They're lightweight and cheap so it doesn't matter what happens to them. I never lock them either. Locks are no good. Anyone can break a lock. Makes going through customs faster, too."

She waited outside the main door while I ran for the car. "It's nice to see you, Pat," she said as soon as she sat down beside me. "After the way I treated you in Toronto, I wasn't sure you'd ever speak to me again. Scold me if you think I deserve it."

"No problem, Margaret."

I squinted my eyes toward homebound, snow-topped traffic and talked matter-of-factly to an icy windshield. "A person's got to be able to explode to somebody occasionally. Relatives or friends are about the only ones who'll take our tempers and come back for more. Yours make you unpredictable and totally challenging. I'm never bored, that's for sure, and I'd rather be challenged than bored any day."

"I wrote Marshall McLuhan a note and apologized to him too," she confessed.

"Oh, no! I forgot what I made up to tell him when I got back to where he waited in the coffee shop. I only hope your story sort of jibed with mine."

"I didn't write you because I knew I'd be coming to Milwaukee and would apologize in person if you'd listen."

"I wasn't at all prepared for his wanting to return to the hotel with me that afternoon," I said. "On the way down, I became so involved in figuring out how to get you two together that I didn't give a thought to what you might have had on your agenda. Afterward, I saw that your particular symposium was international in scope. You couldn't possibly have left it with no more notice than I wanted to give you."

She searched my face for signs of insincerity. When she saw I wasn't about to nurse a grudge, such a feeling of mutual regard filled the car you'd think we'd scratched our fingers and mingled the blood. "Is there anything I can do for you now I'm in Milwaukee?" she asked lovingly.

"Yes, I do have one little favor." I'd put off bringing the matter up and here she handed me a silver platter chance. "With luck, we'll be home by 5:00. I'll show you up to your bedroom right away. Whether you're tired or not, I want you to lie down and have some time to yourself until almost 6:00.

"I know how much you like being with young people and my favor is this: The graduate students in my Education and Anthropology seminar want to meet you. We have to eat somewhere anyway. They'll be bringing out their favorite dishes between 5:30 and 6:00 and will set up a buffet dinner in your honor.

"Everything will be ready when I waken you. All you'll have to do is come downstairs and eat with no more than a dozen young people. I hope you won't mind."

"Is there any particular message you want me to pass along to them?"

"Play it by ear," I breathed a big sigh of relief. "They've been thinking up questions to ask you and have a bunch."

Rain and slush made visibility nearly zero. Passing cars splashed salt on my windshield. The fluid I turned on to clean off the salt froze as it landed.

"I don't want to sound like the Chamber of Commerce, but you're hitting the worst two days of weather this winter." I gripped the steering wheel with half-frozen hands.

"I heard the forecast on the *Today Show* in the hotel this morning," she replied calmly, "so I knew what kind of weather to expect."

"It's so much worse than when I drove to the airport two hours ago," I bit my lip. "At this rate, we'll have to start back for the university twenty or thirty minutes sooner, too."

"Did any mail come for me?" she asked.

"Yes. Something's come. United Parcel delivered two different large brown envelopes from the Museum just as I left. They're on the dresser in your bedroom."

"Which do you think looks better?" She held up a plain and a frilly white blouse with ruffles around the neck when I tapped on her door at 5:55.

"The ruffled one."

She slipped into it and backed up to me saying, "Zip me up."

She flicked a brush through her flouncy curls and applied some lipstick.

Twelve students milled around on the first floor.

"Margaret Mead! You're here! I can't believe it!" A pregnant anthropology major with a month to go put a plate of freshly cut raw vegetables on the dining room table and hurried over to us as we started down the stairs. "I want you to rub my belly so I can someday tell my child about it."

Margaret rubbed her midriff and greeted students as they came up to her. She chatted pleasantly and helped herself to the variety of ethnic dishes on display. We sat on the sofa in the living room. Students knelt, stood, or sat around as Margaret ate and held court. Very much aware of our time limitations, they fired their questions fast. A bewhiskered graduate student pressed her for her theory of logic and of learning.

"There is no one theory of learning." She swallowed a bit of cannibal sandwich made of raw beef and sliced onion on rye. "People learn in hundreds of ways. And I'm not willing to say that there is only one kind of logic and that that comes from the Greeks, either. As anthropologists, you should be ashamed of yourselves if you do not leave yourselves open to discover kinds of learning and logic that you've never even thought of before."

"What do you consider the difference between training and education?" inquired a bespectacled blond.

"One trains dogs and circus animals and some anthropologists," she answered. "Too many anthropologists are trained just as one would train a dog. Schools which permit that to happen shouldn't be allowed to operate. Too many graduates in anthropology don't know any more than their professors do or what's in their professor's books. You've got to be widely read and widely reading to be truly educated. Take care not to get frozen into one specialty. If you haven't read what the psychologists have written about learning, you should. Also, look up Gregory Bateson's essay 'Deutero Learning' too. Then go out and observe how real people actually do learn."

"How do you find time to do all the things you do?" a newly married student–parent queried.

"First of all, I have a keen concept of time. I plan at least a year ahead. I already know what I will be doing between now and next February. I know where I will be going. It's already booked. I go to an Arapesh resettlement for two months in April. I'll stop for a conference in Port Moresby while I'm in the Pacific. I'll be in Europe for more conferences this summer, and so on. I sleep when there's nothing else to do."

"What did you think of the presentation of *The Chariot of the Gods* on TV?" one of the single males interrupted her.

"I didn't see it, but I've heard about the archeological astronauts in the program," she replied as she washed down sliced turkey with Cold Duck. "To my mind, it's nothing more than science fiction. What surprises me the most when I say something like that is a whole generation of you young people has never read any science fiction. That's part of what I mean when I talk about how narrowly educated some specialists, like anthropologists, are these days. Don't ever let your studies dull your curiosity or curb your capacity."

She got up to go in for Valentine cookies and coffee. She stopped in the kitchen to thank the students there who were helping my neighbor, Barbara Consigny, with all the touches that make a gathering like this run smoothly.

"I don't think there'll be much of a crowd at school. It's a good night to just stay home," one of the young men declared as he cleaned off his boots after moving his car clear of the garage door so I could back out.

I held her fur-trimmed leather coat as she slipped her arms into it. "I thought this coat was much too frivolous when I bought it last winter," she said. "I feel more comfortable in it this year because I see more coats like it around now." I helped her with the bottom buckle. "How about a hat? It's blustery outside."

"I have a fur hat somewhere but I didn't bring it because I can't find a thing when Rhoda's not home." She tied a little see-through scarf over her head and slipped into some rubber protectors for shoes that she had found on one of her annual January consulting jaunts to Cincinnati.

As soon as we were alone in the car, she asked if there were anything political that she should know inasmuch as we would be attending a small party put on by the Department of Anthropology after her lecture. I didn't recognize her veiled concern for my employment. "What will you do if you don't get a job here again next year?" she asked me next, and then I sensed her motives.

"There're other colleges in the area," I answered. "This Department of Anthropology is small and largely male. I don't think worrying about what the department does to me jobwise next year will do any good one way or the other. I'm thinking of moving over to the School of Nursing, but keep that under your own babushka."

Her speech, "Thoughts on Ethnicity," was one of fourteen Melting Pot Myth lectures sponsored by the College of Letters and Sciences. We high-stepped through accumulations of sloppy snow between our parking place and the Student Union. When she told me she'd broken her ankle four times, I kept a firm grip on her arm.

She shared a view of herself as a public speaker: "In city after city I find audiences most responsive," she said. "They are ready and willing to appreciate anything I have to say, no matter what it is. Especially, I notice, they appreciate humor. Audiences want to laugh."

As we stepped inside the doorway, a big clock indicated two seconds to go. After a brief introduction, she stalked onto the stage alone. "Mr. Chairperson," she began. Just as she'd informed me moments before, those two words brought down the house. "Ladies and Gentlemen and Others." Once again, she had to wait for the applause to subside. "If I'd said 'others' a few years ago at the beginning of a speech like this, it would have been considered insulting. Now it's not so."

She took a drink of water and looked her audience over. "I must explain this stick right away because Americans are so curious about things." She stepped out from behind the podium and held it out at arm's length. "It's not a water wand, nor a snake catcher, nor a big sling shot. It's not a giant's hairpin, a comet's hair catcher, a scarecrow's or King Neptune's staff. A letter Y. A stirring stick for a witch's cauldron. A rescue flagpole. It's not any of those things. It's what the British call a thumbstick and it's very good for toppling toilet paper off the top shelf in the supermarket. Now we've got that out of the way." She stamped the stick once and let it loose to bang on the floor.

She referred briefly to the title of her speech on ethnicity by saying, "There is so much diversity in the United States today that we have everybody here except the Australian aborigines. Americans like diversity. They are very unhappy with conformity.

"The American Negro is as American as I am. We can both count back ten generations to our beginning in this country. I think of James Baldwin. His father was a preacher. One of my great-uncles and my grandfather preached. James Baldwin read through two libraries by the time he was seventeen. So did I and so did some of you. He grew up in an environment of words. So did I and so did some of you. He speaks American English. So do we.

"Negro Americans are just like any other Americans. They don't sit still. That's really what happened to Mike Rockefeller, you know. When his father, the governor, came back from the Pacific, he made a hero out of his son by saying that Mike dared to swim back. Still, a Dutchman who just sat there was rescued. Mike wouldn't sit still. He was probably eaten by sharks or piranhas."

She welcomed interruptions. The first one she received challenged her stand on marijuana. "I get asked that question so often," she replied wearily. "Far too many people only know about my stand on marijuana and absolutely nothing else about me.

"I'm against making pot illegal. When you make pot illegal, young people go on and experiment with harder drugs. They often have to steal to support their new habits. If marijuana were accepted without fuss in the first place, youth might never have felt the need to try harder drugs."

Another person wanted to know whether she thought it was best that the Vietnam POWs who were returned that weekend had it better by being imprisoned abroad and thus missing out on the turbulent 1960s. "No," she snapped. "The 1950s would have been a better decade to have skipped. I wouldn't have missed the 1960s for anything. The POWs are really out of it for having missed the 1960s. I like your question. Thanks for asking it. It's not very often that someone thinks up one that I've not been asked before."

A woman down front wanted her opinion on electronic listening devices. "These days, it's best to assume that everything is bugged," Margaret bent down to retrieve her thumbstick. "The only way you can disarm eavesdroppers is by being completely open. That's all you can do."

She topped her speech off with a pitch for the Scientific Institute of Public Information. She revealed that she would be donating her week's lecturing fees to that institute in order to help further its campaign to get more of us using biodegradable goods. "Changing habits as small as using biodegradable goods by each and every responsible, caring person adds up. We must cherish and protect life. We belong to one world now. The concerns of any of us should be the concerns of all of us."

Very few suburbanites stayed for the reception. They battled their way homeward before the storm worsened. When she began to yawn after half an hour, I suggested we follow suit.

Once home, she sat on the bottom step in our hallway so I might help pull off her rubber overshoes. She preceded me upstairs and was already in bed when I brought in a glass of ice water.

I would have chosen the bed closest to the door and to the bathroom, so I expected to find her there. But she surprised me. "I always preferred corners when I was a child," she explained. "And I'm very much at home in this corner bed."

I opened the window and tucked her in with a goodnight kiss to her forehead. "A participant–observer mother is something new in anthropology," she looked up at me with a big smile. I turned off the light and tiptoed out.

"Good morning, Merry Sunshine," I knocked on her door and peeked in at 7:55. She was dressed in the clothes she'd worn the night before. I noticed she'd piled the blankets of the other bed on her corner one. "How did you sleep?"

"Comfortably," she answered as she folded her nightgown into her suitcase, "but I was a little cold. I see more snow fell last night too."

"Yes, travelers' warnings are out. We've got an hour and a half to eat breakfast and get to school. We'll have to move right along to do it."

"I'll be down in five minutes," she promised.

"This is the first time I've stayed overnight with you when there weren't any little boys around to wait on me," she placed a handful of new pictures of her granddaughter next to my orange juice as she sat down to breakfast.

"I remember how much alike Vonnie's and your smiles were," I said. "Now I see another similarity. You have the same rear view, both in hips and legs."

"You caught that," she exclaimed. "It's true of Cathy, too. You know, I've already lost the batch of pictures I showed you in Toronto. The negatives are somewhere so they're not entirely lost."

Between forkfuls of Canadian bacon and scrambled eggs with cheese, she gazed out of the window at a busy landing platform where birds feasted on sliced apples and teaspoons of peanut butter. "You have a beautiful home here." Her eyes met mine. "Did you furnish it?"

"My father's sister did most of it. She was Eddie's first wife. I married my aunt's husband."

"You never mentioned that to me before. I think marriages of relatives like that are the best kind. My brother married his first wife's sister. They are very devoted to each other." She poured a little cold water into her hot coffee.

"No matter who furnished it, mi casa es suya whenever you want to hide away somewhere for whatever reason. I'll keep a lamp in the window for you." She asked about a framed photograph of my one-hundred-year-old Aunt Inga.

"I come from a line of long-lived females myself," she said. "My mother's mother lived to ninety-five. If my mother were alive, she'd be 102 next August. Both of her sisters are still alive. Aunt Fanny is ninety-nine. As a young woman, she worked for a while in Hull House in Chicago. In her retirement years, she got bored with women who hire out as companions so she's gone into a rest home in La Jolla. She has lots of friends there and knows all the inside dope on the lives of the nurses and the residents."

"You have an Aunt Fanny," I interrupted her. "So do I! My kids used to giggle so at that name, 'Fanny,' and I never would have thought of another meaning otherwise."

"I've also got an Aunt Beth." Margaret continued without comment. "She's eighty-five. She's my mother's youngest sibling and she lives in Michigan. She's just had a devastating experience. Another car ran into hers when hers was not moving. When the authorities learned her age, they took her license away even though the accident was not her fault. She drives carefully enough to go for another ten years. Losing her license crushed her."

"I know how that would be. There's something ego fortifying about seeing your own car waiting like a willing Pegasus in your garage or driveway. A car represents mobility and mobility is a necessary component of competent adulthood. When those cops took your Aunt Beth's license away, it was the same as telling her she was too old to be any good. No wonder she was crushed by it."

"I'll never have to go through that experience in my older age," Margaret pinched together the last crumbs of her caramelized pecan roll as she spoke. "I don't own a car and I don't drive, as you know. I did drive a Ford a little, years ago, but my arms were too short to reach the emergency brake, so I quit. I've never had a desire to drive since."

"Well, somebody's got to do it and it's high time we hit the road on the double." I scooped up as many empty dishes as I could and toted them to the sink. Margaret carried in the rest. We dipped the dishes in water to soak through the day.

The Department of Twentieth-Century Studies had invited me to sit with its members when Margaret was to lead a "discussion" on the merits of conferences. On the way to the meeting, she told me that smog in the different cities she visited ruined her hair. "It always looks okay to me," I said. "It's so naturally curly. You've got less gray in your hair than I. In fact, it even looks blond under some lights. Not bad considering you're sixteen and a half years ahead of me in age."

We pulled into the university with ten minutes to spare. I spent them searching for a place to leave the car. Finally, in desperation, I parked it in a spot where I risked having it towed away when we returned for our dash to the airport two hours later. "You don't estimate your time very well," she chided me when we walked into the meeting room five minutes late.

The professor who introduced her said what he had to say and then sat as still as a judge with his eyes at half mast. Only two men opened their mouths to say anything during her two-hour discussion turned monologue on the merits of conferences. "The rest of them were just so many pegs sitting there," she complained as we walked down the hall. "I need a drink of water and have to make a telephone call before we go," she added.

She refreshed herself at a drinking fountain. "They let me talk for two hours without a glass of water. I don't know why it is, but water is usually provided for a speaker who stands at a podium and not for speakers who sit at a table. It's strange, isn't it? Amazing, in fact, because we eat sitting down."

"I was disappointed in that seminar," she continued as she fished in her purse for her telephone credit card. "Nobody asked any questions. People who don't ask questions aren't thinking. I didn't learn a thing all morning."

She called her office in the Museum in New York City. It was past noon there and nobody answered. "My three secretaries are probably having lunch together," she reasoned aloud. "They are very compatible. I'd much rather have them compatible than have them fraternizing with the rest of the Museum personnel and getting involved in the gossip that you always find in an institution of that size. I'll try again, if there's time, at the airport."

Boy, she's sure mellowed from the time she tried to call a bunch of us and we were all at lunch when I was a volunteer at the Museum, I thought to myself. "Who pays your secretaries?" I asked as I held the door to the outside open for her and was relieved to see that my bright yellow bug had not been moved.

"I do," she responded. "I am allowed one-twelfth of one secretary but that is hardly enough, so I pay them. There are always plenty of volunteers around too. I have a half century's worth of ex-secretaries, ex-volunteers, and ex-assistants all over the country."

"Some of us overlap," I said, "because I fit into two of those categories myself. Wouldn't it be fun to get us all together some day so we might share memories? I'd really like to do that."

On the way to the airport, we talked about how different drivers handle their cars and how that might furnish a clue as to how they handle other aspects of their lives as well. "Once, years ago, on the main road between Northport and Huntington, Long Island," I reminisced, "I recognized the man in the Cadillac ahead of me as a local judge. The single-lane road meandered as sinuously as a snake. That judge's brakes flashed red all the way. And I found myself wondering how in the world he ever arrived at any decisions in court. He certainly didn't seem to be able to make many on the road."

"When I was in Samoa in the twenties," she said, "I stayed with a family named Holt. One of their daughters was a dancer named Claire. Whenever she drove anywhere, Claire was always fascinated by the people in the car ahead of her. Particularly the person at the wheel."

"I've heard that the driver to pay most attention to is the one behind the one ahead of you," I looked over at her with a smile. "There's always an exhilaration in driving, though. A freedom. A sense of independence."

"All of which dovetails with the American personality," she said as we turned into the parking lot at General Mitchell Airport. "Americans thrive on being independent and free to get up and go, go, go."

We parked and entered the main building, hungry for the restaurant. The only sign that offered a clue read "To gates and concessions." "No one from another country would have the slightest idea where the restaurant is," she declared. "Airports are international these days. Signs in them should be simple and to the point—To food and gates."

Once we began to circulate inside, the effect of the visibility that television had brought through years of her appearing on it surprised me at every turn. A young traveler in line at the ticket check-in counter saw her, stepped aside, and let us in ahead of him. Minutes later, the waitress at the lunch counter caught my eye as I held a copy of *Blackberry Winter* open for her to autograph: "To Pat in affectionate remembrance, Margaret Mead, 1973."

"Is that Margaret Mead?" the waitress mouthed silently and pointed to the person in question. I nodded. "I thought so," the waitress nodded back with obvious pleasure.

We each ordered a Reuben sandwich and a glass of dark beer. While we ate, patrons approached us with the eyes of moonstruck cocker spaniels. They asked her to autograph slips of paper, the margins of newspapers, magazines, or front pages of books. She obligingly scribbled her hieroglyphic M . . . t M . . . d on all but the books. "I won't put my autograph on a book that somebody else wrote," she turned the book bearers away. "I often come out with an extra pen when I sign autographs," she winked at me and pocketed another one.

We stood in line to have her bag and purse inspected. Her shopping bag always contained basic "survival items" should her luggage go astray; extra night gear, toothbrush, hair brush, comb, and reading material. She asked if I had any extra cash. "Just a twenty-dollar bill. Do you want to borrow it? I'll be home in half an hour and you still have to get to Buffalo."

"Yes, thanks. I don't have a dime. You can have all the credit cards in Christendom, but you're helpless while traveling if you don't also have some cash."

The woman in front of us glanced at Margaret when we got in line. She listened to some of our talk. Then she turned around and asked the perfect question of someone with a well-worn passport. "Where in the world are you off to now?"

"Buffalo," Margaret chuckled. "I'm to give a speech there tonight at 8:00."

As we stepped in front of the inspector, Margaret reached for her carry-on shopping bag. "No," I pulled it away. "He just wants to check the contents. He doesn't care which one of us hands it over to him."

"Pat, you've got the kind of bossiness I like." She went on through the gate door that buzzes if you're carrying any more metal than the fillings in your teeth.

"Wasn't that Margaret Mead?" the young inspector asked me as he rooted through her shopping bag and purse. "I've seen her on the *Jack Paar Show.*"

"Everybody around here knows who you are. How do you go for all this recognition?" I asked as we walked down a hall that led to the waiting room.

"It opens a lot of doors," she answered. "I worried through my childhood fearing that I'd not be recognized. Now I don't have to think about it anymore."

Ten minutes later, a voice over an intercom announced the grounding of all Milwaukee flights because of drifting snow on runways. Margaret and I joined a group gathering at the ticket counter. An officer said that one American Airlines flight would be leaving from Chicago for Buffalo in an hour and a half. "Do you want to chance it?" I asked her. "If we run into too much snow on the highway, we could miss the flight. Chicago's eighty-five miles away. If the highway's clean all the way, we might just make it."

She looked up at me. "Even if we did miss that one, there's always a greater choice of flights from Chicago than Milwaukee. It's worth a try, if you think you can spare the time."

"Let's go."

She reserved a seat on the next flight for Buffalo from Chicago. "I'm getting $40 per day expense money from Bantam Books," she volunteered as we hiked back to the car. "I might as well spread it around. Find out what the taxi fare to Chicago is and I'll see that the office reimburses you for gas and parking."

"I appreciate that," I said. "The trip down will give us another hour to visit too." Somehow I sensed that our times alone were numbered. We talked about her autobiography, *Blackberry Winter.* I wish now I had been more specific in my questions about that book. Her Toronto tirade terminated my desire to read any more of it at the time.

"I wrote that book in ten weeks," she disclosed. "Five two-week sessions. Of course, I was thinking about it between times, as well as talking and writing about everything else that I do in the interim, too."

"The more you have to do, the more you get done," I praised her. We had bounced that compliment back and forth like a tennis ball for years.

"I named my first book *Coming of Age in Samoa,*" she recollected. "The next one never should have been called *Growing Up in New Guinea.* It was so similar to the first title that people have twisted them into 'Growing Up in Samoa' and 'Coming of Age in New Guinea' ever since. The publisher suggested *New Lives for Old* for my second book on the Manus. *And Keep your Powder Dry*—that one was my idea. Cathy liked "Other Side of Eden" for a later book on New Guinea, but the publisher turned it down."

We drove along in concentrated silence. Driving through snow monopolized my attention. She sensed my concern and watched the stuff for me. "I don't usually travel first class," she volunteered at one point. "But I am this time. Bantam Books is paying for it, so why not?"

"Eddie and I traveled first class all the time," I loosened my grip on the steering wheel and sat back smiling at the memory of it. "I don't go first class any more but I liked it then. Gave me an idea how the other third lives."

"I never look out of the window in airplanes. I always bring along something to read or to work on," Margaret commented.

"That's not so with me," I said. "Riding in an airplane is a sensual experience. Except when they're feeding me, I press my nose flat against the window and scrutinize the cities as my plane leaves or lands. I pick out line patterns fashioned by nature or farmers or engineers. Lines are ruler-straight here in Wisconsin because of our township system mainly, much more curvaceous in southern states like Louisiana or North Carolina. When it's cloudy or the plane's flying too high for me to watch the land, I do everything but get wet experiencing the insides of clouds."

"I'm going on to the Carolinas after Buffalo. Remember Nora Holland? She's had a bad bout with cancer. I want to spend all day with her, if possible."

"Doing what?"

"I want to know her thoughts about having cancer and about how she's learning to cope with having it. As far as I know, her illness hasn't cramped her style nor stopped her activities. She keeps going and she doesn't let herself get disheartened."

I wonder if Margaret thinks she might have cancer? I thought to myself. If she does, one of her ways of coping would be to talk the predicament out with others who have it. After all, it's not cancer, but life that's terminal.

"Nora's an associate professor now with tenure," my talkative little friend looked askance at me. "You, on the other hand, keep running into bad luck. You always manage to transcend it though.

"I wish you'd gone to Merrill Palmer. You would have been perfect. They never got anybody else." We passed a few farms, a filling station, and a bridge before either of us said anything.

This time Margaret broke the silence. "Might you marry again?" she asked as she took a handkerchief out of her oversized black purse to clean her glasses.

"Who knows? I'm in no hurry and I'm not looking. I like the freedom of single bliss. For the first time in my life, I'm nobody's daughter, wife, or everyday mother. I don't have to account to a soul for where I go, what it will cost, or when I'll be back. That's why I could just take off and bring you down to Chicago. I still have one marriage to go before I catch up with you anyway. Reminds me, I was interested in what you shared about your trio of husbands in *Blackberry Winter* even though it was skimpy as hell."

"Luther and I became secretly engaged after I graduated from high school in 1918. I was sixteen and a half and he was twenty. We married in September 1923, a few months after I graduated from Barnard College. We divorced in 1928.

"So we were five years engaged and five years married. We weren't together throughout either of those periods though. Luther was majoring in military science at Penn State when we became engaged. I'd always said I wanted to marry an Episcopal minister."

"Could someone named Luther have been brought up Episcopalian?"

"His parents were Lutheran. He switched to my church and studied for the Episcopal ministry at Union Theological Seminary in New York City."

"But in the mid-1920s, could an Episcopal priest who had been divorced give Communion? Wouldn't a divorce force him to leave the priesthood?"

"He did leave the ministry and he became, instead, a very good archeologist. He married again, very happily, to a woman he met at the British Museum in London. They've been out at the University of Oregon in Eugene for many years now and have a daughter."

"I suppose everybody who picks up *Blackberry Winter* is very curious about what you have to say about your marriages. But you skirt the juicy stuff and quote from some of the writings of each of your husbands instead. Readers want to know more, especially today. Your first was the only American in the lot, a native Pennsylvanian, like yourself, right? And then came a New Zealander and last of all, an Englishman. What was the New Zealander like?"

"I met Reo on the ship returning from Samoa in 1926, when I was still married to Luther."

"Was Reo the one you told me about once who didn't want a wife of his doing housework? So, whenever the maid had a day off, you bootlegged minimal households tasks like pulling up a sheet on the bed and coming in to smile at him and going back to pull up the other sheet and perhaps a blanket and coming back to smile at him again? Or washing one cup and pretending you weren't really doing dishes that had to be done?"

"Yes, Reo was the one."

"The maid's day off must have been a pain. When you had to hide the fact you were doing housework at all, the work must have taken three times as long."

"Reo was also very jealous. I met Gregory Bateson in New Guinea while I was still married to Reo. Gregory has married twice since we were divorced. I'm a little annoyed at his third wife right now. She hasn't answered my last letter. I think his marriage to Lois will last. He and I were married for eight years. He and Betty, his second wife, the mother of Cathy's half-brother, John, were married for ten years. His third marriage is already twelve years old. Gregory and Lois have a daughter, Nora, who is Cathy's half-sister. I sometimes visit either Luther or Gregory when I go to the West Coast. Reo lives in England and has remarried too."

The date was Thursday, February 15, 1973. Margaret planned to be back in the apartment she shared with Rhoda Metraux some time Sunday. "Rhoda's getting in tonight. I hope there's time to phone her when we get to Chicago. I want to tell one of my secretaries to buy some flowers to put in the apartment. Rhoda's son, Daniel, leaves tonight for Vermont. He's going to feel miserable because he has to go and Rhoda's going to be miserable because there will be no one to meet her. The flowers will show her that I'm not vindictive. If I were, I'd send cabbages."

"It's none of my business, but 'cabbages' doesn't sound as though you two are getting along very well."

"She's been acting just like her mother lately. She's a chain smoker. She's going to get emphysema. She should quit and she won't or she can't. I smoke sometimes in her presence in self-defense, but I can do with or without a cigarette nowadays."

"I like to hear that because I remember you smoked on one of the last visits you made to me in California."

I turned off the interstate highway at an O'Hare exit sign. "Don't look now, but we're entering O'Hare Airport. Watch for American Airlines signs. If we park too far away, we'll have to traipse all over the northern tip of the state of Illinois to get inside the airport and we've only got fifteen minutes." Together, we peered through the windshield.

"Just let me get out," she directed. "It's silly to come in with me. I'll check my reservation and make that phone call. I'm going to give you your $20 back too. I can cash a check in the airport but you're a long way from home. Remember to send the office a bill."

"Greet Rhoda and Tulia for me," I said as I brought the car to a stop. She hopped out. A curbside redcap threw her bags in a luggage cart. I watched and waited until she entered the station and the big glass doors automatically closed behind her. She did not look back.

Margaret traveled to southeastern Wisconsin in mid-November 1974. Barbara Sperling, then her assistant, wrote me from the Museum informing me that I was to be invited to a dinner, a reception, and her talk at Carroll College in Waukesha on November 13. Margaret planned to stay overnight with me. Someone from Marion College in Fond du Lac would pick her up at my house after breakfast in the morning.

My youngest son, Kent, now as skinny as his skeleton and as long-haired as a Navajo, had recently hitchhiked from the Elysian peaks of Colorado with a broken-stringed banjo and a sleeping bag. He wanted to participate in the flurry that a visit from Margaret always roused. He shopped for her breakfast, vacuumed and dusted her bedroom, and scrubbed down the guest bathroom.

He balked at cleaning the tub. "It's not necessary."

"It is too," I insisted. "Margaret loves the soft water of that tub. She's not a person for favorites but she likes the baths she has here, as much as any in the whole wide world. Come on, now. Why not make things as perfect as possible?"

"Well, in that case, okay, but I'm going to pay attention and listen for whether she takes one or not."

"I hope she does. She'll be seventy-three in two weeks and she doesn't come so often any more. Any sudsy soft-water soak in our tub may be her last one there."

I taught on the day she arrived. Dana Raphael happened to call from Connecticut to confirm our hotel reservations in Mexico City for the seventy-third meeting of the American Anthropological Association over Thanksgiving weekend. She and I would be sharing a room again.

When Dana learned of Margaret's visit, she suggested that I ask for permission to take turns following her around in order to make some anthropological observations on the rhythm of her conference interactions. "I'll bet she has one hundred contacts a day," Dana whipped up enthusiasm for the scheme. "We should get all the information we can on her while the getting's good. She'll be in Africa when we meet in 1975 and who knows how many conferences she'll be able to attend after that. Any conference could be her last, you know."

Margaret kissed Kent and me when we met before dinner at Carroll College. "I've not seen you since I was fifteen," Kent lit up. Her greeting kiss warmed every cell of his six foot four inch frame. "Either you're shrunken or I've grown."

Members of the sponsoring Cultural Enrichment Committee commandeered each side of her at dinner. Kent and I sat at the far end of a table of assorted faculty members. We were served a squab, a salad, and some beans with slivered almonds. A squab would be an ideal main dish for Trappist monks. It's almost impossible to carry on an intelligent conversation while attacking one.

A gaunt professor with leather patches on his tweed jacket sleeves took care of his squab by wolfing down the chunkier parts and then jabbing for more tantalizing tidbits in Kent's private life. "You're twenty-four years old and only a second-semester freshman? What have you been doing since you finished high school? Where have you been? Why are you back in school again when you're so old?"

Even if Kent were willing to take up these issues one by one, a full reply did not lend itself to either the social situation or the squab. I squirmed in embarrassment for him. Kent denuded the bones of his bird with studied diligence.

During the reception between dinner and her main speech, Margaret sat on a loveseat and let assembled collegians in on her reactions to a recent U.N. World Food Conference she had attended in Rome. "The year 1973 will go down in history as the year we pulled in our belts," she began. "Seventy million people are going to die from starvation this year. Hardly anybody realizes that only twenty-nine days of food supply stand between any of us and worldwide famine. Most of us are dismally ignorant of the fact that there's no such thing as unlimited agricultural resources anymore."

She chastised Wisconsinites for news stories about their burning calves after shooting them in such times of acute food shortage. "There isn't much meat on a newborn calf," a farmer's son defended the action.

"There's enough meat on a newborn calf to feed some folks their ration of protein for a year," she retorted. "If the farmers didn't see the selfishness of their act, the community should have stepped in." Margaret didn't mince words.

"In New Guinea, where I have done most of my fieldwork, the pigs eat garbage and what they can forage. That's okay. Pigs provide protein for human beings. It's unwise and nonsensical to feed any pig or cow grain that humans could eat. Let the animals eat what human beings can't eat. Grass, for one thing.

"It's also inhumane in our present world food crisis to use fertilizer on lawns. Fertilizer should be used to increase human food production. We send powdered milk around the world instead of fertilizers. Wisconsin's one of the dairy states, but do you realize that very few adults in Wisconsin, or in any other state, drink milk? Adults in the rest of the world don't drink it either. They haven't drunk milk for so long that whole populations of people have lost the enzyme to digest it."

Kent and I hovered nearby, holding on to her purse and her cape. Her lecture scheduled for the evening, "Limitations of Growth and the Quality of Life," was open to the public. At a prescribed time, we followed a large crowd into the auditorium. Kent and I found seats in the first row directly in front of the podium. When it came time to introduce Margaret, someone turned the auditorium lights down low. "Turn those lights back up," she called out. "I want to look this audience in the eyes. And vice versa." She held her water glass in her hand and waited until the lights went on again.

"I've lived long enough to remember back when everybody was impressed with how big the world was," she began. "It took space travel to show us how fragile and how small it really is in the whole solar system.

"Space travel makes us one world. We're beginning to find out that the common resources and dangers of any one country are the concerns of all countries. Since the end of World War II, we have been changing our mental set about the environment. Whether thinking internationally comes easy or not, the situation today demands that we accept the fact that there is no necessary contradiction between loving one's own country and loving the whole world." Kent bobbed his head in approval. I took notes as usual.

"We are entering a period in history in which we've got to throw out nationalistic plans. They're already anachronistic. National plans are done on the wrong scale. We've rooted nationalism in land. For centuries we've fought and died defending frontiers. But today, the most important thing is not land, it's air. Contamination of the air goes on right around the world. No border stations nor boundary lines can stop it. If everybody does not protect the air, no one will be safe. The commonality of air necessitates developing an acute awareness that concern for nations and concern for the world have got to be the same." She stopped for a breather and downed half a glass of water.

"Take energy. We didn't even begin to talk about energy until there was a shortage of it. The world as we know it today was built on cheap oil. No one knew that twenty years ago. They thought it was built on something called progress. The limits of growth lie in the limits of resources. We simply didn't think like that twenty years ago. We have to make some sweeping changes in our use of energy. The United States was the first country in the world that built an entire urban system on gasoline. Now it's time we take the lead in changing the present state of affairs.

"Since World War II, almost every country has come into the civilized world and joined the United Nations. The U.N. is like the U.S. Whether a country is as big as Texas or as small as Rhode Island it still gets only two delegates or senators in an assembly in which every nation is represented equally. Through U.N.-sponsored conferences on world food, population, pollution, nuclear energy, and the like, we are beginning to plan together for improving the quality of life on a planetary scale. It's got to be done that way or it won't be done at all."

She grabbed at the far corners of the podium and held on so that her arms extended openly toward her audience. "Since World War II, the people of the world have witnessed the decay of their cities, an increase in juvenile delin-quency, the loneliness of people who know nobody, death from malnutrition, and the breakdown of young marriages."

She reached for her water glass again and looked deliberately at her host suburbanites as she proceeded. "Each one of these problems can be traced to cheap oil. Cheap oil enabled responsible people to flee from the cities to the sub-urbs for their children's sake. That left the disenfranchised young, the old, the poor, the ethnic, and the technically unskilled behind. There lies the cause of the urban crisis. The things that are wrong with our civilization are related to the way we have been using gasoline since World War II.

"To improve the quality of life, the people in every society in the world will have to do some serious revamping. It means we here in the United States are go-ing to have to sacrifice some of the luxuries we've become used to. In World Wars I and II, we showed that we can pull in when circumstances call for it. To a peo-ple with our history, anything we really want to do is possible."

After her formal lecture and informal repartee with individuals who invari-ably came to the edge of the stage to question or to congratulate, we took her home with us. Kent drove our bright yellow VW bug. Margaret sat beside him and I settled down behind her and rested my chin in the space between the front seats.

"I was at Marquette University all morning," she began to wind down, "Car-roll College most of this afternoon and evening. Someone will take me up to Mar-ion College in Fond du Lac tomorrow until after lunch, and then I will go to the University of Wisconsin at Stevens Point for dinner and another speech."

"Four talks and four meals at four colleges in two days," I counted aloud. "Not bad for a septuagenarian who can't quit."

"Besides these lecture tours," she said, "I still write and hold down assign-ments at the Museum and at Columbia. I've had a regular visiting professorship in the Department of Psychiatry at the University of Cincinnati for sixteen years now too."

"Where do you think you get your stamina?" Kent asked.

"I've had an abundance of energy all my life. My mother was the same way."

"I remember the people I used to see sitting around the lobby in wheelchairs waiting for someone to come and visit with them in the nursing home where my dad died," I reminisced. "And then I think of the momentum you maintain. You are older than many of those people and look at you. Listen to you, in a speech like the one you just gave, for instance."

"Those people in the nursing home would be dead if it weren't for modern medicine."

"Each time I see you, you seem to be shifting into an even higher gear. You're off to the Pacific, or South Africa, or Europe so often your passport must look like an old-fashioned post office ink blotter. No matter which college campus you speak on, capacity crowds come to hear. Your books sell well, and they're still coming out. Even strangers know who you are in places like airports. How much credit do you give to television for that?"

"Providing a person has written, there's no denying TV helps. So does my age. I've lived so long, my memory makes me an asset. I started young and I studied children. Those children are grandparents now. I intend to go on exploiting that fact until I have both feet in the ground," she sniffled.

Kent turned off the ignition and hustled around to open her door for her. "Do you have a cold?" he asked.

"Not really. I'm allergic. I'm allergic to life, but I'm not about to give it up." She wiped her nose with a tissue and followed me from our attached garage into the house.

"Sit down and relax. Unwind," I said. "Kent's got the fireplace ready in the den and the bar's open." I took her coat to the closet. Kent carried her suitcases to the bottom stair. She ordered a scotch and soda and sat back in the same chair in which Eddie died.

Kent brought in three glasses of scotch and soda. He lit the fire. We gazed into the flames as newspapers ignited twigs and twigs ignited chunks of an old tree. We sipped nightcaps and chatted. "I hope I never outgrow fireplaces," she mused aloud.

"Me neither," Kent said, as he stretched his full length out on the couch and propped his head on his elbow.

"I look into fires and find new colors springing up, dancing a while, and then disappearing," I said as each of my feet pushed the shoe on the other one off.

"Remember my telling you about writing a sequel to *Blackberry Winter*?" Margaret talked into the fire nostalgically. "Well, I've given up the idea. Life becomes too routinized as one gets older. The younger years are much more interesting."

I asked about the people closest to her.

"Cathy's an associate professor already. She speaks Persian and Arabic and Tagalog, and she teaches Hebrew. She can get a job teaching that anywhere because there are always Jews around.

"Vonnie's growing up fast. She has my smile as you remember. She's also got my legs and hips. So does Cathy. All three of us look alike from behind," she grinned and gulped more scotch.

"Is Vonnie her real name?" Kent got up to push glowing wood back with a long-handled iron tool.

"Her real name's Sevanne Margaret, half for a town in Armenia and half for me. You remember my sister Elizabeth?" Margaret continued. "She's still in Cambridge. Has been for years. Her two children have grown up and she has a granddaughter, Melinda, who's Vonnie's age.

"Rhoda's gone to New Guinea three times now. After I'd introduced her around, the natives wanted to keep her and send me, whom they call 'Missy Fella,' away because I know too much. I try to go back there every other year. I have foster great-grandchildren there, you know."

The cuckoo clock chirped twelve times.

"I'm getting so tired I need suspenders to hold up my eyelids," I yawned. "We've each put in a full day. What say we go to bed so we can get up in time to have a leisurely breakfast before the advance guards from Marion College whisk you away?"

"Yes, Mother," Margaret reached over and placed her glass beside mine on the serving tray.

Kent chuckled.

Margaret raised her eyebrow and spoke to him. "Your mother's a general, isn't she?"

"You noticed!" Kent's eyes twinkled. He banked the fire to prevent sparks from flying onto the rug during the night.

Margaret and I climbed the stairs together.

"I remember this room," her eyes darted around, as I turned on the lights.

"I'm thinking of engraving a plaque for the door, 'Margaret Mead slept here,'" I joked as I opened the window an inch. Kent brought her suitcases in after us.

"Good night," he smiled as he departed for the refuge of the room next to hers.

"That fresh air's just chilly enough for me to dive into bed. I'll take a bath in the morning."

"Fine. Kent gave the tub a special cleaning just for you."

She was in it when I went to waken her at 7:00 a.m. She woke up ready for action, as I do. She was definitely not one of those 'I've got to have a cup of coffee before I feel human' types. "I hope I never outgrow bathtubs," she announced as she came down to breakfast.

I looked at Kent. He grinned from cheek to cheek.

I asked her if it would be okay if Dana Raphael and I followed her around to do an ethnographic field study of her conference behavior during the meetings in Mexico City. "I'm used to it," she assured me. "Reporters and newspaper photographers trail me all the time. Write Barbara Sperling in the Museum and tell her, as she'll be going with me."

A frazzle-haired sociology instructor and a long-haired student body president knocked on our door at 9:30 a.m. Kent helped Margaret with her coat. "Do you like dogs?" Kent finally dreamed up a question for her. All he endeavored to do from breakfast to the moment of her departure was listen.

"I live with Rhoda's two cats, Mimi and Mr. Gold," she said. "We kept dogs and horses when I was growing up and we named them all Josephine. My mother and father kept a dog in their later years. It used to greet me whenever I went home to Philadelphia."

"I hope you can come again very soon, Margaret," Kent said, as he held the door of the Marion College car open for her. Kent and I stood together in the driveway and waved as she headed down our hill. She did not even see us. She was already thoroughly engrossed with two brand-new people.

When we went upstairs to straighten her room, we found two envelopes with brightly colored English stamps lying on the dresser. "I'll save these stamps. They're too pretty to throw away."

Kent read the return addresses. "They're from the same guy! Who's Geoffrey Gorer?" he asked.

"He's another anthropologist who worked in the Pacific; they've been friends for years. He lives in England."

8

SHADOWING HER IN MEXICO

Dana Raphael and I synchronized our arrival from Connecticut and Wisconsin so that we might take the same taxi to the conference hotel. Four thousand anthropologists were congregating in Mexico City for the seventy-third annual meeting of the American Anthropological Association in late November 1974.

We had arranged with Margaret Mead's assistant, Barbara Sperling, to follow her around during the second and third day of the meeting. Well we knew the demands of our self-imposed assignment. Even though we were younger and would be sharing shifts, trailing this woman would be as rigorous as two days on a national political campaign.

For this reason, we decided to take time off on arrival to adjust to changes in altitude, diet, and pace as well as to see some of the city's sights. Although I had driven to Mexico once or twice when my sons were California schoolboys, this was Dana's first trip there. I suggested that we spend most of our free afternoon at the Museo de Antropologia.

"I love museums," Dana reacted positively.

"Good. I promise you'll be overwhelmed by this one. This museum is one of the most beloved of its kind in the world. It embodies the very soul of Mexico! Every group, from the past to the present, that ever lived in Mexico has contributed to the spirit of the place. And you'll feel it. We have the whole afternoon.

"Let's go on foot. It's not too far from here and that way we will be able to watch the people and smell the flowers on the way."

Two fiftyish college friends who only saw each other when we roomed together at annual anthropology meetings giggled like schoolgirls as we walked from the hotel through Chapultepec Park to the museum. We were in the mood for doing something crazy and a row of wheelchairs just inside the lobby inspired me.

"Follow me," I whispered, as I limped toward the wheelchairs and sat down in one. "Put your purse and camera on my lap. You push first. We're going to ogle this place in style." Instantly Dana caught on and complied.

As either one of us steered the other from one colorful exhibit to another, we noticed a correlation between age of passersby and behavior toward perceived impression of our handicapped condition. Children stared at us. Young adults glanced and turned their eyes away quickly. Older visitors looked on us with compassion and smiled benignly.

"You know," Dana remarked as we sought out unpopulated corners in which to exchange roles, "I can't remember ever hearing Margaret Mead laugh."

"Me either," I answered. "Let's try to remember to ask her about that in the next two days."

"You're right," Dana commented as she rolled along. "I'll never forget our visit here, Pat. It is a special museum all right."

"A lot of planning went into bringing this one from dream to reality," I said, "and the love of millions of Mexican people keeps it well visited. Remember that poem Emily Dickinson wrote about her church being in the out-of-doors? Well, this museum is my church. I get that feeling every time I come here."

"This has been perfect." Dana's eyes sparkled as we abandoned our peculiar chariot at the foot of a flight of stairs near the exit at closing time. We took our time getting back. We stopped in a movie theater and sat through an old comedy from the States. We lingered over a late meal.

When we returned to the hotel, Margaret Mead had not arrived. We left a note for her at the desk. It read:

> Jubilant that you have given us permission to make an interaction analysis of your conference activities.
>
> We're convinced your life after forty is every bit as interesting as the years before.
>
> Please call Room 1107 as soon as convenient.
> Dana and Pat

I pulled aside boldly colored floral drapes for an early morning glimpse of Tenachtitlan, ancient capital of the Aztec empire, which we moderns know as Mexico City. Sunrise tipped skyscraper edges with a warm red glow. The gold Monumento Angel statue in front of the Hotel Maria Isabel–Sheraton glittered in the new light of our first day of conference activities.

The telephone rang. "Pat? Dana?" our human alarm clock inquired. "Did you get the newsletter with the room changes?"

"Yes, we've got it," I answered, as Dana stirred drowsily.

"Which one of you will be with me this morning?"

"I'll do mornings and Dana afternoons," I said. "We'll share evenings."

"I'm in Room 1520. I'll be ready to go downstairs in thirty-five minutes."

"Okay. I'll be outside your door when you open it," I promised. Klunk. She hung up.

I gathered together the program and the sheet of room changes and sat down to study the morning's schedule. In it, Margaret listed herself as being from the American Museum of Natural History rather than Columbia University. Probably because she's employed full time by the museum and she's only an adjunct professor at Columbia, I mused.

The sessions that I guessed she would be most interested in followed head over heels on each other without pause. Considering how supportive she was of relatives and friends (who were, as often as not, ex-students), she would certainly attend the 8:00 a.m. slide show/talk that her seventh cousin and former fellow graduate student, Theodora Abel, would be presenting along with her apartment mate, Rhoda Metraux. She was due at the breakfast for past presidents from 9:00 to 10:00. Bill Mitchell, whose exam essays I remembered correcting, would be talking about medical care in a New Guinea group at 10:00. Ted Schwartz, another former student who had gone to the Admiralties with her in 1953, was scheduled to review the results of various intelligence tests he gave to three Pacific Island populations at 10:40.

We'll have to dash from one of these meetings to the other all morning, I said to myself. It's going to take some going to keep up with her and there won't be a moment to spare! At least she approves of letting us follow her. That's the big thing. "Good luck," Dana called from the bathroom as I left. "Meet me up here after lunch."

I arrived at Margaret's door as she opened it and we rushed to catch the elevator I'd come up on before somebody buzzed for it. "I've got your hot water bottle," I said. "Would it be okay with you if I put it in your box in the lobby this afternoon when Dana's with you? Kent liked your visit," I continued. "You gave him space. You didn't thrust him through a third degree like that insensitive professor at the Carroll College dinner."

"He thinks a lot of you too," she grinned. "In fact, he told me you were 'incredible.'"

"Inedible, maybe; incredible, never!" I bantered back.

"I remember when I met Kent and his brothers at that breakfast in Saratoga Springs," she remarked. "He told me then he wanted to be an 'archy-ologist.' He was such an adorable little fellow." We smiled over our memories of that graduation day at Skidmore. She paused and looked at me solemnly. "I'm going to interview him one day," she said.

She's smart enough to wait until he's ready to talk, I thought. No one can beat her sense of timing.

"Teddy Abel wrote two letters to the conference committee about having a slide projector in the room, but she didn't personally check it out. So that's the first thing we've got to do." She pulled a typewritten green sheet from her purse. It had her personal schedule typed on it. "Nothing goes right unless you check and recheck everything. There may be a projector and no projectionist. If that's the case, Alex Randall 5th will pinch-hit for us. He's good at it and he likes to be useful."

"Alex Randall 5th?"

"Yes. He's a young man who's very wise for his twenty-four years. He is majoring in instructional technology over at Teachers' College. He took my evening course two years ago. Even though Columbia is supposed to provide a projectionist, he has been showing slides and films for me ever since. He's the son of pediatricians and he likes both his father and his mother. That in itself makes him unusual."

We entered the Embajadores meeting room at 7:50. Four people had preceded us. One of them was Alex Randall 5th, who had the projector all ready to go. He was a handsome young man with facial features rimmed in foliage. Rhoda and Theodora brought in their slides. As Alex helped arrange them in the carousel, Margaret planted herself just outside the doorway.

"Eight in the morning is a bad time to present anything," she grumbled impatiently. "I'm going to stand partly in the door and partly in the hallway so people can at least see that someone is here! There are always those who say they'll come and then don't. You go in and save seats for us."

I watched her gaze up and down the hallway. With her shepherd's crook in hand and her cape flowing around her like a body tent, she looked for all the world like an overgrown Little Bo Peep.

In the few minutes before the room filled up enough to merit starting, Alex and I became acquainted. Both of us had taken courses from her. "She had a regular teaching assistant," he related, "but by the time I went to her fourth lecture, I saw she was having trouble with her slides. I volunteered to help with them and have shown slides and films for her ever since. She reminds me of my mother and my father and my grandmother all rolled into one. I told her that too, and she ate it up."

"How far along are you in anthropology?" I inquired.

"I read a lot of psychology books," he confided, "but, believe it or not, I've yet to read a single book in anthropology! I walk to taxis with her. I hang around during her office hours. I sit in on her class. I just listen and bring in information from other fields. So far, that seems to suit her fine.

"I see myself as just another in a long line of young men like Ray Birdwhistel, Paul Byers, Ted Carpenter, Ken Heyman, and Alan Lomax who have put ourselves at her beck and call in the formative years of our career. She attaches herself to us and works through the launching of our careers. Whether we become anthropologists or not, each of us represents some facet of one or another of her interests. She collects us. We're her people but she doesn't make arrangements for any of us to meet each other, darn it."

As Alex spoke, I found myself wondering if Margaret didn't use her female students and aid the males. If so, why? "Wouldn't it be fun to have a reunion of all of us someday, males and females?" I asked. "We'd have to come forward on our own to do it. Nobody would ever be able to find us otherwise." The possibility excited me. "All of us would have to write to one of us. I'd like to hear."

Margaret came in and sat down for the twenty-minute Metraux–Abel talk about their slides, which illustrated cultural and universal regularities in artwork by Pueblo, New Guinea, and Caribbean schoolchildren. She maintained eye contact with Abel and Metraux. She smiled supportively at them as they emphasized their main points. I leaned back, listening to the speakers with one ear and observing Margaret with both eyes.

She was dressed in navy blue slacks with a red and white blouse of a stair-step design that is often described as "stepped fret" in pottery analyses. She sat with legs astride. She grabbed her staff in her left hand and rested her left ear against it. Her fingers were short; her fingernails, not much bigger than those of a six-year-old child. A thin, leaf-patterned gold band, which she had purchased in a jewelry store in England, ringed her wedding finger. Age spots freckled her hands and wrists. On one wrist she wore a small gold watch on a black cloth strap; and on the other, a rubber band and a flesh-colored round Band-Aid that protected a newly removed wart. She was wearing her usual black, low-heeled slippers and her feet looked swollen. The eyes that gazed out through rimless spectacles and the ears that hid under her naturally wavy bobbed hair focused on the business at hand. "Your ankles look a little swollen," I said when I caught her eye.

"It's just fat," she replied, as she swung around her scarlet cape, handmade by Lacette in New York City, to cover her legs. "I'm glad I have this with me. The high altitude here combined with the hotel's capricious air-conditioning gives me the shivers."

I reached over to pull a gray hair off her red cape.

"You're incorrigible," she admonished even as she cast an appreciative glance at the notes I was taking. I sensed that she was studying me observing her. She scratched the left side of her head impatiently and frowned at her watch. The speakers finished at 8:30 sharp.

We left the room immediately and hurried to a lower floor for her slightly late arrival at the past presidents' breakfast. I promised to return in fifty minutes and be ready to lead her to Bill Mitchell's presentation of his paper "Medical Care for a New Guinea Tribal Population."

In the meantime, I walked to the lobby to buy a five-cent pack of peanuts for my own breakfast and to mail four Christmas cards that pictured the Catedral Zocalo outlined in tiny white lights to Kent, Laird, Miles, and Neal. Even though they were grown men, they would remember the sight because we stayed at a hotel around the corner from the Zocalo in 1959 when the last anthropology conference met in Mexico City.

The instant I dropped the cards into the *buzon del correo,* or mailbox, I remembered they lacked stamps. A bellhop told me to wait for an overdue postman, so I sat nearby and watched waves of anthropologists of every possible shape and style of dress mill by.

I recognized some and nodded. Only two of hundreds responded. The rest looked through, past, or blankly at me without really seeing anybody. That mystified me. If anthropologists are supposed to be students of people and their ways, what kind of anthropologist looks at someone without acknowledging a greeting? Might he or she behave that way in the field too?

Then my thoughts sheared off in another direction. If only one could document the scribbled first impressions of a conference as big as this attended by people as educated as these, in a country as fascinating as Mexico. I toyed with the idea that their postcards might serve to register the mood of a conference population. There would be so many legal problems involved in getting at the cards, however, that the follow-through would not be worth the hassle.

The worst resistance to reading these cards, of course, would come from the anthropologists themselves. People who study other people don't particularly welcome having the field glasses turned on themselves. Margaret Mead might and might not be an exception to this general observation. One way or another, these next two days would surely tell.

The letter carrier arrived. He let me affix stamps to my cards with time enough left over to enable me to reach Imperio D just as the past presidents' breakfast group dispersed. Margaret greeted me by summarizing the meeting.

"Jobs are so scarce," she said, "that as many as two hundred people apply for each one. It's killing those who are doing the interviewing. They have time for nothing else."

"Bill's speaking in Caza A-B, which is on the same floor as Embajadores, where Rhoda and Teddy showed their slides," I informed her quickly. "If we hurry, we should be able to sneak in just as he starts."

"I see you've done your homework," her eyes reflected approval. "You're earning your keep."

No matter how much of a hurry she was ever in, someone always managed to fall in step with her. On this sprint, we acquired two student autograph hunters, a middle-aged woman who'd shared "a lovely long lunch" with her in Cleveland in 1934, and a young, anthropologically inclined law student.

"For reasons known only to himself," she said as we opened the door to the ongoing symposium, Systems for the Delivery of Health and Medical Care, "that young man has dogged my steps at conferences for years." Ken Frietas revealed his name to me when he brought each of us a glass of ice water.

"I learn more listening to her in five minutes than I do in a year of ordinary course work," he beamed. Margaret nodded reassuringly at Bill Mitchell when he walked to the podium to read his paper. I looked around and saw that Alex and Rhoda had also come to hear Bill.

The Iatmul people Bill studied lived up the Sepik River in New Guinea. They attribute sickness to sorcery. Their health and curing rituals consist of pacifying or exorcising malevolent ghosts and demons who, they believe, bring disease. They engage in these activities with an interest so passionate that it borders on religious fervor.

"Look at curing in our own world," Margaret interrupted Bill to reinforce his statements. "We build hospitals with chapels in them. Prayer is an open acknowledgment that there are forces older than modern medicine we call upon to intervene in the disease process."

Without waiting for the questions following his session, she motioned me to leave as soon as Bill sat down. Ted Schwartz, another student who did New Guinea fieldwork, was due to speak in yet a different room in another seven minutes.

We boarded an elevator for her room on the fifteenth floor. An embarrassed young couple held a toddler who reeked with the unmistakable odor of a full diaper. "How universal that smell is," I whispered to her. Her face broke into a sunny smile; then it clouded over just as suddenly. "What's the matter?" I asked.

"I just remembered that we've only got one key to our room and Rhoda has it." We hunted down a chambermaid who let us into her room. Once inside, we saw that the bathroom door was open and the light was still on. "As a child my mother trained me to save energy," she said as she walked over to flick off the light, "and that was long before anybody ever thought of energy shortages."

The phone rang. I took the call while she disappeared into the bathroom. Ted Schwartz wanted to make sure Margaret intended to be on hand to listen to him read his paper. "People depend on her," Ted's wife explained to me as she greeted us at the door of the meeting room two minutes later.

A look of relief spread over Ted's face as Margaret entered. She had been his teacher at Columbia. She introduced him to the Manus people when he was a graduate student twenty years previously. Once he saw Big Mama sit safely down in the front row, Ted seemed to feel better about reading his report. She placed her walking stick flat on the floor and pushed it back slightly out of people's way. Students came over and sat down next to her or knelt in front of her.

She took out a diminutive leather-covered notebook. It was about the size of a credit card and was constructed with a sheet of carbon paper between the pages similar to grocery store receipt pads in the days before supermarkets. I remembered coming across boxes full of such notebooks when I cleaned out her office in the Museum. She told me once she bought them in London. "I've carried these notebooks to conferences for years," she remarked. "I keep reminders like names and addresses in them. As you probably remember, I store them at the Museum. Sometimes I wonder why because no one else will ever be able to decipher them." I watched her date the top of each page and outline the notations she made on it.

Ted apologized for using what he called "slash and burn" techniques to pare his paper down to the allotted twenty minutes. He reported on his attempts to document culture change by administering various intelligence tests to primary school children, high school graduates, and unschooled adults over an entire South Pacific archipelago. "He's tested all these people without my knowing a thing about any of this," she muttered. "Sometimes I think he plays his research cards too close to his chest."

Ted read falteringly, scrutinizing her reactions as he proceeded. She led the clapping when he finished. As the applause subsided, she stood up, licked her lips, and flashed her tongue a time or two before making a comment which, in retrospect, would have been better timed had Ted heard it before he began his study.

"We know by now every population we look at has a range of intellect," she declared, "but what we don't know and what we most need to do is to find the breakthrough individuals. Time after time, it's possible to pinpoint who they will be when they are still children. And such youngsters are always at the high end of the IQ scale."

I looked up at her as she spoke and realized what she said about early recognition of leadership qualities might also have been true of herself in her childhood. I shared this insight with her when she sat down. "You're supposed to be playing the role of my ubiquitous shadow," she reprimanded me even as I suspected the insight tickled her.

"You know darn well that I'm no more shadowy than you are," I responded. "Henceforth, I'll try to contain myself."

A woman and two men followed Ted on the program. Margaret folded her hands in her lap and looked straight at each person with an I-mean-business mien as each one spoke. "When I haven't read the papers beforehand," she later divulged, "I see what the speaker is like and I hear the voice. Twenty minutes isn't too long to hear an important voice."

Noon arrived. Eleven different presentations had been squeezed into four hours in the psychological anthropology symposium. Probably because of time, no discussants had been assigned the session. Richard A. Thompson, the coordinator, stepped down from the platform and approached Margaret. He asked her if she would take over the chair for him and do the windup. Even though she later asserted that the chairman "should have stayed on the platform where he belonged," she took over without hesitation.

The switch happened so fast that most of the people in the room were caught unawares. Suddenly Richard Thompson disappeared; just as suddenly Margaret Mead appeared.

Someone accused her of usurping the chair. "I'm not usurping anything!" she retorted. "I'm just as much a member of this audience as you are! The chairman simply had something else to do."

At the close of the session, the usual assortment of admirers clustered around her like moths drawn to a light on a summer night. She extended her sensory antennae into their midst. Her feelers reached out in every direction for a buzz of comments. Alex Randall walked over and stood beside me. We stepped back to give her fans freer rein. Participant–observers can't always grasp the whole picture from too close a vantage point; distance adds perspective. "Hundreds of people come by and tell her how wonderful she is," Alex said, "and she smiles sweetly, but let one individual ask her a few good questions and she's all attention."

Rhoda walked by on her way to lunch. I noticed her companion's hair was dyed as black as her shoes and stockings. The two of them nodded without speaking.

A tall black man with leather dangles and embroidered mottoes on his jacket sauntered up to her. He must have been descended from the Maasai of

Kenya, some of the tallest people on the planet, because he towered over both of us. He took a small camera from his pocket. "Naturally, I've heard of you," he said, "and I'd like to have a picture of the two of us together so I can hang it in my office back in Detroit."

He asked me to take it and she posed alongside him. There was as much difference in their heights as there is between a teaspoon and a carving knife stood on end.

"I enjoyed your books *Strawberry Statement* and *Growing Up in Samoa,* hiccoughed a portly man with a slight odor of last night's partying.

"Remember me? We were both at the World Food Conference in Rome," a short woman in slacks shoved close enough to get within speaking range.

"You look so distinguished," said a red-haired, freckle-faced graduate student from Texas reaching out to shake her hand. "I'm just getting old," I heard her answer.

Margaret juggled her admirers in her own way and at her own pace while Alex and I waited. He told me he'd taken a trip with her the day before. Six people, including Rhoda, graduate student Nancy McDowell, Dr. and Mrs. Ted Schwartz, and he, journeyed to Tepoztlán.

"I drove," Alex reported. "Margaret rented the car and she gave me hell because I forgot my international driver's license. The Schwartzes were supposed to know the way but forgot some of it. They kept telling me turns to make after we passed the place to make them. We missed a couple of towns that way but we got there and back. It was a day!

"I felt I was chauffeuring the smartest traveler in the world! She bargained in the markets just like any other tourist! She complained about the food just like any other tourist! It was great!

"In the car coming home at sunset, Rhoda happened to mention that the sky looked as big and beautiful as it does in Iran. Margaret jumped her because Rhoda has never been in Iran. That set the two of them off!" he smiled as the scene ran through his mind again.

"We returned so late that none of us got more than five hours' sleep. I've been pooped all day. But look at her! She's three times my age and she's not acting a bit tired."

"Don't say she's tired. She never gets tired," Mrs. Schwartz overheard us. "Ted and I worked near Tepoztlán when the anthropologists last met in Mexico. Margaret goes to villages whenever she can, no matter where in the world she is," Mrs. Schwartz remarked. "She's always and forever an anthropologist. She can't imagine any other kind of existence. It's partly the role of the stranger, you know."

"She's a stranger who cares about people she works with," Alex added. "All of us former students and coworkers make up her intellectual family. We're as much a part of her family as Cathy is. She thinks we should support and help each other the way blood relatives do too."

"That's right. She doesn't use students and then trash them like some anthropologists I could mention." Mrs. Schwartz looked around but only young people remained in the room. "My daughter is twenty-four years old now and she has known Margaret since she was ten. Fourteen years. 'She hasn't changed a bit,' Debbie says about her, and I think most of us who have known her a while could say the same. She doesn't change."

"We'd better stage a rescue or she'll lose weight and have to go to her next session lunchless," I said when I saw her yank her green cue sheet out of her purse. "Can you get lunch in this hotel?" she asked as Alex and I together nudged her out of the Embajadores meeting room.

"Yes, but it will be too crowded. Let's go to Sanborn's instead. It's next door and we could use the fresh air," Alex recommended.

Margaret suggested that we sit at a table instead of a counter. "That way we won't take up some workman's seat when he is on his lunch hour." We each ordered a small bottle of mineral water that never came. "Have you noticed how full of chlorine the water in the hotel is?" Margaret said. "I washed my hair in it this morning and nearly asphyxiated myself."

The waiter handed each of us a menu. "I want something with beans," she declared as we looked it over. "I learned to like spicy foods from our Italian neighbors when I was a little girl." All three of us ordered the same thing. It sounded good but turned out to be a nonentity on a bun.

"Eat what's put in front of you," Margaret said as she cut hers into bite-sized pieces with her knife and fork. Alex and I picked ours up and ate them like hamburgers.

Doctors Abel and Metraux entered and chose seats near us. I jumped up to shove our tables together but Margaret signaled not to so I sat down again.

Alex noticed that Margaret held her coffee cup in her left hand. "I always hold a cup this way when I travel," she explained. "Since most people are right-handed, you use the cleaner side of the cup by acting like a left-handed person in restaurants."

I sat silently pondering Margaret's not wanting me to push our table closer to Rhoda's. I narrowed my eyes in Rhoda's direction. Neither Dana nor I had consulted her when we made arrangements to follow Margaret at this conference. Should we have? Could she snag our plans? Dana's or my presence at sessions and at meals like this one would certainly rouse whatever jealousy Rhoda harbored, if she had any.

In a way, I mused, I'm glad the two of us share this project. If either one should fall into bad graces, the other one might come through unscarred.

"How did you meet Rhoda?" I wondered aloud.

"I worked on a project with her second husband, Alfred Metraux, first," Margaret replied. "Then she wrote me a letter. I don't go looking for helpers, as you know. They come to me. Rhoda started as one of my assistants."

I read the clock on the wall. "Dana's probably wondering what's taking me so long. I'll go up so she can get down here," I excused myself.

"You'll be free for the rest of today," Margaret said as I got up. "Barbara Heath has invited me to dinner."

"Okay, I'll meet you outside your door at 8:00 tomorrow morning then." I tapped her on the head and waved good-bye to Alex as I left.

When Dana returned to our room at the end of her afternoon stint, she disturbed my nap. "Can you believe it? Someone asked me if I was CIA?" she exclaimed. "We're going to have to expect a lot of questions as to what we're up to from now on."

"Nobody has asked me any questions," I said. "But I've got one for you. Who is Barbara Heath? Margaret is dining with her tonight, as you probably know. Her name is familiar but I just can't place her."

"Margaret has invited Alex and this Barbara to come with her when we take her to dinner tomorrow night!" Dana mentally counted our money.

"Margaret told me that Barbara has invited the four of us to her room for cocktails beforehand. We can save some money there."

"Great," I winced. "I sure hope the restaurant across the street accepts credit cards. If we're going to have to feed Margaret and two others besides ourselves, I won't have enough cash to call home from the airport."

That evening I participated in a gathering of nurse anthropologists. Dana attended the annual business meeting after her session. I returned to the room at 9:00; she, not until midnight. Once again, she roused me from sleep.

"Margaret's getting annoyed at us. People are calling us her shadows! She came over to me at the business meeting and asked, 'Are you kids mucking things up for me?'" Dana laughed. "Imagine calling two women in their fifties kids."

"I didn't get any flak from her at all," I sat up. "She's sometimes short-tempered, as you know. Probably more so late at night."

"I think she picks on me more than she does you anyway. Nobody talks to her as you do."

At fifteen minutes past midnight, the phone rang. It was Margaret! "Dana, why didn't you come back to the room with me? There's nobody here and I feel abandoned," Margaret complained. Then she took a breath and asked, "Which one of you will be with me in the morning?"

"I'm so sorry. I thought the best thing I could do at the end of a long day would be to leave you alone," Dana apologized. "Pat expects to be outside your door again at 8:00."

Klunk. She ditched us. We reassured her. Conversation ended. Dana placed the receiver on its hook. Her big eyes glowed in disbelief. "Can you beat that? She wants us and she doesn't want us! In spite of all her scolding, she's eating up this attention! She loves it!" Dana grinned from ear to ear.

"Sometimes I think she likes to get hot and bothered for the excitement of getting hot and bothered," I mumbled as I snuggled down to tackle a third installment of a highly interruptible sleep. "I've told her two separate times today when I'd meet her. She should know by now."

I stood sentry duty outside her door a few hours later. Two voices raised in high dudgeon startled me. Eavesdropping was the last sin in the world I wanted to be caught doing; that would turn Margaret against our shadowing her for sure. I sped to a spot in the hallway nearer the elevator but still close enough to watch the door of Room 1520.

In seconds Margaret stormed out at such a pace that she resembled an irate witch braking for a landing. She spied me, stomped her stick, and demanded, "Pat, what in hell are you and Dana up to?"

Her angry words spurted out through gritted teeth. I'll bet she wore off a lot of tooth enamel that way.

My whole body stiffened defensively. "Margaret," I answered calmly while I groped for just the right order to pronounce the words. "You're smart enough to know you attract a lot of criticism. Many people consider you a controversial character, if not a kook. Dana and I are just trying to get a minute-by-minute analysis of all that you do for people at a conference. We want to be able to show you as a very warm and wise human being. I think the more people learn about your basic humanity, the more you'll enjoy their reactions while you're still around."

She slanted the stick against her shoulder and put her hands on her hips. "Rhoda says you're keeping people away from me."

"We've only been at it since yesterday," I countered. "I can't speak for Dana, but I step back whenever anybody comes near you. I step back so far I don't always catch a name or the message.

"You know, the Koreans are supposed to have a saying that there are at least three ways to interpret anything; your way, my way, and the right way. I don't think it's fair to jump to negative conclusions about what we're doing just on the basis of Rhoda's say-so."

She melted. We walked to the elevator together. The new president of the American Anthropological Association, Ernestine Freidl, waited there. Freidl expressed regrets that no one had thought about providing translation services at the business meeting the evening before. "I conducted the meeting with a most uncomfortable impression that the Spanish speakers present sat politely for hours without understanding one word," she said.

"Thanks for the tip. I'll insist on a translation microphone for my session this afternoon," Margaret pulled her green sheet from her purse and tore it as she did so. She held the two pieces together and read, "The psychoanalysis and anthropology session will be in the Independencia Room. That means I'll be there all day. At noon I have to go down to the registration desk in the lobby to find out where the committee on committees meets for lunch."

"I'll go over and grab some reprints for both of us at that time if you'd like any," I volunteered. She handed me an order sheet with 108 entries checked off.

"You'd better get there as soon as possible," Dr. Freidl warned me. "They only printed twenty copies of each speech and there are 4,000 of us here. You'll be lucky to get any of the ones you want."

"Now it's my turn to thank you for a tip," I said as I pocketed Margaret's list. The elevator doors opened and we squeezed in.

"Izzat Margaret Mead?" someone behind me asked her companion.

Margaret turned her head just enough to glimpse at them out of the corner of her eye. "Why? Does my slip show?" she surprised them with a question that any woman might ask another. She caught almost everybody in the car unaware. I reached for a piece of paper and was making note of the incident when the elevator stopped and we were the first to walk out.

"What are you going to do with all those notes you're taking, anyway?" Margaret worried aloud as we marched toward the Independencia Room.

"Don't know. Got to gather a bunch of them first." I put the note in my purse.

"Are you going to write about me as a scientist or as a human being?"

"Remember the study you did after Sputnik in which schoolchildren depicted scientists as bald, bespectacled, and bony? Well, I'd add benighted. I'm increasingly turned off by the media's quoting 'scientists this' and 'scientists that' as though scientists were modern magi whom we should all adore. No. It's the human qualities that endear you to me. Most of the readers of the world don't know anything about that part of you. That's what I want to write about: you as a very human, human being."

"Frankly, I can't be hurt by what others might say about me but I worry about what anyone might write about my friends. One columnist referred to them recently as 'superannuated women serving time volunteering for me in the Museum.' That hurt."

"Never fear. I'd be inclined to do unto others as I would be done by. Besides, you've told me what your mother learned after her study of Italian immigrants in Hammonton: Never write anything about somebody who would resent what you wrote if they learned English and were able to read it."

"Just the same, promise me you'll let me see what you write about me or my friends before you show it to anybody else."

How much anthropology would never have been published if primitives exacted the same promise from anthropologists who followed them around? My shadow self prodded my social self.

Alex sat between the two seats he'd saved for us. I greeted him and took Margaret's green sheet out of her bag to mend it with some Scotch tape from my carryall. She stopped briefly to exchange a few words of greeting with a beloved friend of forty-two years, George Devereux. He had traveled from Paris to be a panel discussant for the morning session on psychological anthropology. Margaret herself planned to take over in the same capacity for the continuation of the session in the afternoon.

"George has his own apartment in another hotel," she reported when she rejoined Alex and me. "He wants to take a nap after the meetings. Pat, would you mind walking over to his place with me about four o'clock? I want to see him away from conference noises and alone."

"Okay, I'll window shop while you two talk. Who is he?" I asked. "I seem to remember having read something by or about Devereux when I took one of your courses."

"He's a very satisfactory mythological living legend. George has embodied in his personality two different disciplines. He's both an anthropologist and a first-class ethnographer as well as a practicing psychoanalyzing clinician."

"He's cross-disciplinary then," Alex said. "That's remarkable."

"It is," Margaret answered. "Anthropologists who criticize psychoanalysts don't know anything about psychoanalysis. And the flip of that is also true! Psychoanalysts who criticize anthropologists don't know anything about it, either."

"How old a man is Dr. Devereux?" Alex asked.

"Sixty-seven and he looks eighty-eight. He's not feeling well, either. Lots of people are having respiratory problems. This is high country, you know." She caught me putting her mended green sheet back in her bag. "Pat, you're being compulsive," she upbraided me.

"That's one way of looking at it," I replied. "You tore it and it needed mending. I had the time and the tape. So, why not? I could have just sat here and counted light bulbs in the chandelier but that wouldn't have been as productive."

"I see you've already lost your identification badge," Alex changed the subject.

"Yes," she patted the place where hers used to be. "I usually wear out about two or three identification badges per meeting."

"I'll get another for you at lunch if you want one," I offered.

"Why bother?" Alex shrugged. "Of the 4,000 people who are supposed to have registered, Margaret Mead's probably the last one who needs to tell the rest of us who she is."

"Pat, would you confirm Rhoda's and my flight out of here the day after to-morrow? Rhoda's at the Museo this morning so she can't do it and somebody's got to." As she talked, she pulled copies of the half dozen papers to be presented at the next session out of her bright yellow plastic bag. She spread them in a semi-circle at her feet. I could tell by her markings on them that she'd read them. In this session, she would reread each paper along with the author's oral presentation.

The meeting began with six panelists and two discussants at the table. "Louder, please," she bellowed in the midst of the introductory remarks. "I can't hear a thing. This is supposed to be the big session on psychoanalysis and anthropology, and they expect us to go all day without earphones," she protested while panelists scampered to check cords and connections.

Alex took advantage of the delay to bring both of us some ice water. At the same time, he delivered a note from two newsmen who asked to do a videotape of her sometime that afternoon.

Before the reading of the third and fourth papers, the chair declared a break. Margaret wanted to go to the bathroom. Alex and I would have visited in her absence but I went along after she stood up and asked, "Aren't you coming? I thought you were supposed to be my shadow."

She found her way to the ladies' room with the accuracy of a homing pigeon. I commented on this evidence of her memory for spaces. "I walked a lot when I was a child," she said. "When you walk over an area enough, you don't even have to think about the route after a while. Your feet know the way."

Six or more women waited in front of each of the two booths in the room Para Senoras. In less than a minute, Margaret realized there weren't any feet in one of the booths. She astounded everybody in front of her when she sailed past them with cape at full mast and opened the door to the empty booth!

On the way back to the windup papers in the morning session, a series of people stopped her. Joan Rosenfeld Eggan breezed up and embraced her. Joan wore a richly colored handwoven jacket from Guatemala and tinkly jewelry. Joan was Margaret's youngest sister's roommate at the University of Chicago in the 1930s.

Joan's tall husband, Fred, thanked Margaret for having advised him to buy a camera. "I'm surprised at the pictures we're getting—they're so good," he enthused.

"Photography tells each generation of anthropologists more than we know enough to look for, you know," she acknowledged. "Why don't you put more emphasis on photography in your curriculum?"

"Easier said than done," he smilingly stalled. "It would take fifteen years to change our curriculum."

"You want to meet Ted Carpenter?" she asked a young man who waylaid us at the door. "Send me a postcard to that effect and I'll get the two of you together, providing you'll let me listen to the conversation."

"You want the sources of the homosexuality studies that I cited in that symposium yesterday afternoon?" she reacted to the query of another. "Write your name and address in my notebook and put down exactly what you want to know. I'll see the information gets to you."

A tall young man from the University of Capetown and his shorter, bearded companion cornered her at noon when she emerged from the Independencia Room after the morning meetings. She seemed to know they would be looking for her.

We sat together on a stair step. The Afrikaners stood in front of us and hid her from the easy view of conferees, who passed by without interrupting her for a change. I suspect, however, that she saw most of the passersby because her eyes darted from face to face like a lost traveler in Grand Central Station even as she carried on her conversation.

"I'm leaving for Paris for four days," she told the young men. "I'll be stopping off in Holland to give a talk on the radio. I'm going to say I think the rest of Europe turned against the Netherlands because of how they treated Huguenots. The criticism Hollanders got at that time helped establish their feeling of being abandoned, of having to go it alone."

"That's true," the taller one agreed. "You might go even further and make note of the fact that Netherlanders have abandoned masses of people in their vast colonies as well. They just wash their hands of those they leave behind."

"Exactly!" she exclaimed. "And you know the key difficulty in South Africa is the relationship between imperialistic English speakers and colonizing Afrikaners. That's the key! It's nonsense to say the difficulty there is between whites and blacks."

"Uh-huh," the Afrikaners murmured in unison.

"Well, English speakers have always acted contemptuously toward Dutch settlers. I think the English feel some guilt about that. Afrikaners are settlers who feel they have a right to be in South Africa. The covered wagon is their symbol just as it is in our western states. And the United States is no more about to give our country back to the Indians than the Afrikaners are about to give theirs back to the Bushmen."

"That's certainly true."

"The descendants of settlers in the United States should be able to understand the situation with the descendants of settlers in South Africa, but no one in the United States seems to see the similarity. Anti–South Africanism is the cheapest form of liberalism in the world today. I'm going to say I think it is the duty of the Christian Netherlanders to reconsider their whole position; to get back to establishing conditions so that South Africa can continue to be in the United Nations."

"Yes, because if the members of the U.N. can successfully gang up against South Africa's membership, then South Africa would just be the first country in a long line."

"That's what happened in the League of Nations, you know! We cannot let it happen again. Other countries like Russia and Indonesia and Chile have done worse things than South Africa has done and they've remained in the U.N.! We've got to stop this anti–South Africanism! It's essentially terrible!"

"The Afrikaners pay a price personally, too," the taller man recalled. "I was in Amsterdam the other day myself and I felt endangered in life and limb."

"Well, I thought I'd also say something about the Dutch colonial past and what happens when a people repudiate their past. The Dutch participated in atrocities here in America every bit as bad as any committed by any other European power. Now they're trying to pretend that they didn't do anything."

"Our noses aren't all that clean, either," she continued. "We were just as bad as the Dutch when we were a colonial power in the Philippines.

"All over the world people are repudiating their pasts. All of our pasts are dubious. But we must not let the dubiety of our pasts interfere with our constructive activities for the future."

"Dialogues will have to open up in the United Nations instead of having pressure pile up against South Africa as it is right now," the shorter man interjected.

"Now can you tell me in case I'm asked, as I haven't read any recent reports on it, has anything significant happened to the colored in South Africa?"

"They've got a lot of publicity and they're saying they aren't going to fight for South Africa unless they're given decent status."

"I think they'll get some status soon. I have considerable contact with the colored community because my wife teaches in one of their schools," said the taller man. "She notices the families with children in school have become the same kind of upwardly striving middle-class consumers as the whites."

"Sure, and those middle-class blacks are not sympathizing with the blacks back in the bush at all. They're racists inevitably! Each top layer of racism produces a lower layer of racism!" Margaret managed to wave to someone whose sharp eyes spotted her.

"I thought I'd also say something about the fact that there're not three but five different groups in South Africa. And each group separates itself from the other four by all kinds of class distinctions," she continued.

"People have such incredibly emotional propagandized reactions," the shorter man turned to follow her eyes as he spoke. "Who's that man you just waved to?" he asked. "He looks familiar somehow."

"Steve Polgar. I worked with him at the Population Conference in Bucharest," she answered. Then she returned to the subject at hand. "One thing I've noticed about the Dutch is that they're not beyond flipping their opinions in certain circumstances. I'm counting on the possibility of a flip in their current stance against South Africa."

The shorter man stroked his beard. "As Afrikaners, we definitely have the Dutch as part of our past. I've noticed that our being rejected by our past has a curious psychological effect on us as a people. We all feel rejected by our past."

"Being rejected by their past has a terrible effect on people," Margaret looked thoughtfully sad. "It turns them into very funny folk.

"Emotionally, the South Afrikaners have been triply transplanted. It reminds me of what happened to the Scotch-Irish in my Ramsay ancestry. They were in Scotland and then they went to Ireland. From there, they sailed to the coast of the United States and settled down in Appalachia. Then they moved up into Ohio and Illinois, where the Czech and Polish miners rejected them as rabbit-shooting natives."

She fingered her new room key. "Rejection's gone on all over the world and through time. We have to look at the whole picture. The only way to deal with one people's rejection of another is to keep sight of the whole picture, historically, geographically, politically." She stood up to go, already late for lunch with the committee on committees. "If you think of anything else I should mention in the broadcast in Holland next Monday, leave a note in my box for me," she told the young men. "I'll be here until tomorrow morning."

She picked up her possessions and scurried away without a word to her shadow. I stood on the bottom step with my mouth open, feeling like Alice in Wonderland as she watched the busy rabbit hightail it out of sight.

A friend with whom I attended some of the afternoon meetings reminded me that Barbara Heath was a physical anthropologist who specialized in somatyping the human body. Margaret had met her when Barbara worked with William Sheldon in the Gessell Institute at Yale. Then I knew why her name was so familiar. Barbara Heath was the friend Margaret invariably visited in Carmel after her stops with us in Palo Alto when I was still a graduate student at Stanford.

Promptly at 5:30 p.m., as per instructions, I knocked on Heath's door with a water glass in my hand. Margaret, Dana, and Alex had already arrived and brought drinking glasses from their rooms. I liked Barbara Heath immediately. We let the others talk while Barbara and I took the assembled water glasses into the bathroom to mix up predinner cocktails. She produced fresh limes and a bottle of tequila in which floated one well-fed white-green worm. "We can't let Margaret see that worm," I said just loud enough for Margaret's antennae to pick up some of my words.

"What am I not supposed to see?" she demanded. "A mere worm? Don't you think I've consumed something with worms in it before?" she frowned at me disparagingly. "When I'm in the field I eat whatever anybody else eats. It's as simple as that."

"Well, tonight we're going to eat Mexican," Dana, the cohostess, diverted the heat from me. "There's a place across the street that is pleasant and cheap. We won't even have to pay a cab to get there."

"You can't get a cab for less than $5 in this town and I've only got $8 to my name." Alex's declaration dismissed his having to cover any of the evening's expenses.

"I don't go anywhere. That's how I beat cab prices," Barbara disclosed as she distributed the drinks.

"They serve something over there called enchilada molé. The enchilada has chicken inside and then they pour chocolate sauce on top of it, of all things." Dana sampled her tequila.

After one round of cocktails, we walked across the street to the restaurant. Lively Mexican music bombarded our ears as we made our way to a table for five. We sat in a corner lit by one lone candle. I never cease to ponder at the irony of finally being able to afford to eat in a restaurant when physically my eyes have become too poor to read by the dim light in many of them.

"They have delicious gazpacho soup here," Dana informed us as we half-blindly deciphered items on the menu.

"That's not hot, is it?" Barbara asked.

"No, it's a cold soup," Margaret answered.

"I mean pepper hot," Barbara responded.

"Not too much. You'll like it. Gazpacho is a very good soup." Margaret's glasses glistened in the gloom.

"*Tres platos de gaspacho, por favor.*" I practiced my pidgin Spanish on the waiter.

"*Cuatro?*" he asked.

"*Cinco!*" I corrected myself as I caught their cues, "*y cinco botellas de aqua mineral, por favor.*"

Most of us ordered the enchilada molé. The waiter brought so much food on even so simple an order as ours that Margaret recoiled at the sight of it. "This is obscene! Absolutely obscene!" she exclaimed as she surveyed our five orders spreading across the table. "Nobody should be served this much food. There's a world food shortage! Three orders for the five of us would have been plenty. Or two! Waste like this in a time of near universal famine nauseates me."

"It is too much," Barbara, the thinnest among us, hastened to agree.

"Restaurants serve big helpings so they can charge more." I was, after all, one of the two destined to foot the bill.

"So few ever challenge practices like this." Margaret leaned forward so her words could be heard despite the mad music. "Most Americans are oblivious of the world's hunger problem. And that includes most anthropologists, sad to say. We've been at this meeting three days and there hasn't been a single session on the world's food problem, on nuclear energy, on pollution, or on population. It's sickening. I guess we can't expect anthropologists to do anything except talk about their jobs or each other."

"I've heard you say that about other conferences we've attended too, Margaret," I said as I piled the ashtrays atop each other to make more room on the table. "You know, I tried to get the book on conferences that you wrote with Paul Beyers to bring down here. So I don't know yet what you say in it about the choice of topics for sessions. It's not easy to find that book."

"Right! It's not easy to get hold of that book." Barbara savored her multitextured gazpacho. "Mouton published it in 1968."

"Interdisciplinary people virtually have to go to conferences today," Margaret declared. "There's no other way to keep up or catch up with the literature in any field that's moving. When you go to a conference, you get the latest information hot off the fire and from the fire tenders."

"Everybody knows that by the time anything is published, it's out of date anyway." Alex looked up from the last of his soup.

"You can learn more in a concentrated morning listening to people read papers on their work than you can in reading for a month of Sundays." Margaret soothed her throat with a gulp of mineral water. "We need so much more information before we can understand human behavior. As anthropologists, we have always expanded our material. We go to another tribe that has something else, something we haven't even thought of. I'd go to any conference on the brain right now. Some decent biochemistry should provide us with new kinds of material."

"What's more, you'd attend all the sessions, too," I pitched in. "I can't say that for at least a dozen of your peers. They hold confabs in their rooms or talk to people in the hallways and lobby and miss all the scheduled sessions."

Except for the click-click of the silverware on dishware, we ate in silence for several minutes. It was easier to listen to marimba music than carry on a conversation either above or below the sounds of it.

"The core of any conference should be some people who have worked together before. They know how to talk to each other," Margaret reminisced. "We were together for a month at the Dartmouth Conference in 1935 and then we all went home and wrote books.

"The Doxiadis cruise conference went on every summer for ten years. The people who attended them communicated. We knew each other. They've been called off now because they got too expensive," Margaret continued.

"This enchilada molé is excellent. Very fascinating. Imagine having chocolate on chicken." Dana smacked her lips approvingly. "Or chicken on chocolate."

"I couldn't stand a dish like this when I was in the hospital here with pneumonia six years ago," Barbara recalled. "They served me combinations I'd never heard of."

"I can't eat Mexican food every day," Margaret acknowledged, "but I think it's marvelous once a year."

"You can't believe the notes I've taken on this conference," Alex said between bites. "Would you believe I got twelve pages on the homosexuality session you were the discussant in yesterday afternoon? I may never read them again but at least I have the notes."

"It's essential for any good conference that those who come do not get paid. They should come out of their own interest. Then they're really committed. Once you pay people, and that includes those who come to read their own papers, they lose a certain commitment and then it's not comparable." Margaret pushed the last of her molé to one side of her plate.

"This conference has frustrated me," Dana sighed. "I've not been able to go to any sessions of my own choice except when Pat's been on duty. Then I'm confronted with too many choices every hour on the hour. It's very frustrating, really."

"A conference should have good secretarial help beforehand and during," Barbara volunteered as she put down her fork with half her meal uneaten.

So that's the secret skinny people have for staying thin, I thought. They don't clean their plates.

"And it should not have mediocre quarters," Margaret chewed words and chicken together. "Either poor ones in which to feel noble or elegant ones in which to feel comfortable. I'm never bored at a conference, either," she continued. "If the subject or the paper under discussion begins to bore me, I can always sit and study the process." Dana's and my eyes met in a shared memory we did not voice.

"She makes process happen," an older brother anthropologist had told us at dinner the night before. "She barges into a session, sizes up the situation fast, and spits out her comments in no uncertain terms. She kills egos all over the place and seems to like to pounce on the underdog. This is an interesting necessity for the oldest of five, is it not? I used to wonder why she thinks she has to do this. But over the years, I've come to realize that she's more bark than bite."

Dana and I sat on each side of her. In deference to our hostesshood, Barbara diverted Alex's attention by telling him about somatyping family members in the village of Pere where Margaret did much of her New Guinea fieldwork. Barbara's thoughtfulness left Dana and me free to close in on Margaret and question her randomly about her more Secret Self.

"Everything you want to know is in *Blackberry Winter*," she hedged. "If you'd only sit down and read what I've already written, you could answer your own questions."

We hedged in return. "*Blackberry Winter* is full of holes," I protested, "and we'd like to fill in some of them while the filling's good."

Her eyes darted over newcomers entering the darkened restaurant.

"For example," I continued, "on the afternoon before Dana and I started following you around, we pushed each other in a wheelchair through the Museo laughing all the way. We couldn't remember ever hearing you laugh. Do you ever laugh?"

"Cathy makes me laugh."

"You chuckled at least twenty times during the homosexuality symposium," Dana reported.

"I laugh with some people and in certain situations." Margaret looked over at Barbara and Alex, half-listening to their conversation.

"The two of us giggled like schoolgirls when we walked across Chapultepec Park yesterday on the way to the Museo," I added. "But somehow, I simply can't imagine your giggling."

"I don't giggle. I doubt if I ever did."

"Were you very playful as a child?" Dana asked.

"Children are kittenish, I know, but I'd say that by the age of ten, I was a very sober little lady."

I slumped down in my chair and let Dana take over for a few minutes while I asked myself what could have slowed Margaret the child down to be always so solemn. She was born playful and she became serious. What in her nurture changed that part of her nature?

"How do you handle jealousy?" I heard Dana ask as I came out of my momentary reverie. We suspected Margaret had run into a good dose of jealousy on the part of her roommate at this conference.

"If the jealous person were someone I loved, my first response would be to identify the affection that roused the jealousy." Margaret stirred restlessly. "But if that led to conflict, I'd leave."

"Would you consider marrying again?" I wasn't too sure how she'd receive this question even though she'd asked it of me a time or two.

"Heavens, no!" she huffed. "Whatever gave you that notion? I've got other things to do and I'm not lonely anyhow."

"You could still get a lot done and at the same time have the pleasure of having a man around to kiss you on the ears," I teased. "Why not?"

Dana caught her breath and her eyes sparkled mischievously. I got the fleeting impression I should have kept the kisses out of it. Margaret stood up, grabbed Barbara by the arm, and waltzed her off to the Columbia University party without a please, thank-you, or good night.

Dana and I sat stunned. Then we came to enough to tell Alex what precipitated her departure. "Your questions probably took more energy to answer than she'd counted on," Alex explained. "And she's too nice to tell you when she's had enough."

In retrospect, I think our questions grazed that Secret Self so carefully encrusted by the many conference interests of Margaret's Public Self. If Margaret Mead, who constantly studied other people in her own life, demonstrated that she didn't appreciate being studied, then would anybody?

Dana and I left that question forever unanswered as we combined our cash to pay the bill. I took my shoe off to get at the last dollars hidden there. Alex waited and accompanied us across the street to the hotel and the Columbia Party. "Margaret'll probably be gone when we get there," he said.

"That's right." Dana took him up on his guess. "She mainly just makes token appearances at conference parties. She comes late and leaves early."

"She has told me her father used to do the same thing when he taught at the Wharton School at the University of Pennsylvania," I remembered aloud.

"You really can't blame her," Alex, who was the same age as my youngest son, playfully announced. "Conference parties are dullsville and anthropologists are so uptight. Wouldn't it be great if they'd just once take off their clothes at the door, take a little snort, and smear each other with vegetable oil?"

"Margaret would definitely disapprove," declared one of her abruptly retired ubiquitous shadows. "That's much too physical and she's too serious. I can see her scowl and stand in the doorway with her hands on her hips, grimly deploring such antics when the future's at stake and the world's waiting to be saved."

"And besides," echoed the other, "novel as your suggestion may be, Alex, we're all on such ego trips with our esoteric specialties that it would take a helluva lot more than corn oil to enable even one anthropologist to get to know another any better."

9

SHE REFUSED TO BE LABELED TERMINAL

"Would you please autograph this copy of *Blackberry Winter* for me?" I led the pack that pushed in on Margaret Mead after an evening session on the last day of the annual conference of anthropologists at Houston's Hyatt Regency Hotel. "The eight-year-old daughter of one of my gerontology students says she's going to be an anthropologist someday," I talked fast. "You're her model and her parents want to give her this copy of your autobiography for Christmas."

Margaret reached for the book with one hand and passed a clump of white yarn to me with the other. "December 2nd, 1977," she scratched her pen across the flyleaf.

"Her name's E-r-i-n K-e-y-e-s," I spelled out the letters.

Margaret wrote the letters down as fast as I said them and glanced up. "Erin Keyes is the same age as my granddaughter," she thought aloud. Then she looked down again, hesitated, and added her own comment.

I had detected a slight waddle in her usually purposeful stride when she entered the room at the beginning of the session. I scrutinized her now as she obliged me. Her nose and mouth appeared thicker than when I saw her at the 1976 conference in Washington, D.C. Toward the end of his life, her father's features became spongy and spread out over his face in the same way. Her skin wasn't quite the same shade. Her head bobbed. She didn't exude her usual high energy. "Thank you." I reached for the book. "Erin's mother will be very pleased with this."

"I hope Erin sticks to her goals." The woman who'd stuck to hers as much as any anthropologist in the field retracted the point of her pen as she shoved it back into her black, voluminously pocketed purse. "Societies need anthropologists and anthropology needs all the dedicated people it can get."

"You're certainly one such," I said as I returned her yarn and secreted the book in a side compartment of my own voluminously pocketed handbag. She gave me the number of the room that she shared with Rhoda Metraux across the street at the Sheraton.

"This is the first time I've ever seen you kah-licking away with kah-nitting needles. Makes you look positively domestic. What's the knitting all about?" I queried.

"Rhoda's trying to give up cigarettes. Knitting gives her hands something else to do. We're knitting together. I find it helps me concentrate."

"That's good news." I looked into eyes that responded with more pain than twinkle. "We've all read about the connection between smoking and cancer. It seems to be catching up with more women too. The experts say at least three in ten of us will get it and that's scary. Reminds me of the dragons and witches that haunted our medieval ancestors."

We both knew that the next conference would begin in Los Angeles, the City of Angels, on November 15, 1978. One of us knew that cancer had caught up with her over a year before and that she had been given two months to live. Neither of us could have predicted her demise on the precise morning of the opening of the seventy-seventh annual gathering of American anthropologists, nor the extent to which that eerie coincidence would shroud registration procedures.

Ours was just a snatch of conversation seized in a swirl of seconds before the crowd around her caved in on us. In retrospect, I find it comforting to remember that one of our final face-to-face interchanges involved her doing me a favor that enabled me to do the same for the parents of a little girl who aspired to follow in her footsteps. Like candles that burn at both ends, passing favors along lights up the lives of both givers and receivers. Margaret Mead continuously received and gave favors. In the jargon of her day, she referred to this aspect of her life as "networking." Networking resembled knitting. One intertwined threads; the other, people.

The doors of an almost completely empty elevator slid shut just as I bolted into it with the prized Christmas present. The best way to guarantee not leaving it somewhere was to hide it in the bottom of my suitcase post haste. On the way to my floor, I peeked at the inscription on the flyleaf: "For Erin Keyes, with the hope that she will someday become an anthropologist. M . . . t M . . . d"

"Margaret's not going to live long enough to get to Milwaukee again." The voice startled me. I looked up at the only other person in the elevator. It was John Dowling, a red-headed peer from Marquette University.

"Don't kid yourself. She's only seventy-five," I countered. "She's told me one of her grandmothers lived to be eighty-two; the other, ninety-six. As I recall, her mother didn't quite make the eighties, but both of her mother's sisters did. One's nearly ninety and the other died at one hundred only a year or so ago."

"She'll never make one hundred." John pulled a pipe out of his pocket and looked wiser. "She leads too fast-paced a life to make it."

"She said she doesn't want to, but she'll come close," I boasted even as other thoughts buzzed through my brain.

She was born two weeks before the end of 1901. If she stuck around until the year 2001, wouldn't that be something? Imagine having a hundred-year-old anthropologist of her stature loose in the world! Making whirlwind visits everywhere and passing out advice as if it were fortune cookies! A sage like Margaret Mead could wind up as almost everybody's expert on nearly everything. She said that older females, even in prehuman groups, carry the culture.

"Well, who knows, John," I said aloud. "You might be right, but I hope you're not." We both stepped off the elevator on the same floor and headed in the same direction. "When I took my first class from her in the 1950s," I recalled as we clip-clipped along, "she had just returned from her second trip to the Manus people in New Guinea. She stressed the fact then that the ones who raced around the most died first. Only those who slowed down and took life easier survived to tell tales about those who spent themselves trying to hasten change."

"That figures," he grinned as he unlocked his door.

I fumbled for the key to mine a few steps further down a garishly carpeted hallway. Dana Raphael and I had not roomed together since Mexico. Rather than follow Margaret around again, we had agreed to collect anecdotes about her instead. Dana suggested calling them "Meadiana." Between the first afternoon and evening session on the initial day of the Houston conference, about a dozen old and new acquaintances were lingering in the Hyatt Regency lobby. We decided to eat together, hailed three taxis, and set out for a reasonably priced restaurant with "atmosphere."

I remember groping, Indian file, through a maze of smaller tables to a larger one on a platform near a wall. The lights were low, the music loud, and the seating helter-skelter. On either side five others sat between Dana and me. This happenstance mixing heightened our chances for gathering Meadiana. Missy Makarit was one person about whom most anthropologists had a comment to make or a tale to tell.

"Did you see *Newsweek*?" Dana set the wheels of conversation in motion almost as soon as the waitress disappeared with our orders. "MM got a stand-up ovation when she addressed the Women's Conference at the Sam Houston Coliseum here nine days ago."

"Nine days ago?" A dyed blond of uncertain vintage arched one eyebrow. "So this is the second time she has been in Houston in nine days? My God!"

"When I registered this morning," Dana continued, "the desk clerk said, 'Anyone who'd been to the Women's Conference wouldn't want to come back. It was mad.' I told him Margaret Mead was back and she's almost old enough to be his great-grandmother."

"She's on the go all the time. Go. Go. Go." I chipped in. "I think she loves it. This afternoon she introduced me to a couple of secretaries she brought down here with her. The friendlier one told me she went to Brazil and Europe in January and February; to Iran in May; to Bali and Indonesia in July; to Canada in August; to Sweden in September and even took a cruise to the Pacific when there was an eclipse in October. Can you beat that? Seventy-five years old and she's taken six trips out of the country this year."

"She must carry one of the most worn-out passports in the world," exclaimed an older woman next to Dana.

"I can't figure out how she keeps up the pace: writing, lecturing, traveling, plus God knows what else." The brunette turned blond balanced a long, thin cigarillo between red-nailed fingers.

"She brought two secretaries down here, did she?" queried a svelte, pleasant-faced college professor who was dressed in an attractive fringed leather outfit and the latest eyeglasses. "Traveling secretaries enable her to get a lot more done at least."

"Forgive me," I butted in. "She doesn't refer to them as secretaries. They're usually pre-Ph.D.s, so she calls them assistants. The way she figures, there's a two-way profit in the relationship. She uses their talents, yes, but the opportunities that open up to them through working with her help get their careers off to a healthy start as well."

"By the time most of us reach our middle sixties, we've collected some noticeable maladies." A tight-lipped older man with a shoulder tic twitched his chin whiskers and surveyed the lot of us. "Margaret passed sixty-five ten years ago and she doesn't show any signs of wear and tear yet. She's tough as hell. Reminds me of my mother."

"She doesn't take proper care of herself, but who does?" Dana, who routinely stretches at a ballet bar and polices her calories, commented on another thought that occurred to her. "She's been breaking an ankle off and on for at least fifty years, but I don't really know for sure if it's always been the right one."

"Maybe she wants to be the richest person in the graveyard," quipped a balding man whom I recognized from another conference somewhere.

"She is not as rich as you might think." I looked up from my note taking. "She has told me that she won't leave enough to help a sick dog."

"I don't believe it," pronounced a meticulously dressed black-haired New Yorker as he fingered the edge of his napkin. "She's even got her picture on the packets of sugar they serve in hotels and restaurants these days. That measure of success is sweet." He licked his lips, pleasured by the vision of it.

"Impossible," chimed in a middle-aged archeologist who sat beside his anthropologically astute wife. "With the books, speeches, radio and TV appearances, consultantships, monthly *Redbook* column, she's got to be loaded. She probably sends one of her secretaries over to the bank every time the mail comes in."

"Not necessarily," I argued. "I know for a fact that she has all or most of her larger checks addressed to either the Institute for Intercultural Studies or the Scientists' Institute for Public Information. She helped set both of those organizations up, so she has a parental as well as a professional interest in them."

"She pays some attention to her body," declared a square-faced fellow who ran up and down the corridors to escape pouring rain during a noontime jog. "I don't know the details, but the scuttlebutt out in San Francisco is that she took several private sessions with Moshé Feldenkreis last June."

"She did?" I interrupted. "I must ask her about that! I enrolled in a Feldenkreis course last summer myself! Drove up from my house in Palo Alto to a little college in San Francisco once a week for eight weeks."

"Who's Moshé Feldenkreis?" Dana asked from the far end of the table.

"He's a physicist turned physical therapist," the San Franciscan answered. "He teaches you how to move more than you ever thought you could. His book, *Awareness through Movement,* tells about it."

"Hmmm," grunted an older woman of Margaret's stature. "Maybe I should go to this Feldenkreis fellow."

"Make it in the summer," the Californian warned. "Unless you want to fly to Tel Aviv. He lives there and comes to the United States summers. He's about the same age as Dr. Mead, I'd guess."

"My grandparents heard Dr. Mead speak at an adult summer school last August in Chautauqua, New York, of all places," the black-haired best dresser changed the subject slightly. "After the way she stood up for smoking pot a few years ago, they hated her. But they were at Chautauqua anyhow, so they went to hear her and she won them over. They say she's coming back next August and so are they."

"She's got dozens of projects like Chautauqua going all the time," Dana declared. "She's on the board of the Human Lactation Center and I happen to know that we will be meeting the day after her birthday on the seventeenth."

"Too many people stop everything when they reach seventy-five," I summed up what I'd learned leading death workshops for the University of Wisconsin in Milwaukee. "But she'll die before she stops! I've always had the impression that her work was her hobby and her hobby was her work. She seems to think that she'll die if she stops. So she keeps moving and generating projects with people. One overlaps another and then she's got to see each one through. She's built up too much momentum to stop. She'll keep going."

"Did any of you read *Blackberry Winter*?" questioned the stocky woman with a full face and matching bust. "According to that, when she was a teenager she wanted to be the wife of an Episcopal priest and have six kids. Had she not gone to Barnard and met Benedict and Boas, she'd probably be the kind of woman we all know who fears she's got cancer and immediately starts to needlepoint the seats of all the dining room chairs. I think women live longer than men because they feel they do have to finish needlepointing the dining room chairs or filling up the family photograph album or spending a month with all the married kids before calling it quits."

"She does finish things." Dana fingered a fountain pen that hung on a chain around her neck. She had presented its twin to Margaret some weeks previously. "No matter what it takes out of her, she does finish things."

"Or what her projects take out of her helpers," the wife of the middle-aged archaeologist said. "When Ted was in graduate school, I worked in her office myself for a while. It flattered us to be called assistants to Dr. Mead rather than mere secretaries or gofers. I think she's savvy enough to know that she squeezed more work out of us when we were titled too."

"Oh well, I remember," her husband's dark eyes gleamed as he winked at her, "Margaret's good at finding people who can do things well and then she puts them to work doing things well."

"She's been that way for the twenty-five years I've known her," I said. "You don't even have to be named one of her assistants. I've heard innumerable stories of friends, relatives, students—her own or somebody else's—who have stepped into her office and had her pull what I've come to call 'a Margaret Mead' on them. That is to say, they found themselves roped into helping get something that Margaret wanted done now, done now. Or sometimes even yesterday."

"Have you considered collecting elevator stories about her for your Meadiana?" asked one of our former Columbia classmates.

"She's amazingly friendly in elevators," the chic college professor in two-tone leather and tinkly costume jewelry recalled. "You're temporarily immobilized in elevators anyway, so Margaret takes the time to be friendly. We were in an elevator together at a conference just like this and we overheard a couple of teenagers whispering back and forth. 'Izzat Margaret Mead?' She grinned at me broadly, glanced over her shoulder at the two kids and asked them, 'Why? Does my slip show?'"

"That was in the days when she wore dresses. She's no clotheshorse," the older blond stated flatly. "She graduated to slacks some time ago. She'll wear the same pair two days in a row, so I suppose she's traveled enough to travel light."

"I was in an elevator with her once too," Margaret's former student grabbed space to tell this story. "It got stuck between the eleventh and twelfth floors in a hotel when a dozen of us were on our way to a party. I like to think that the car was a microcosm of Margaret's world. One woman started to tell Iatmul stories when Rhoda Metraux wailed, 'I'm claustrophobic!' The woman shouted for help, hoping rescuers would respond more quickly to a female voice. Margaret then ordered the bearded man in the car to stand out of sight in the back because, as she explained it, 'We've got to look like we're worth saving. Until we get out of here,' she sized the situation up correctly, 'we'll just waste energy unless we stay calm, cool, and collected.' About the time we tired of pretending to be calm, cool, or collected, the elevator started to move. 'Remember! Act middle class!' she belted out her last instruction as the doors spread open.

"I still chuckle over the look of absolute amazement on the faces of the workmen who stood by when we barged out of that elevator. Margaret led the pack, cape flying, staff stalking, eyebrows scowling impatiently, and teeth clenched into a smile that would have scared Theodore Roosevelt."

We laughed at the picture of middle-class bearded anthropologists stampeding for the closest comfort station until our meal arrived at the table and it became inefficient to converse further except with the person at either elbow.

Fourteen days after the American Anthropology conference in Houston dispersed but only six days after her return from a lecture trip which included that event, Margaret Mead turned seventy-five. Her birthday the year before, at the end of the nation's bicentennial, had been happy but hectic. It began before she got to the office. A full-page advertisement in the New York City morning papers announcing the establishment of a $5 million Margaret Mead Fund for the Advancement of Anthropology set the condo phones buzzing with congratulations. "They've convinced me," she joked, "that I'm of more use to the Museum alive than dead."

During the day, her department at Columbia University put on a party. Later that afternoon the American Museum of Natural History hosted a reception in the Hall of the Peoples of the Pacific to celebrate her seventy-fifth milestone as well as her fiftieth as a museum curator.

Soon afterward she and Rhoda flew to Georgia to spend Christmas week with Austin Ford, an Episcopalian priest and director of Emmaus House in Atlanta. The pair then sped back to New York state in time to engage themselves in a two-day Margaret Mead gala at the Tarrytown Executive Conference Center on the Hudson. She and entrepreneur Robert L. Schwartz, chairman of the board of the Tarrytown conference center, filled the place with activist friends of multidimensional experience and expertise. She loved parties. This one capped them all.

It opened with a black-tie birthday ball Wednesday evening that included salutes to her as a "national treasure," a formal dinner, dancing, drinking, and socializing. For a day and a half guests were encouraged to don blue jeans and wrangle in small groups over such discussion assignments as citizen participation in network models, and ends and means.

A free-time task of each guest was to write her a letter on pieces of paper preprinted as follows:

> Dear Margaret Mead:
>   If I should pick one area of concern to work on with you and the others at your party in the coming year, the area in which I feel really great passion is this: *
>
>   *Please be militantly specific. It will add to the chemistry of the interchange.

On January 20, Georgian Jimmy Carter assumed the presidency of the United States. He invited MM to his inaugural festivities but she declined. She did not feel chipper enough to go but sent along a bundle of Tarrytown birthday letters that contained what she considered helpful suggestions for him to keep in mind as president.

On February 28 he thanked her:

> To Margaret Mead
>   Thanks so much for your kind letter and for the very useful recommendations which your friends offered in celebration of your birthday.
>   I am trying hard to find ways to maintain an intimate relationship between myself and the American people and your suggestions are most helpful.
>   Sincerely,
>   Jimmy Carter

Certainly her seventy-fifth birthday found Margaret Mead at the peak of her powers. She was a world-renowned scientist who lived each working hour to capacity and enjoyed it immensely. She could wing off to Paris or the Punjab with the flash of a credit card. The world rolled out its red carpet to her. At least half of the media-listening or reading public had read about or heard her. Many prominent leaders admired her wisdom and sought her out for advice.

The years spent achieving success in any field inevitably exact their price in physiological aging. Although it was not at all characteristic, Margaret Mead, the private person, was accumulating signs of slowing down. She tolerated macular degeneration in the right eye, extreme dyslexia, and attendant reversals of color memory. She couldn't recall proper names so well anymore. She dozed off easily. She was in the care of a podiatrist. She'd been fitted for a hearing aid. She'd had her teeth capped. For those parties that she'd previously promised to attend, she sometimes requested that yogurt be substituted for banquet fare and that her cocktails come in the form of sparkling water with the bubbles stirred out.

In contrast to the hoopla of her seventy-fifth, she wanted her seventy-sixth birthday to be informal with a few old, old friends from the past and some younger ones of the present. Rhoda made plans for a birthday breakfast. She invited friends from Margaret's special group from her undergraduate days at Barnard, the Ash Can Cats; women who'd worked with her on books or projects over the years; nearby relatives; the office assistants.

Before her apartment mate returned from her Houston–Dallas–Washington–New Orleans lecturing and conferencing, Rhoda phoned prospective guests: "It's going to be a surprise," she cautioned.

Time after time, on Friday morning, December 16, 1977, another woman buzzed the doorbell to apartment 16-J, the Beresford, 211 Central Park West in New York City. Margaret answered the bell. Time after time, another startled friend stepped back at the sight of her framed in the doorway.

"Didn't Rhoda want this to be a surprise?" the next ones asked.

"It is a surprise," Margaret responded as she reached for each guest's wintry apparel. "I just found out about it ten minutes ago and I'm helping Rhoda by answering the door." Rhoda presided at the festivities and Margaret occupied center stage.

Once the party disbanded, concerned citizen and letter writer Margaret Mead sat down at her typewriter. She pecked out at least four letters: three to Washington, D.C., and one to Cincinnati.

In her first letter, she thanked Margaret (Midge) Costanza, liaison staff member for the president on women's issues, for taking her to the airport and for listening to her expound on how important it was that the people of the United States realize the interrelationships between all of the president's proposals and himself. On the heels of Watergate and Vietnam, grassroots Americans were not yet convinced that presidential proposals emanated from his office, and that this situation must be changed PDQ.

She addressed her second missive to Dr. Peter G. Bourne, a psychiatrist who also served on the presidential staff. In her note to Dr. Bourne she repeated her concern: "At present," she wrote, "the people see each program as unrelated to the others—hurled into space and cut down or injured by necessary compromise."

The third epistle was to President Carter, who had been in office almost a year. It began with a pair of drawings. In diagram A, she depicted Carter shooting out directives every which way in torpedo-shaped capsules. She titled this sketch: "Each initiative partly destroyed by necessary compromise."

In diagram B, she drew a wheel with nine spokes labeled antiproliferation, energy, human rights, Panama Treaty, Social Security, and so on. She affixed Carter's name to the center hub. The second illustration she explained, "President Carter's purpose clear and glowing with compromises on the periphery of a total plan on which all the presidential initiatives are related." The rest of the letter read:

Dear Jimmy,

Please consider these diagrams carefully. Diagram A is how people perceive you're attacking problems sequentially. Diagram B is how you can make them see your initiatives as part of one central purpose. Undoubtedly, if you had tried too many initiatives at first, you would have been criticized. But now, I think you can present the American people with a central purpose and the necessary compromises will look like mere nibbling on the periphery. But they have to see you at the center of each initiative as part of the whole and your program incandescent and worthy of their trust.

Working with you and for you.
Sincerely yours,
Margaret Mead

A public relations agent in Cincinnati received her fourth communiqué. In it, Mother Margaret announced that she'd chosen her daughter, who planned to be in the United States the following summer, to be her companion while at Chautauqua. She also expressed a desire to have Cathy be given an opportunity to participate in that institution's century-old summer program as well.

My daughter, Dr. Mary Catherine Bateson, Dean of Social Studies and Humanities, Reza Shah Kabir University, Iran, plans to be in the United States in late June and July. She would like to come to Chautauqua and herself play some role as a lecturer. She would plan to do some writing also. Catherine is an excellent public lecturer. I am enclosing a Curriculum Vitae. As you can see, she has taught at Harvard, North East, the Philippines, and the University of Teheran. She is a specialist in the Near East, culture, language, and religion. I believe Chautauqua might enjoy her speaking on comparative religion. She spent a year in Israel and has taught Hebrew, preparing little boys for their Bar Mitzvah, and is now planning the new graduate university in Iran, which is to be the highest institution of learning in Iran. It was talking with her god-mother, Marie Eichelberger, who was my companion last summer, that gave her the idea. So please advise me how you think this will fit in.

Yours hastily,

Margaret Mead

I do not know whether Margaret allowed herself any time other than break-fast that day to escape her customary preoccupations with counseling public fig-ures on national or world problems and promoting her daughter.

Far removed from New York City, I sensed somehow that this birthday might be her last. She had hovered gently on my mind since I saw her in Hous-ton. I had begun a series of death-year dreams. Ordinarily, I would have tried to phone her as soon as the rates went down. But I became distracted.

My third son, Laird, called from the West Coast. He had followed his two older brothers into the ranks of fatherhood. By supreme coincidence, my newest grandchild, David Nathan, a full week late in arriving, introduced himself on Margaret Mead's last birthday at 5:00 a.m. California time. Another generation. Another Sagittarius. Twenty-one inches long, eight and a half pounds heavy with black hair and square hands. A boy child destined to scamper if he were to go one-hundredth as far as that girl child born seventy-six years earlier to the day.

Between December 16, 1977, and January 13, 1978, the media announced that my home state senator Hubert H. Humphrey was terminally ill. Whenever he then appeared on television, I stared at his talking visage without compre-hending a word. I sat transfixed with thoughts like, You're terminally ill. You could be dead and buried the day after tomorrow. You'll never blow out the candles on another birthday cake.

I wonder now how Senator Humphrey felt about being so blatantly dis-missed. Might the description have compelled him to oblige the public's imme-diate expectations and not make liars out of the broadcasters? He must have re-alized that people tune out the terminally ill.

With the clear sight of hindsight, I now look at this situation from the sen-ator's perspective. Hearing oneself referred to as terminally ill must be terribly demoralizing. I am ashamed to admit that I didn't see the senator's side of the announcement then and tumbled right into the morbid trap unwittingly set for me. I regret not having made any attempt to hear Senator Humphrey's last and most fervently uttered words to his fellow Americans.

All people present had given him their full attention only six months earlier when he delivered the keynote address at the symposium for the bicentennial at the Smithsonian Institution, Kin and Communities: The Peopling of America. Margaret chaired the meeting. She recognized the drastic change that occurred in his appearance between June and January. She determined not to let her health be similarly speculated upon publicly, nor to be ostracized by otherwise welcoming audiences.

For half a century, she had been known as a strident and triumphant sharpshooter, ready to fire lightning-fast advice on almost anything to anybody from the president on down. She was not about to alter this vigorous image or have it altered for her. As far as she could control information about her physical condition, media people would be the last to know.

At staggered months before Humphrey's funeral, Margaret had picked up and dropped internists like knitting. Independently, they diagnosed her persistent abdominal pain as cancer of the pancreas. Specialist and patient sat across the desk staring at each other in the silence that usually accompanies such a disclosure.

"Ridiculous!" Her words ring in my ears. "Anthropology's a profession in which one expects exposure to all sorts of diseases. This is some bug I picked up on one of my field trips. Or another bout with malaria, and I thought I'd had every kind. It could just be a case of diverticulitis. Oh, fiddlesticks, it's more likely to be ordinary everyday exhaustion."

Each internist had been flattered when she approached him about her discomfort. It was no easier for him to have to tell Dr. Margaret Mead that she probably had no more than months to live than it was for her to accept it.

"In my mid-seventies?" I can imagine her angrily denying the death sentence. "Nonsense! It's true my brother died of cancer of the pancreas and my father thought he had it, but I've got my mother's Lockwood stamina. No adult female on either side of my family who died naturally gave up living this young. Pancreatic malignancies occur in only 3 percent of all cancer cases and nobody can prove I have an inoperable cancer of the pancreas without an operation. You're not considering the whole person. You're only looking at one part. There's more to me than two ounces of tissue. My schedule's full for the next five years, and I'm a person who makes and keeps commitments."

This feisty little fighter reminded each internist of some strong woman in his own background. He could have proposed that exploratory surgery, a laparotomy, might pinpoint the source of her trouble.

"Totally unnecessary," she would have retorted. "I don't agree with the medical profession's quick cutting up of people. Surgeons tend to treat patients as mechanics do cars. A big overhaul. They chop you up and put you back together again in a new way. They don't seem to think that anyone should ever adjust to anything."

Medical training does not include much time for teaching future doctors how to talk to patients. Nobody likes having to be the bringer of bad news. One of her internists solved the problem by speaking to Margaret as though she were his mother, but he misjudged his patient.

"What are my chances?" She leveled her gaze at him.

"There aren't any beyond the next two months at the most," he said. "There's every indication the growth is malignant. You're going to find it increasingly difficult to get food past the obstruction or to keep it down. It's possible that you are about to lose the ability to swallow. So have all the fun you can now. Live it up. Eat, drink, and be merry as long as you can."

Well aware of alcohol's toxic effects on the pancreas, she reacted as his mother might have. Margaret Mead stomped out of his office in righteous indignation. So much for specialists. They were too specialized for her. She would look for a good generalist, someone who considered the whole person, environmentally, physically, psychologically, and spiritually. Someone who included the will to live in his medical armamentarium.

What should she do otherwise? Curl up in some corner and feel sorry for herself? Blab a diagnosis like that to friends and bask in the warmth of their sympathy? Or shut up and keep on going? She'd seen enough of life and death in civilized and primitive societies to know that a person is more than a disease; that miracles do happen. Medical literature abounded with cases of unexplained remissions; why shouldn't hers be another? Wasn't "Lucky" one of her middle names?

She resolved to pretend nothing and conduct business as usual. She'd continue to reach out to interesting new people. She'd start more projects. She'd cope with the pain and find a compatible faith healer. She'd search for a holistic practitioner who was secure enough to entertain both ancient and modern ideas about maintaining wellness. She'd reduce stress in her living arrangements.

Grow or die! That had been her shibboleth even before fieldwork with the Arapesh in New Guinea showed her how they see all life as an adventure in growing. Growing emphasized the positive, and she was a positive person. She had too much going for her to give anything as uncompromising as death a fling.

Margaret collected friends as little girls collect butterflies. Once caught, she held on to them. Older ones, whom she saw intermittently through the spring and summer, accepted what she tossed off as her "slight decrepitudes" without prying. The holistic inclinations of a trio of newer friends actively assisted Margaret in her fight for life.

One of these, Jean Houston, was the same age as Margaret's absentee daughter. Mary Elder, another, was slightly younger than Cathy. Carmen de Barraza, somewhat older, was herself a practicing psychic healer. Margaret gained strength in the company of each of these women and they, in turn, showered her with the remedial gifts of laughter and love.

Margaret had met Jean Houston at the International School of America's Conference on Women's Education in Bath, England, in July 1973. Margaret's career lay largely behind her and Jean's ahead when these two Barnard College alumnae struck up their friendship. The flair, flamboyance, and flounce with which Jean swayed audiences in her "possibility thinking" workshops entranced Margaret.

"I need a daughter. Mine's in Iran, so you're it." With those words Margaret installed Jean as Cathy's surrogate.

"Hot dog, thou art!" Jean acknowledged her instant parent. Then, as newfangled daughters are wont to do, Jean set about remodeling the mother figure.

Margaret Mead had taken her body for granted all of her life. With Jean's encouragement, together with some welcome treatments from Jean's psychophysiologist husband, Robert Masters, and Israeli friend Moshé Feldenkreis, the customarily cerebral anthropologist learned to become more acutely aware of her bodily state. Together, the three guided her into a realistic program of low-key exercising.

Jean also taped Margaret's reminiscences. The two friends planned to use this material for a book on MM, though Jean would take major credit for authorship. Margaret aimed to live long enough to hold that book in her hands.

Mary Elder—short, broad, and light haired—met Margaret in the Museum on a spring day in 1977. Mary was a graduate student and nurse–midwife. She sought Margaret out to be one of her advisers for a photographic analysis of interactive behavior between Puerto Rican parents and their newborns.

Margaret had sailed to the South Seas to do her fieldwork. Here was an enterprising young woman conducting research as close to home as the South Bronx. She wore a beeper to keep herself informed of imminent birthing events, toted videotaping equipment that she had taught herself to operate, and jounced from tenement to tenement in an inherited jalopy that she affectionately called the Blue Lemon.

Margaret mentioned having to get to Columbia University for a tightly scheduled meeting immediately after their introductory interview. Mary offered to give her a ride. On the way the Blue Lemon had a flat tire. Margaret scrambled out and hailed a cab. A very shaggy jogger stopped by and volunteered to change Mary's tire. She offered him a $5 tip. He said he was insulted. She raised it to $10.

Then he identified himself as an anesthesiologist at Mt. Sinai Hospital who wouldn't take a nickel.

When Mary repeated this story to Margaret, the two of them laughed like third graders. At this time in her life, Margaret craved the kind of laughter that shook the belly of Santa Claus. Her fame put people too much in awe of her to laugh with her. When that happens, fame's no fun.

When Margaret learned that Mary's mother had died six years after her birth, leaving her to be reared by a professional woman, a lawyer–grandmother, she recognized another reason for their affinity. "A professional woman, a teacher–grandmother, helped raise me," Margaret divulged, "and all my life I've been attracted to women who have been close to their grandmothers."

Needless to say, Dr. Mead accepted advisership on Mary's dissertation committee. She anticipated paging through a published edition of her completed research. She also encouraged Mary to think about a second doctorate, this time in anthropology.

Jean Houston and Mary Elder did not know each other, but they were like daughters to Margaret Mead, who adopted daughters all over the place. It was one of her "networking" techniques. Those who nurture, however, also require nurturing. Margaret was always on the lookout for surrogate mothers too.

The more doctors Margaret saw, the less hope of renewed health she got. She knew she needed hope as well as the support she received from Mary and Jean. She also realized that nothing would happen until she took control of her own rehabilitation. She remembered a Chilean faith healer named Carmen, whom she'd met socially a few years back at the Tarrytown conference center. She called Robert L. Schwartz. "I think I should see your friend Carmen," she said. "What is her full name and how do I get in touch with her?"

Margaret had often told me that psychic phenomena intrigued her. Two relatives in the family of her father's mother possessed psychic abilities: her great-grandmother Priscilla Rees Ramsay and her great-aunt Louisiana Priscilla Ramsay Sanders. Residents who lived around the Winchester, Ohio, area a century ago spread word that this mother–daughter team diagnosed illnesses, read people's thoughts, and levitated tables. Margaret herself had been what her Ramsay kin called "a psychic child."

The more stories her cousin Callie Sanders Hunter in Cincinnati told the grown-up Margaret Mead about these two strong Priscillas, the more Margaret toyed with the notion that she herself might very well be her generation's reincarnation of this pair of psychic predecessors.

When Bob Schwartz provided her with the name and number she sought, she phoned the Life Energy Chapel of Rev. Carmen Loyola de Barraza of the

United American Free Will Baptist Conference of New York and made arrangements for an early appointment. This time Margaret Mead's middle name was indeed "Lucky" because Carmen turned out to be exactly right. She was a happily married wife, mother of three, and grandmother of five with all the earthy resilience and wisdom associated with these universally humanistic roles. Carmen was another person who became important to Margaret who had lost her mother in childhood and had been raised by a grandmother. Margaret rallied under Carmen's treatments. She learned more about relaxing. She laughed. She garnered hope. Even though everybody must subconsciously realize that no recovery is ever permanent, she gained support for her belief that some recovery was possible and most certainly more pleasant.

Carmen was ready to die anytime. Margaret definitely was not. She envied Carmen's easy feelings about dying. She knew full well that her deep-seated fear of death dated from the night when she was three months past four years old and the little sister for whom she later named her own daughter died in the bedroom they shared.

Carmen sometimes worked with Margaret twice a day. With Margaret's encouragement she taped all of the dialogues that transpired between them during their sessions. Patient and healer intended to have these tapes transcribed for publication against the time, as Margaret expressed it, "when we know more about nonmedical approaches to healing than we do now." And she planned to write the introduction. "You'll be able to earn enough money on the book to buy that little cottage in the country that you've dreamed about," she said, "and then I can come to visit you."

Rhoda Metraux, the anthropologist with whom Margaret had shared an abode for over twenty-five years, objected to the time Margaret spent with these "Johnny-come-latelies." Especially Carmen. A faith healer! To think that a scientist as sophisticated as the great Margaret Mead had resorted to so primitive a practitioner! Were news like this to leak out, how people would talk! What would happen to Margaret's image as a scientist?

But Margaret protested Rhoda's protective precautions. Like her anthropologist mentor Ruth Benedict, Margaret separated friends by compartmentalizing her relationships. She saw no reason to condone Rhoda's making inroads on this one.

Carmen led Margaret to a handsome, open, relaxed, and loving grandfather named Dr. Goodrich. Charles Goodrich had once augmented his formal medical education by an informal apprenticeship to a psychic healer. Later in the year, when at least one newspaper learned that he was the doctor Margaret eventually settled on, a reporter interviewed him. "In this day of high-tech medicine, why in the world do you work with a faith healer?"

"You're asking the wrong question," Dr. Goodrich replied. "The real question should be, 'Why is the healer consenting to work with me?'"

On January 1, 1978, knowing that she had outlived by fourteen months the shortest time predicted for her, Margaret Mead turned to the first page of a new calendar. It was already chock-full of appointments and commitments. Even though racked with pain, she would force herself to keep every one. Such was the secret for staying alive. No one can afford to coast on a reputation. One must deliver to keep in demand.

Sheer traveling in and of itself is harrowing, yes, but groups of interested people energized her. Her pain subsided before the eyes and ears of an audience. These last few years increasing numbers of public appearances ended in standing ovations, blurred visions of happy faces, and the sound of clapping hands. Even though the topics she was asked to speak on sometimes stretched her ingenuity, she thrived on the exhilaration of the applause they brought.

On Thursday, January 5, she flew to Georgia to deliver a speech entitled "Aquaculture in a Changing World" at an aquaculture conference for commercial fish farmers. Mary Elder's Blue Lemon got her to the plane early one morning and picked her up late the next afternoon. Margaret took along thick and thin sheets of yellow paper and a folder to read in her spare time that contained data pertaining to upcoming speeches and consultations for a thirteen-day trip scheduled to begin two days after her return.

On Sunday, January 8, faithful Mary Elder dropped her off at the Eastern Airlines terminal at LaGuardia airport shortly after 1:00 p.m. Four hours later, Margaret's plane arrived in Miami, where a limousine from the Food Marketing Institute waited to take her to the Boca Raton Hotel and Club. She arrived in time for a half hour "rest" before she was due to appear in the Galleria room for a dressy, but not formal, dinner. At 8:30 Monday morning, she spoke to a conference session of the Food Marketing Institute for forty-five minutes in a talk she called "The Future Is Now."

Part of the agreement form sent from her office in New York City included these instructions:

PLEASE NOTE: Dr Mead is only 5'2" and therefore prefers a small table to any form of lectern. If a lectern must be used, a heavy, immovable one would need a riser behind it (for Dr Mead to stand on). Dr Mead does not need any reading lamp for notes.

She didn't need a lamp to read by because she always spoke extemporaneously. A latter-day bonus was that this practice hid her dyslexia. After answering questions previously submitted on written cards, she was interviewed by the press and had brunch. Then she left for Cincinnati.

Two doctors, one from the University of Cincinnati College of Medicine and the other from the Jewish Hospital, met her that evening at the Alben W. Barkley Airport just over the Ohio line in Kentucky at 9:35. They drove along the Buttermilk Pike to the place in Cincinnati that would be her headquarters for the next eleven days. Shortly before midnight she was at last able to slip into slumber in her bed at the Queen City Club. She liked Cincinnati. It was one of her favorite cities.

For twenty-one years, during semester break in January, Margaret Mead had served as Visiting Professor of Anthropology at the University of Cincinnati College of Medicine. She came originally on the invitation of Dr. Maurice Levine, director of the Department of Psychiatry. She and he had met as graduate students at Columbia University in the 1920s. He invited her because both of them believed that experts in various branches of science should meet to exchange ideas. "The education of psychiatrists has got to be many sided," she asserted in her association with the department, "because the causes of the problems that patients bring with them are many sided. We can no longer attribute any problem to any one cause."

Her appointments in Cincinnati were always multifaceted. This year at least a dozen professors had arranged time to discuss concerns with her as varied as a drug dependence treatment program, a life-cycle course, the preverbally deaf patient, and psychosomatic medicine.

She was scheduled to lecture to the staff of the Children's Medical Center on the battered child. She spoke to the personnel at the Children's Psychiatric Center twice, first on understanding adults through insights from child development and second on the effect of violent parental death on children.

Her visits put the local medical community in an annual bind. She gave them all a shot in the arm and each unit wanted a piece of her act. At the same time individual heads of departments hesitated to crowd her too much too many times because they wanted to keep her coming back to Cincinnati.

Since she had expressed a desire to be kept informed of the progress of a newly established geropsychiatry unit at Cincinnati General Hospital in 1977, the head of that unit ventured to invite her to lead the final session of an education/sensitivity seminar. She managed to comply.

Requests from the community at large poured in to this spunky little woman who found saying yes irresistible. She gave several newspaper and at least two television interviews. She taped one of the latter for national broadcast on the *Today Show* two days after her return to New York City.

One of the civic groups she usually obliged with a speech was the Women's City Club of Cincinnati. This year, instead, she gave a single lecture to the general public. Probably without ever giving a thought to how much the title she chose described herself as a workaholic cancer victim, she named it "The Battered Woman."

On evenings when she wasn't dining at the home of a faculty member of one of the medical complexes, she visited local relatives. Margaret looked forward to her annual stopovers to this city of seven hills for sentimental as well as professional reasons. Long-lost relatives on both sides of her family living in Cincinnati read about her in the newspapers when she began coming to town. They made contact with her and built up a tradition for renewing their acquaintanceship year after year.

Margaret's mother had been Emily Fogg before marriage. Margaret's first cousin, the son of Emily's brother, Lockwood, lived in Cincinnati. He was a lawyer and his wife was an eighth-grade social studies teacher; they had five children.

"Dinners with Margaret, the one celebrity in our lives," reported Marjorie Fogg, "stimulated us so much that we couldn't get to sleep after she left. I used to lie awake thinking about all the things she talked about. She was like fresh air, like electricity! Sparkly!

"The last time she was here, I invited one of those once-in-a-lifetime students teachers get every now and then (as was Margaret in her day) to have dinner with us. He went on to Harvard after high school and even ate dinner with Henry Kissinger once. I saw his mother today in the grocery store and she said he still remembers vividly the meal with Margaret at our house."

Margaret's paternal grandmother, Martha Adeline, was the seventh child of nine children born to Priscilla Rees and Richard Ramsay. They lived in Winchester, Ohio. The village was an old-time bicycle ride away from Cincinnati. Each day when she combed her hair, Margaret's live-in teacher–grandmother, Martha, gleefully recollected a pre–Civil War childhood for her granddaughter's amusement. Martha was such a vivid storyteller that Margaret grew up feeling she could find her way around Winchester with her eyes closed.

After her young husband, Giles Meade, died unexpectedly in January 1880, Martha Ramsay Meade supported their one child teaching school in either Union City, Indiana, or Youngstown, Ohio. She and her son, Edward Sherwood, the boy who would become Margaret's father, returned to Winchester each summer.

When Martha's mother died in 1890, one of Martha's sisters, Louisiana Priscilla Ramsay Sanders, kept open house in the family homestead for visiting siblings.

Martha and an older brother, Rev. William Warwick Ramsay, took summertime turns reading McGuffey's schoolbooks to Lou's tiny daughter, Callie (Caroline). At Margaret Mead's birth, two days less than thirteen years after Callie's, Martha transferred tutoring activities from beloved niece to bright granddaughter using the same readers.

In Cincinnati in the late 1950s, Margaret Mead and Callie Sanders Hunter found each other. In nothing flat, they recognized that their minds were as alike as though they had been born homozygous twins: stern, sharp, quick, with a tremendous capacity for memory.

Callie's store of family lore engendered two more projects. Margaret made arrangements with a young psychiatrist at the University of Cincinnati to tape Callie's memories. She asked him to think about doing some research comparing the intelligence of family members who did and did not leave small towns for big ones. She also discussed the prospect of having him write a historical novel about the Ramsays of Winchester. Of course the real identities of the characters would be disguised, as well as her kinship to them.

Margaret also developed a particular fondness for Callie's daughter, her grandmother's namesake, Martha Hunter Glardon. Margaret considered the social service agencies in Cincinnati to be some of the best in the nation. Martha Glardon worked in one of them, Talbert House, headquarters for the International Halfway House Association (IHHA). On this visit Margaret agreed to speak to the assembled members of the IHHA when they convened in Portland, Oregon, the week of August 22. The two cousins made plans to fly there together.

With Martha as social engineer, Ramsay descendants and the young psychiatrist gathered for an afternoon tea on Sunday, March 27, 1977, at the nursing home in which Callie spent her older age. Margaret made a special stop on one of her cross-country trips to attend this reunion.

Here she commenced dialoguing with another newly discovered cousin. He was John Gibson, executive vice president of an architectural and design firm in Indianapolis. Gibson anticipated sharing with Margaret his enthusiasm for applying knowledge he had gleaned from readings in the behavioral sciences to architecture and design.

Their grandmothers were Ramsay sisters. His eighty-four-year-old mother, Alice, attended the reunion too. Margaret immediately pictured Alice Ramsay as a resource person for her sideline genealogical research. Mrs. Gibson might be able to draw in and label some of the phantom branches in her ongoing project of filling in a family tree. So yet another undertaking got going when John Gibson entertained her at dinner on one of the last evenings she stayed in Cincinnati on this, her final, heady stopover.

Early Monday morning, January 23, two days after her return from Cincinnati, NBC broadcast the interview that Margaret taped there for the *Today Show*. I grimaced at the sight of the dress she chose to wear for the broadcast. The horizontal stripes on it widened her figure. I scrutinized her face as she talked. She looked older already. She had aged noticeably in just two months. She darted her tongue out less often. Or did her many quick glances toward the cameramen signal them to aim elsewhere?

Not a hint about her physical condition came out in the interview. After an introductory mention of her latest book, *Letters from the Field,* she focused on her lifelong interest in children: "I've always been a carriage peeper." She stared straight into the red eye of the camera and pleased a legion of eavesdropping mothers who knew her through monthly columns in *Redbook* magazine.

I sat in the solace of my breakfast room and sensed the charm of this simple statement. Whether she was one of the world's most famous anthropologists or not, this particular carriage peeper looked and sounded like anybody's dumpy next-door neighbor. "I'm sure having your own child is your most authentic link to the future," she told her public what it wanted to hear. I squirmed uneasily as I privately recalled that she got her own career off to a rolling start before she gave birth sixteen years and three husbands after her first wedding. And she told me about advising her sole offspring to follow suit.

She related how she had hired Helen Burrows, an English nanny with a teenaged daughter, as a live-in helper. She said she rented an apartment large enough to accommodate an extra mother and child. "Most people would have begun with the baby and worked backward," she stated. "I started with the nursemaid."

It didn't sound like that to me at all. The way I heard it, she behaved exactly like most people. Who hires a nanny ten months before there's an infant on the scene? She would have been more believable had she initiated parenting preparations by moving into a larger-than-otherwise apartment in order to accommodate a mother-and-daughter helper team, just as her mother used to do in Margaret's younger years.

"People blame parents when children do something wrong," she rehooked the fans listening in at the end of her instant interview. "But when a child does something right, then that's taken as the child's own doing." I pensively bit into a piece of partially scorched whole wheat toast. Margaret's daughter, Mary Catherine Bateson

Kassarjian, was in Iran for a stint as dean of the School of Social Studies at Reza Shah Kabir University. Would she have acquired such a prestigious post in her mid-thirties were she simply Jennie Jones?

The same with Margaret a generation earlier. She admitted that her professor father, Edward Sherwood Mead, "defined" her place in the world. From what I already knew about her roots, he, his wife, and his mother fully prepared Margaret for getting where she got when she did. I remember her saying that she "paid her parents back" by her thirtieth birthday, undoubtedly on the proceeds from her first book, *Coming of Age in Samoa*. Did that remark insinuate that she considered her impressive accomplishments from thirty on as her own doing?

If so, how Anglo-Saxon of her! Between the ages of ratiocination and retirement, many middle-class do-it-yourselfer Americans, I suppose, egocentrically figure that they did indeed create themselves. Financial independence tends to toss nature/nurture arguments into universities or pressrooms for academicians and journalists to pick over.

On Tuesday, January 24, Margaret Mead became the first woman to receive the Franklin Award for Distinguished Service. It is the highest single honor of the nation's graphic arts industries. Twelve hundred people gathered in the miniballroom of the Waldorf Astoria at 5:00 p.m. Formalities, festivities, and dinner (which included remarks by the governor of New York and the mayor of New York City) followed. Finally, at 8:50, the long-suffering award recipient was presented with the Franklin citation and medal. She heard herself described as follows:

> Guidance counselor to modern America, orchestrator of change in our culture and consciousness, and catalyst for new global understanding, she continues today to stalk change as social scientist and humanitarian. Like Franklin, she is a great American and citizen of the world, intent on providing a contemporary perspective of enormous value in preparing our generations for a better tomorrow.

Compliments like this momentarily erased pain. She capped the evening off with a wearied and welcome fifteen-minute response.

Wednesday, January 25, Harper and Row, which published *Letters from the Field* (already named an alternate choice of the Literary Guild) hosted a promotional dinner at the Museum. One snowstorm and one WOR-TV television appearance later, on Thursday evening, January 26, the Lotus Club staged a state dinner in her honor.

Before she retired that Thursday night, she wired two identical mailgrams: one to Governor George Busbee of Georgia and the other to his wife, Frances, who headed a committee called Citizens against Hunger. Margaret sent one of her mailgrams to the statehouse and the other to the governor's mansion. As her Franklin Award citation had indicated a few days earlier, her words were those of a humanitarian fighting to prepare our generation for a better tomorrow:

> I am deeply concerned by the failure of the Georgia legislature to alleviate the alarming poverty in which poor people in Georgia live, especially for welfare families. Women should be supported in their efforts to work. They should not be cut off from welfare before they can care decently for their families.
>
> It is not yet too late for you to rise courageously to this desperate need among your people.
>
> The protection of parents and children is a sacred national obligation.
> Margaret Mead
> Formerly Visiting Professor at Emory University

Bright and early next morning, Friday, January 27, Mary Elder shoved Margaret's red plaid overnight bag into the backseat of the Blue Lemon. She transported her friend to the Eastern Shuttle Terminal at LaGuardia for a flight to Logan Airport.

Margaret arrived in Boston at 9:30 a.m. A limousine waited to whisk her to an appointment with a doctor in his office near Harvard Square in Cambridge. Next the driver sped to station WBZ-TV back in Boston for a 12:30 promotional broadcast for *Letters from the Field*.

An hour later, she caught her breath long enough to board the same limousine and head for the Ritz-Carlton Hotel. She left the driver to his own devices for lunch while she looked around for a special table in the main dining room, where she was to meet with Marian Christy and Joseph Dennehy of the *Boston Globe*.

Photographer Dennehy caught her flouncy hair, deep frown, finely crinkled face, and jowled neck encircled in a priestly-looking elliptical white collar. Margaret complained of "gastric pressures" and proceeded to order two halves of a toasted English muffin, each topped with a slice of ham and a poached egg peeking from under a sauce composed of egg yolks, butter, lemon juice, and seasonings.

She sighed to reporter Christy about the unpredictability of life, her daughter, her marriages, and her parents. "My mother was a sociologist," she said, "who did the first study on Italian immigrants. In fact, we moved to Hammonton, New Jersey, so that my mother could be near the people she was studying.

"How many husbands would move so that a wife would be close to her work?"

"My parents were two generations ahead of their time and so am I."

Interview over, the man in the limousine finished his day by taking her to 3

Langdon Street in Cambridge, the home of her only surviving sibling, Elizabeth Mead Steig. The sisters spent three hours together before Dr. Babette Weksler, chairperson of the eastern section of the American Federation for Clinical Research (AFCR), picked them up. They drove to the Isabella Stewart Gardner Museum in Boston for a reception opening the annual meeting of the AFCR. An hour and a half later in the large music room on the second floor, Margaret lectured to the assembled biomedical investigators from eastern medical school faculties. She addressed her speech to social issues relating to clinical research in a talk entitled "Losing the Gap between Scientist and Citizen." After a dinner as guests of the officers of the federation, she and her sister were returned to Elizabeth's apartment.

Margaret Mead was the oldest child of the three daughters and one son born to her parents. At four and a half, she had been allowed to name her first baby sister, who later died. On the day she turned seven and a half, June 16, 1909, her second sister, Elizabeth, arrived to take the place of the little lost one.

The friendship between Margaret and Elizabeth strengthened after the rest of their immediate family had died. With the two of them reinforcing each other's memories, Margaret wrote much of *Blackberry Winter* in Elizabeth's apartment. In that book she referred to the sister relationship:

> Sisters, while they are growing up, tend to be very rivalrous and as young mothers they are given to continuous rivalrous comparisons of their several children. But once the children grow older, sisters draw closer together and often, in old age, they become each other's chosen and most happy companions. In addition to their shared memories of childhood and of their relationships to each other's children, they share memories of the same house, the same homemaking style and the same small prejudices about housekeeping that carry the echoes of their mother's voice as she admonished them, "Never fill the tea kettle from the hot water faucet," and "Wash the eggs off the silver spoons at once," and "Dry the glasses first."

It was a strong family tradition. For generations, pairs of sisters on both sides had been close friends. On visits when they were children, Margaret's maternal grandmother, Elizabeth Lockwood Fogg, regaled them with stories of her sister, Antoinette Lockwood Rowe. They raised their children together on the same block in Chicago. Their other grandmother, Martha Ramsay Meade, idolized her sister, Sarah Elizabeth Ramsay. Sarah never married because her sweetheart had been killed in the Civil War, and she moved in with Martha in her widowhood to help bring up Margaret's father. Whenever visiting them in New Jersey or Pennsylvania, they saw the affection between their mother, Emily Fogg Mead, and her younger sister, Fanny Fogg McMasters. After Emily Fogg Mead died, Margaret and Elizabeth corresponded with, and paid visits to, their childless Aunt Fanny as though she were their mother until she died in California at the age of one hundred.

United in common memories of these ancestor sisters, Margaret and Elizabeth were poles apart in temperament. Artist Elizabeth bubbled over with a magical child's freshness of perception. She relaxed and laughed more easily than her usually serious older sibling. Blithe Elizabeth endlessly buoyed up Margaret's spirits; she felt better around her.

Since Elizabeth had converted what would have been the bedroom into a studio for teaching and painting, the sisters bedded down in the living room—Margaret on a convertible couch in a corner by the window and Elizabeth on a davenport by the door. They chatted back and forth across the room into the night. Probably because she refused to believe it herself, Margaret did not mention the possibility of her having cancer. She did say that she wanted to reduce stress in her life by making a change in her living arrangements.

After nearly three decades sharing apartments, fieldwork, and writing projects, Margaret and Rhoda Metraux had become overly work oriented and interdependent, mutually critical and crotchety. If anything, they knew each other too well.

Margaret's frequent absences from the apartment helped some, but not enough. She still had to come home to argumentative incompatibility. Would Elizabeth mind if Margaret put her name on a waiting list for renting a suite of rooms that they might share together? Considering the housing shortage in New York, the sooner they got on a waiting list, the better. They wouldn't be able to find a place right away anyway, so Elizabeth still had plenty of time to think about possibly vacating an apartment that had been her home for over twenty years.

At 10:00 the next morning a representative from the University of Rhode Island in Kingston stood in the small vestibule downstairs and pressed the buzzer labeled Steig. Margaret was ready for Dennis Gonsalves, who was to take her directly to a luncheon at the Memorial Union on the university campus. There followed a press conference after which she entertained the students on one of her more popular topics: the changing roles of males and females.

As usual lately, because she wasn't able to hear that well anymore, she asked for written questions from her audience. Four of the responses that she took back to New York City with her were:

1. Do you really feel parenthood and a career is an either/or decision for women? You were able to work this out. How did you do it?

2. When you were eagerly pursuing your own career in a world in which men prevailed, how is it that you got such strength to continue against what must have been resistance? Can you share with us a little about this experience?
3. What were the influences that made you able to accomplish all that you have in your life?
4. What is your opinion on homosexuality?

Thoughtful, honest answers to questions like these called for more introspection than Margaret relished taking time for. They did, however, provide her with clues about what questions students had as they listened to her. Sometimes she gave their questions the Mead touch and recycled them in the monthly columns she sent over to her editors at *Redbook* magazine.

So went January 1978.

Letters from the Field had been launched. Her column in *Redbook* that month permitted the magazine's readers an early peek at some of her letters from faraway encampments. She was updating *World Enough,* a book that had come out in 1960 with former student Ken Heyman, for republication. She had purchased three round-trip airplane tickets, delivered at least a dozen speeches, and engaged in that many professional consultations. She had coped with the usual and sometimes annoying adulation that accompanied her live appearances as well as the correspondence that flooded her mail after local or national broadcasts. She had renewed contact with Midwestern kin and spent a folksy evening with her sister.

She had begun another semester at Columbia University as a full-time adjunct professor. Also, she met with one class Monday evenings from 8:10 p.m. to 10:00 p.m. The 1977–1978 Columbia catalog identified it as Anthropology G4143:

Culture and Communications: (With instructor's permission) Principles of cultural analysis applied to such primitive and modern media of communication as oral and literary materials, film, stills and records. Students may concentrate on creative projects or on cultural analysis of finished products.

On Tuesday afternoons from 4:10 to 6:00 she taught an old favorite that was almost unchanged from when I took it in the 1950s:

Methods and Problems in Anthropology: Open to selected graduate students with permission. Field work experience to be determined. Methods of studying homo- and hetero-geneous societies among primitive and modern people with emphasis on the various methods of field work; observation, interviewing, use of photography, and other technical recording devices. Qualitative content analysis of stills, films, projective and verbal materials.

The catalog listed Professors Herbert Passin and Walter Slote as coprofessors for her third course. It was cross-indexed as Sociology 09311 and billed as Seminar on Psycho-Cultural Dynamics: Personality, Society, and Politics: "An individual research and tutorial for graduate students preparing doctoral theses on problems relating to the study of culture and personality."

Except for bursts of exhilaration before audiences at Columbia or elsewhere, she suffered pain every hour. As much as she could will it to be so, she separated herself from acknowledging that pain. "I've been sick all month," she wrote a friend in California, "but I'm feeling better."

She loved food and found remembering Carmen's dietary restrictions very difficult, especially when temptations were placed in front of her. Whenever she left the apartment, she was wined and dined at lunches, dinners, or receptions. She battled bouts of nausea. She made appointments with at least four different medical doctors. She lost ten pounds.

However preposterous some of her assignments seem in retrospect, the grim little Spartan fulfilled each and every commitment on the first sheet of her New Year's calendar. She tore off the page for January and prepared to tackle February.

In February, her nonstop schedule jolted to a near halt. She granted five interviews and delivered the same number of speeches. She sent out complimentary copies of *Letters from the Field*. She whipped up an article to be published later in the year by *TV Guide*, which she called *The American Family: An Endangered Species*. She attended one board meeting, a press conference, an award ceremony, and flew once across the Mississippi. She kept up with her courses at Columbia.

In Margaret's lexicon, the word "will" wasn't so much the noun for dispersing her comparatively few possessions after death as it was the dominant verb for what tasks lay always ahead on her daily schedule. She had strong-willed her way through January. She intended to dispose of February's commitments similarly. But her body, for a change, took charge. Recurring cancellations finally forced her to cease making promises.

The cancellations began on February 1. She simply lacked the energy to fly to Minneapolis to autograph her book at Dayton's Department Store or speak at a Minnesota conference. For these hardy northern conferees, she had chosen a subject most pertinent to her present stage in life, "The Zestful Generation: Exploding the Myths of Age." The irony of having to cancel that one must have nettled her. Not being able to go to Minneapolis automatically ruled out her stopping in Chicago on the return flight to tell a national audience on the *Phil Donahue Show* about her new book. She rallied enough by Wednesday of the second week, however, to be interviewed at home in New York City on *Paths to the Future* for a New Zealand film project.

On Thursday, February 9, she braved the snowdrifts between New York City and Greenvale, Long Island, to give a "lively lecture" at C. W. Post College. "You scored some really good, fresh points for an audience that I thought too dull to merit them," a Long Islander friend complimented her by letter a week later.

Meanwhile, back in her office at the Museum, the mail brought accelerating requests for public or private appearances at commissions, committees, conferences, classrooms, or lecture halls from inside and outside the United States. When she was not chipper enough to hike over to her tower herself, a sturdy assistant lugged shopping bags with scheduling folders and mail from the Museum to her.

One of the pieces that she received in mid-February was from me. In lieu of a Christmas card eight weeks earlier, I sent out Valentine letters that spring. I imagine she smiled when she learned of the grandchild who arrived on her birthday. But she must have snorted disdainfully over my announcement that I intended to retire in June in order to tackle a writing career. Shortly thereafter, my turn to smile over what she thought about slackers who retire came when I chanced upon a line in a newspaper article. "Sooner or later," she was quoted as saying at her seventy-fifth birthday party, "I'm going to die, but I'm not going to retire."

Sessions with Carmen de Barraza during this month enabled Margaret to postpone her retirement by death. Sometimes she stepped up her treatments to more than two a day. She ran into static from Rhoda because of it. Rhoda became increasingly solicitous as she watched her apartment mate of nearly a lifetime grow more spindly. Margaret systematically resisted what she perceived to be erosions of her power. The verbal tiffs between these two battlers became the most disruptive of Margaret's life and of Rhoda's. Both women were valiantly concerned about Margaret's optimal well-being. They just disagreed on procedures.

At 6:15 Wednesday morning, February 22, Margaret escaped and drove with Mary Elder to LaGuardia Airport. At 11:26 that same morning Eileen Lieben, associate vice president of personnel at Creighton University, greeted Dr. Mead in the Omaha Airport and took her to the Hilton Hotel. One half hour later Margaret met the local press in a student center on campus. Reporters bombarded her for opinions about the family, society, world hunger, women's rights, and abortion. They described her answers as "insightful, fresh, and personal."

"We should not be permitting abortion as a way of life," she advised. "To argue for a woman's right to abortion is absurd. Women have a right to institutions which will see to it that they never have an unwanted child." She dubbed abortion "barbarous" and deplored the underlying cause—insufficient sex education. In regard to forbidding abortions by law, she drove home a cogent point: "America was founded on the principle of religious freedom. That doesn't mean that any religious group has the right to force its ethical ideas on others."

She was scheduled to talk in the Alumni Library at 2:30 p.m. on the changing role of males and females. Her presence on the campus thrilled so many Creightonians, however, that the seminar expanded to the size of a lecture. Nevertheless, she carried on with "abundant charm, wit and energy."

Henry Badeer, a microbiology professor at Creighton, arrived to take her home with him for a quick reunion and dinner with the Badeer family: his wife (sister-in-law of Margaret's daughter, Mary Catherine) and his Armenian mother-in-law, Mrs. Kassarjian. After dinner she and the Badeers drove to the Brandeis Student Center for her well-advertised evening lecture. "The auditorium was packed," reported a university official. "People were hanging off the window sills. It was by far the most overflowing of all the events we've ever had. It was just marvelous."

Margaret had been invited to Creighton, a Jesuit university, for the part of its centennial called Kate Drake Week. In 1892, Kate Drake became the first female to enroll at the previously all-male school. Margaret's speech, in partial homage to this medical student pioneer, had been billed as "Twentieth-Century Faith: Hope and Survival." But in her weariness she unwittingly surprised some and amused others by extending her afternoon remarks on the relationship between the sexes and women's contributions to culture.

She held audience attention anyway and listeners surged up on the stage afterward to ply her with comments and compliments. At 10:30 p.m., when people decades younger would have headed for their hotel, Margaret accepted an invitation to join a group of freshmen in the recreation room of a new all-women's dormitory. She sat in a big chair, obviously pleased with the admiration of instantly adopted daughters who clustered close. "Were you to do it all over again and she were our age," one of them asked her, "what would you have your daughter study?"

"Business administration." Mother Margaret astounded them. Then she went on to assure the young women that "the last thing my daughter ever wanted was my undivided attention."

They sought her views on the Equal Rights Amendment (ERA). "I favor it," she replied, "primarily because it assures women of more status. ERA will help divorced, widowed, and abandoned women borrow money and handle their own affairs. Were husbands perfect models of rectitude," she winked at them wisely, "women wouldn't need an Equal Rights Amendment."

At midnight, 2:00 a.m. Eastern time, Lieben gave her a ride to her hotel. Margaret had answered questions and had listened to stories about other people's concerns all day, maintaining a facade of personal strength. I learned that Carmen shared most of her confidences these days, but she was fast asleep in New York City. I imagine that Margaret Mead, migrant campus lecturer, restlessly passed the remainder of the night alone, a bit frightened and in pain in a hotel room in the middle of Nebraska.

Promptly at 8:30 a.m., Betty Green (who proved to be a delightful companion for the jaunt) called on Margaret to take her to the United terminal of the Omaha Airport for her flight to Newark, New Jersey, where Mary Elder waited with her faithful Blue Lemon.

The next day, Friday, February 23, Margaret ignored the jet lag resulting from her thirty-two-hour jaunt to Nebraska long enough to write an apology to Lieben for having accidentally switched titles on her big speech.

"It was so charming of her to do that," Lieben told me later, "but she didn't have to. We were just thrilled by what she did say. We wouldn't have got so many men with the other title, and her topic was so timely. We all learned from her too, so it was a most fortunate mistake, if you could call it a mistake."

February was a comparatively slow month, but on seven days in that month Margaret Mead nevertheless willed herself to do something for somebody somewhere. Unwillingly, she lost another ten pounds.

Thanks to ministrations by Carmen and her own determination, she kept on going and growing. She slowed down considerably, but she made it, and with some of the same old gusto. She yanked the second page from her calendar and tossed it into the wastebasket beside her sawed-off rolltop desk. She would have stomped her staff and sputtered vehemently had anyone attempted to convince her that she would only be able to do that eight more times.

Thirty-three years earlier, in March 1945, Margaret wrote to her younger sister, Priscilla, then in California:

> These last six weeks have been rather nightmarish here, for I had two upper teeth out, which resulted in sinus and eye and what not infections, on top of two weeks of malaria. I've gone right on with my schedule and done the things which had to be done, but I've not had much spare energy.

By March 1978, Priscilla had long departed this world, and Margaret's maladies had changed. Her grim determination to fill each day full to the brim with committed as well as casual meetings had not changed. Her agenda ruled and she invariably stuffed more person-to-person contacts into each scheduled day than ever showed on the calendar.

March 1, in observance of International Women's Year, she addressed the Women's International Forum in the United Nations building in New York City. She named her speech "Women in the International Community and the Challenge of the U.N. Decade."

On Thursday, March 2, she was a special guest in the third of an eight-week Anthropology through Film course at the Museum. She discussed *Trobriand Cricket,* a fifty-minute documentary that had won the Prize Blue Ribbon for Anthropology in the 1977 American Film Festival. In her speech she claimed that no individual could maintain a false front for more than forty-five minutes. A letter sent to her by one of the students who listened that evening attested to trouper Margaret Mead's ability to contradict herself in keeping with the tradition that the show must go on, no matter how the performer felt: "I want you to know that I enjoyed your talk and I would like to suggest that you consider being a comedian. Your timing was perfect and your control of the audience was excellent."

After this performance, she reached the apartment early enough to wrest a few hours' sleep before Mary Elder picked her up in time to catch the 10:00 a.m. shuttle Friday for Washington, D.C. A car from the A-One Limousine Company met her on arrival and took her to the Sheraton Park Hotel for a book and author luncheon sponsored by the *Washington Post.* She talked briefly about *Letters from the Field,* which some of her readers liked to think of as her sequel to *Blackberry Winter.*

She returned to New York City by 5:00 p.m. Mary Elder sped her through rush hour traffic to a gathering of psychologists, psychiatrists, and psychoanalysts who belonged to the New York Consultation and Referral Service. She had been selected to play the role of their distinguished lecturer for the evening. Her topic was female psychology. "I was intrigued by your statement that women who anticipate becoming mothers tend to inhibit their creative endeavors," a Freudian psychoanalyst in her audience wrote her later. "In my post meeting discussions of your talk with other analysts, I found that they too found this idea to be a novel but fascinating one."

Even a robust person would have looked forward to a recuperative weekend after four speech-making appearances in three days. In the busiest of her healthy halcyon years, she would have maintained that momentum over the weekend. Instead, she landed flat on her back. But only for Saturday, March 4, 1978.

This happened also to have been the day when her third ex-husband, the father of her only child, had exploratory surgery at the University of California Medical Center in San Francisco. His third wife, Lois Bateson, and he learned that he suffered from an inoperable malignancy in the lung. Gregory Bateson was in intensive care by the time Margaret got the news. Nobody knew whether he would pull through or not.

Whenever dear ones get sick enough to die, we die in part. Margaret's good friends and collaborators Edith Burton Cobb and Martha Wolfenstein had slipped away in the past year. Dorothy Cecilia Lock, the second wife of her first husband, Luther Cressman, had also died in 1977 at home, with Luther in loving attendance.

News of the demise of her second husband's wife came to her just as Gregory was hospitalized. She wrote Reo Fortune, the man whom she'd divorced more than forty-two years previously, with wifely concern:

> I was very sad to hear of Eileen's death and I know how lonely you must be. How will you manage? Can you eat dinners in the hall of your College? This has been a bad winter. I have been more or less ailing since early December and it seems as if everyone I know has been ill. I am barely keeping my head above water with all the obligations that have piled up. I hope you can work out a viable life without Eileen, but I know it will be difficult. All the best, Yours,

Even in her own immense discomfort, Margaret Mead genuinely cared for people, including her ex-husbands and their subsequent families. In one of her dreams of this year, she, her daughter, her son-in-law, and her grandchild joined her three ex-husbands, their four wives, and several children for one mad, memorable "extended family reunion."

On the day after Gregory's operation, Sunday, March 5, she awoke nauseous but attended an open house on 93rd Street at a school established for five- to thirteen-year-olds with special learning problems. She had been a personal friend of the Reece School's founder since the 1940s. They had met when her daughter attended the Downtown Community School, which Ellen S. Reece then directed. With stalwarts like Margaret Mead to serve on her board of directors, Reece later branched off on her own to establish the first nonpublic elementary school in New York City. It was designed to help children who learned better in classrooms in which the student–teacher ratio was as low as 2 to 1.

On the next day, March 6, she forced herself to do a personal favor for a former student turned friend who followed me as her Columbia University graduate assistant twenty-two years earlier. Warren Swidler was teaching in the Department of Anthropology at the City University of New York in Brooklyn.

His institution had previously arranged with her to speak in a Social Sciences of Food lecture series in the Gold Room of the College at 12:30 p.m. Lunchtime. She named her talk "Food, Hunger, and the Environment." She had been asked to discuss general problems of world hunger, food distribution systems, and food within the context of culture. She was also expected to draw on her World War II experiences as executive secretary of the Committee on Food Habits of the National Research Council in Washington, D.C. But she had lost twenty pounds since Christmas and would have had to disassociate the reality of her own slow starvation to have been able to regurgitate intellectually palatable thoughts on either food or hunger for that lecture.

Her cousin Martha Glardon called from Cincinnati to report on developments with Talbert House on their proposed trip to Portland together in August. Margaret "talked sick" when she answered the phone. "Have you had your coffee yet?" Martha attempted to open the conversation with a pleasantry.

"I'm too busy and I can't eat much."

"Well, Margaret, how do you feel?"

"Like hell," came the gruff response, so deep and odd sounding that Martha wondered if her cousin were under some sort of sedation.

Margaret proceeded to explain that some obscure bug she'd picked up years ago in the field had lain dormant in her system all that time and was now ruining her appetite.

"She told me that and then she hung up," Martha reported afterward. "I didn't know what to think. She must have been really hurting because she'd never hung up on me before."

Margaret Mead was hurting. I expected to see her at the visual anthropology meetings at Temple University in Philadelphia on March 8–11. But she canceled that appearance and stepped up the pace of her visits to the statuesque and *muy simpático* healer. Carmen de Barraza supported Margaret's intensely positive hope that she was going to overcome whatever was wrong with her physically. Carmen's energy, gentle massages, shared confidence, and laughter relaxed her impatient patient more than anything else.

Margaret craved large doses of relaxing because she wasn't getting much, if any, back in the apartment. The more she depended on newcomer Carmen for comforting, the more old-timer Rhoda objected. Protestations from Rhoda stirred up stress for both of them and feathers flew.

Some birders have classified humans as either larks who stay up all day or owls who stay up all night. Rhoda often worked so late into the night that she was fast asleep when Margaret got up before daybreak to peck away at her typewriter. As disagreements pushed them farther apart, Margaret would often awaken in pain to find herself alone in the apartment.

Rhoda suffered acute pain of another kind. It's not easy to watch the slow demise of a once cooperative, now increasingly recalcitrant apartment mate. Often Rhoda's only comfort came from leaving the place for a few hours, or, for that matter, several days. This time she departed for her private hideaway, a converted schoolhouse beside a country road in what is called the North East Kingdom of Vermont.

Margaret prepared to make her annual pilgrimage to the Menninger Foundation in Topeka on March 11, the beginning of the academic spring break. As lecturer, friend, and consultant, she had been visiting there for thirty-six years. Since 1973, when the foundation appointed her a trustee, she had tried to time her visits to coincide with the meetings of the trustees each spring as well.

Her intersession seminar this year was entitled "Violence and Aggression in Modern Society." Weeks before her arrival, her staff sent a bibliography of her and Rhoda's writings on these subjects to the library in Topeka to afford staff members the greatest possible opportunity to read over her old remarks before listening to her newest ones.

Although she made every effort to appear otherwise, sharp-eyed cronies could see that she was quite ill. She confided to at least one of them that she might have a touch of something serious, and, for that reason, she would cut her Kansas consultantship short and not attend the trustee meetings.

Carmen de Barraza had flown to Mexico City in the company of another patient and his wife. Margaret, in this month's heightened misery, didn't want to be deprived of Carmen's energy or tender touch-healing treatments for a week. She spent a full Saturday, Sunday, and Monday lecturing and meeting with staff in the various buildings of the Menninger Foundation. Then she flew to Chicago in the early evening of March 13 in order to be ready for the first flight out to Mexico City in the morning.

During that same academic spring break in which Margaret flew to Kansas and then Mexico, I joined a conference cruise on holistic healing in the Caribbean. It was sponsored by the Association for Humanistic Psychology. As an anthropologist about to retire from teaching in a university school of nursing, I was ripe to learn more about changes taking place in medicine: from authoritarian to humanistic; from emphasizing dis-ease to wellness; from a physician curing someone's illness to a patient not getting sick in the first place; from the Occidental left-brain focus on physical structure and technology to the Oriental right-brain evocation of universal energy, or ch'i, and pure states of consciousness.

The idea of taking charge of my own wellness appealed to me immensely. I say "wellness" because the word "heal-th" or "stage-of-being healed" seems to assume that human beings start out sick. Meanings sometimes somersault inside of words and most people rarely take the time to think about contradictions hidden within them.

"Too many of us live and die *un*consciously." One of the initial daily lecturers startled me. "They bumble through life unaware of awareness. Holistic healing requires the recovery of consciousness, unbounded willingness, and deliberate choice to participate in one's own well-being."

"If you're ill, dare to become involved in your own rescue. I warn you, it'll take courage, discipline, and rebelliousness. Be prepared to put up with the objections of friends and family," challenged another speaker as I privately recalled running into antagonism many times when friends or family pressured me to quickly call a doctor and I wouldn't.

"Nobody will know quite what to do when you set out to overcome a disease on your own," he continued. "It's more fashionable to let the disease overcome you! Average Americans don't yet understand holistic healing alternatives. They're still doctor happy. They don't pay any attention to their own well-being. Whenever some part needs to be fixed, they expect doctors to fix them. Which do you choose? The passivity of being treated, symptom by symptom, or becoming actively involved in staying well in the first place? Or, if ill, by personally taking an informed course of action toward getting better?"

Dr. and Mrs. Carl Simonton of Fort Worth, Texas, took turns describing their success in having cancer patients apply the cognitive process of imagery to what was going on in their own insides. "Holistic healing, by definition," they contended, "combines the whole: the body, the mind, and the environment. We humans possess untapped powers to activate recuperative energy. A person doesn't have to be rendered a victim when informed of undifferentiated growth. You can elect to perceive the news as an opportunity to marshal physical and psychical coping mechanisms for attack."

The Simontons don't accept just anyone who has been diagnosed with cancer into their program. They refuse skeptics and quitters. They select right-brained fighters. Their patients must be willing to imaginatively encourage fight in their natural immunity systems. At least three times a day, in fifteen-minute stretches, they must agree to sit down and deliberately visualize their white blood cells doing battle with cancer cells.

Equally important, "significant other(s)" in the lives of Simonton patients must give wholehearted support to these meditation periods. "The negativity of *one* disbeliever in a patient's surroundings," the Simontons said from experience, "can undermine the entire process." Alas, Margaret had at least one.

I picked up a flyer at this conference, which was called Explorers of Mankind. It announced the First International Congress of Bodily Arts and Sciences. The congress was to convene in Los Angeles over the weekend of June 10. According to the program, explorers Charles Brooks, Barbara B. Brown, Moshé Feldenkreis, Alexander Lowen, Ashley Montagu, Karl Pribram, Carl Rogers, Ida Rolf, Charlotte Selver, Hans Selye, and Margaret Mead were to disclose their vision of human nature and illustrate it with examples of lifetime insights.

I knew Margaret would be there. Invitations to gatherings like this energized her. She'd revel in the spontaneous conversational give-and-take between the live wires in that line-up. She couldn't resist such a meeting. It would get her out of the apartment, expose her to new contacts, and immerse her in zesty conversations. And applause always provided a momentary tonic more exhilarating than any drug.

I talked myself out of Exploring Mankind in Los Angeles. My tonic would come in the form of a celebratory June birthday and retirement bash amid myriad flowers in the garden of my second son, Neal, and his wife, Darragh. Neal's brothers would be pitching in. I intended to spend as much time as possible during the first part of the summer with them and their families because I had purchased a nonrefundable ticket to two conferences on aging to be held in the Orient in August.

On my return, I determined to distill some sixty-year-old learning into a book or three. I too expected to die sometime: at a desk instead of in bed, in comfortable work slacks rather than an open-air hospital smock.

Four days before I returned from my Caribbean cruise, Carmen de Barraza met Margaret at the airport in Mexico City. It was midday on Tuesday, March 14. Carmen's facility with the Spanish language helped Margaret reach the quarters reserved for her in the Hotel International Havre, around the corner from Carmen's temporary residence in the Suites Orleans. Margaret remained in Mexico City all of Wednesday and most of Thursday.

Carmen had traveled to Mexico to undergo a minor operation and to look in on a seriously ill friend–patient and his wife. The demands of Margaret Mead's fifty-one-hour intrusion must have taxed her obliging healer's coping mechanism to the hilt.

In 1978, la Republica de los Estados Unidos de Mexico became the last country Margaret was to visit. The brisk beat of Mexico's plaintive music haunted her spirits during an exhausting return flight. She arrived in New York City close to midnight, Thursday, March 16. Mary Elder waited at Kennedy Airport ready to whisk her back to bed at the Beresford at 211 Central Park West.

Margaret had left Mexico to spend an evening with anthropologist and friend Barbara Honeyman Heath Roll and her new husband, Fred, who lived in California and were visiting friends in the East. Over a fish dinner on Friday, the trio talked about their next field trip to New Guinea, planned for December. Margaret looked and felt under the weather, but she expected to be long recovered by December. She thought her problem might be diverticulitis. Through a combination of antibiotics, Fred told her, he had been able to avert an operation when he came down with diverticulitis some years back. He couldn't remember the name of the doctor, but he promised to send it on to her later.

In the meantime, her personal outlook remained positive. Her very obvious weight loss might be merely a warning that she should cut down on her "accumulated and inescapable obligations" and cut back on taking too many future ones. But it wasn't going to be easy; it matched no one's image of Margaret Mead. But who said Margaret Mead ever tackled anything easy?

Her most immediate "inescapable obligation" occurred the following Monday on United Nations Earth Day. As chairperson of the event, she read her prepared salute for the occasion:

> Earth Day is the first holy day which transcends all national borders, yet preserves all geographical integrities, spans mountains and oceans and time belts, and yet brings people all over the world into one resonating accord, is devoted to the preservation of the harmony of nature and yet draws upon the triumphs of technology—the measurement of time and instantaneous communication through space.
>
> Earth Day draws on astronomical phenomena in a new day; using the vernal equinox, the time when the sun crosses the equator making night and day of equal length in all parts of the earth. To this point in the annual calendar, Earth Day attaches no local or divisive set of symbols, no statement of the truth or superiority of one way of life over another.
>
> Earth Day is a great idea, well founded in scientific knowledge, tied specifically to our solar university. But the protection of the earth is also a matter of day-to-day decisions. Some taken by individuals, some by national governments, some by multinational corporations, and some by the United Nations. Planetary housekeeping is not—as men's work has been said to be—just from sun to sun, but as has been said, like women's work that is never done. Earth Day

lends itself to ceremony, to purple passages of glowing rhetoric, to a catch in the throat and a tear in the eye, easily evoked, but also too easily wiped away.

Earth Day uses one of humanity's great discoveries, the discovery of anniversaries by which, throughout time, human beings have kept their sorrows and their joys, their victories, their revelations and their obligations alike. But the noblest anniversary, devoted to the vastest enterprise now in our power, the preservation of this planet, could easily become an empty observance if our hearts are not in it. Earth Day reminds the people of the world of the continuing care which is vital to earth's safety.

"I was delighted to hear your statement on Earth Day, a splendid integration," wrote a fan who also thanked her for her continuing participation in the National Commission on the Observance of International Women's Year a few days after her appearance.

Between Earth Day on March 20 and her departure for San Francisco on March 29, Margaret mainly covered her classes at Columbia, met with a doctor and her healer, and socialized with out-of-town and local Easter season guests. She plowed through mail that accumulated at the rate of fifteen pounds per day. She tended to answer the people she knew best by telephone. More likely than not, one of her assistants responded to the others according to her almost indecipherable instructions.

Ailment by ailment, physical attrition weans most of us from life. Sickness had almost loosened Margaret's grip on living several times during the past winter, but by what she called "responsible caretaking" she chose to hang on. Heaven could wait. She had much to think about besides the endless droning of pain.

On March 22, she attended a meeting of the Nongovernmental Organization of the U.N. to assist in drawing up plans for declaring 1979 the International Year of the Child. Since anthropology is about everything that concerns people, it's a slippery science that more dedicated practitioners continually grasp anew. Margaret Mead's memories of fifty-five hyperactive years in the field enabled her to sit down after that meeting and type out an informed statement of compassion and purpose. She named it "On Stigmatized Children." It read:

> No society that we know of cares well for all its children, nor does any society have a monopoly of ways in which children can be especially cherished. In discussing stigmatization, it is important to keep in mind these two considerations, as we explore the way peoples all over the world have cared for those who are conceived but not yet born, the newly born, the infant, the toddler, the

child. In some societies, orphans can never be full citizens; in some twins must be put to death. Many peoples can not find the will to care for those severely deformed or blind at birth. Sometimes an infant whose mother dies in childbirth has no one to care for it. The ways in which stigmatization is followed by death are various. Actual infanticide is far rarer than neglect or later mistreatment. There are societies where the death rate of girl babies is much higher than that of boys. And there are societies where babies are listened to gravely and with respect, where even a small child can not have his or her clothing disposed of without their consent.

The International Year of the Child, participated in by the peoples of the planet, gives a chance to bring together information about ways in which each country has special defects to correct and special gracious customs to the peoples of other nations.

She signed her copy and left instructions for a secretary to retype the piece for presentation to the North American Committee of the United Nations. Then she prepared for an end-of-the-month transcontinental flight to attend the American Orthopsychiatric Association meetings in San Francisco.

Margaret's chief involvement at this conference centered around an all-day session called "Impact on Mental Health Boundaries of Culture, Economics, Government, History, and Social Groupings." She delivered the Ittleson Award Lecture, "Boundaries of Mental Health and the Culture." She was the guest of honor at the luncheon between the sessions at which the association formally presented her with its Ittleson Award.

For Margaret, Thursday, March 30, turned out to be a nine-hour marathon. Soon after Gregory Bateson's surgery earlier in the month, his daughter, Mary Catherine Bateson Kassarjian, secured a professional leave from her deanship in Iran to help her father shape up the first few chapters of his last book, *Mind and Nature: A Necessary Unity.* With Margaret as close as the San Francisco Hilton, Cathy came there to dine and to spend the night with her mother. In the morning, the two women departed for Lois and Gregory's place in Ben Lomond south of San Francisco.

I wonder if, during their short flight down the California coast, she bothered to tell Cathy, or if Cathy wanted to hear, about Margaret's helping her father, E. S. Mead, with a similar task exactly a half century earlier. Together, the preceding generation of father and daughter hammered out an outline and got the first chapters off the ground for a book he called *Harvey Braun.* It was a partly fictionalized report of his running a family farm to augment a professor's salary from the time his oldest daughter was a preteenager through most of the 1920s.

The full-day visit that followed Margaret's and Cathy's return to the senior Bateson must have been particularly poignant. On one level of her consciousness, Margaret at least knew that Gregory was not alone in having some form of cancer. He openly admitted it; she did not. With perhaps equal exposure in their fieldwork to nonmedical approaches for treating disease, each of them independently sought out the recuperative assistance of women healers as well as men in medicine. On this first of three visits to the Bateson household in the next five months, these two Trojans shared complaints about the side effects of medical treatment, which sometimes make the cure seem as devastating as the disease.

Margaret left the Batesons in Ben Lomond at midday on April 1 and arrived in New York City fifteen minutes before midnight. In this year's bridge between March and April, blackberry winter snows succumbed to early spring showers while Margaret Mead, anthropological elder and type A personality, forced herself to keep on going whether she felt up to it or not. During March, she packed her borrowed time with speaking, teaching, visiting, and letter writing. Only seven and a half more months lay ahead. But she had always raced the clock and the calendar. Thus in that respect she wasn't letting this year differ from any other one in her career.

Each April, warming breezes speed the tempo of growth. Young life sprouts. Older life sports spring raiment and sparks plans for fresh activities. This particular season, Margaret needed new clothes in the worst way. She had lost thirty pounds. Nothing fit anymore, but she wasn't the type to take time out for an indulgent pursuit of shopping. Instead she wore the same things, pinning here a tuck, there a pleat, or she borrowed something from Rhoda.

She marked the first day back, April 2, as income tax Sunday. Her friend and Cathy's godmother, Marie Eichelberger, usually labored through the mathematics homework that buffered Margaret from the Internal Revenue Service.

On Monday and Tuesday, April 3 and 4, Margaret presided at the spring meeting of the Institute of Intercultural Studies, met her classes at Columbia, conferred with three students on their projects, saw one doctor, and was treated each morning by her healer.

On Wednesday, April 5, she saw a doctor at 9:30 a.m. and visited the treatment rooms of her healer an hour later. Mary Elder picked her up in the lobby of the Beresford early in the afternoon. Margaret wasn't feeling "too terribly well," but the prospect of a spin up the Thruway toward Albany in the company of a nurse–midwife whose family called her "Go-Go" made taking off on another three-day, three-place lecturing commitment something of a lark.

"Whatever you do, don't touch the dial on the heater," Mary's husband, Brent, cautioned her over breakfast that morning. "We've got to have it fixed. Remember to keep your hands off the dial because it will get stuck wherever you move it." Mary, preoccupied with plans to get Margaret to the Sienna College speech on time that evening and to meet her father and stepmother the day after, paid little heed to Brent's advice.

As her disease progressed, noises and temperatures that Margaret might have laughed off previously became real annoyances. Mary had closed all the windows of the car. They had barely cleared the city limits when Margaret felt uncomfortably chilly. She scowled and clutched at her cape. "Please keep the heat up," she said.

Mary turned the dial all the way to high. Then Brent's warning rang in her ears. Sure enough, no matter what muscle power or wishful thinking she directed toward that heater, the dial refused to budge. Floor heat soon simmered their feet. Mary stopped and helped Margaret get into the back where she might lie down with her feet on the seat. Mary's feet burned too, so she watched for the next exit. She stopped at the first gas station, and an attendant disconnected the heater.

Margaret moved to the front again. To distract her distraught passenger somewhat, Mary turned on the radio. Margaret, fresh from a visit south of the border, demanded Mexican music. Alas, neither the AM nor the FM bands produced anything closer than Puerto Rican. Having exchanged sweltering in an overheated car for shivering in a chilly one, the two squirmed politely over one frustration after another for three desperate hours. The trip, begun as a lark, ended up more like an endurance contest.

About 5:00 p.m., the two travelers checked into a Holiday Inn in the Sienna College area between Loudenville and Lathan. For the first time, Margaret's agreement for this lecture visit stipulated that she be allowed one hour's rest or private activity for every four of paid performance. She also requested that there be no dialogues and no classroom or television appearances.

Her press conference before dinner covered such topics as abortion, capital punishment, and handguns. She called abortion "a necessary evil" and alleged that capital punishment "does not stop crime. It just makes somebody happier in having revenge on somebody else." About the use of handguns, she suggested that "if people had to use their fists or a knife to get at someone, fewer would be killed."

Thirteen hundred students and high school counselors crowded the bleachers of a large gymnasium after dinner to hear the speech Dr. Mead had come to deliver, "Where Today's Students Fit In." In her opinion, students fit into the future and she forever craved more of that. By reaching out to youth through classes at Columbia and other campuses across the country and by capturing the attention of mothers through monthly columns in *Redbook* magazine, she penetrated the future more deeply than one life span would have ordinarily permitted. "A good proportion of the burden of bringing this world together will fall on you young people," she challenged them. "So look carefully at what needs to be done now and what occupations are necessary."

She compared predictions of the 1930s for the destruction of the world through war with those of the 1970s when atrocities to our environment loomed far worse. "It's much harder trying to decide what to do about our environment than it ever was to fight a war," she squinted at them meaningfully, "so figuring out what to do about our environment won't be easy. Maybe that's why nobody seems to be really working at it yet."

As she shared her deep concern for the future, she talked freely and naturally. She was probably more at home with students on a college campus than with any other audience anywhere.

Mary half-listened to the speech, realizing how unwell was the newfound friend whom she preferred to address as "Dr. Mead." She wondered how many people, if any, realized the tremendous effort expended by this five-foot fighter to be up there in front of them in the first place.

Like any show person, Margaret refused to let personal pains have the upper hand or cause a performance to be called off. En route back to the Holiday Inn following a token appearance at a reception afterward, Mary asked whether Dr. Mead might like a backrub before going to sleep. "This is the way it is when I travel," Margaret said as she disrobed. "After delivering a lecture somewhere, all I've got to talk to is four bare walls. Sometimes I phone my sister, Elizabeth. She's alone and up all hours, so my calls make company for her, too. Maybe I'll get her tomorrow night when you'll be gone. Then again, maybe I won't because I'll be visiting her in a week anyway."

Mary, who was not aware that Margaret had cancer, mentioned seeing what looked like bruises on her skin in the region of her pancreas and liver. Margaret made no comment other than that she would tell Carmen about Mary's observation on her next appointment. Mary pulled the blankets up over her patient and suggested that she phone if she experienced discomfort during the night.

In the morning, before she went to visit with her father and stepmother in Ghent, Mary ate breakfast with her traveling mate. Margaret told Mary about the diet Carmen had advised her to follow. It included staying away from citrus fruits, fat, sugar, and foods containing white flour. For someone who eats in restaurants, any diet presents obstacles. Besides, Margaret's willpower did not necessarily apply to what she craved to eat. She liked cottage cheese and bacon, for example, both of which contained forbidden elements. When Margaret ordered that combination for breakfast, her eyes momentarily glinted with mischief. "Should you ever meet Carmen," she said, "just forget to say anything about what I eat."

Mary went on her way. Margaret lingered in the area one more day. She was scheduled to speak at Rensselaer Polytechnic Institute, the first college of science and civil engineering to be established in an English-speaking country, that evening. She delivered one of her more popular lectures, "The Changing Roles of Males and Females."

Next she flew to Philadelphia for a two-day stint in the city of her birth. She had been invited to address the Delaware Valley Society for Adolescent Health at Children's Hospital on Friday, April 7. She entitled her talk, "The Adolescent in Contemporary Society: Coming of Age in America." "It was gratifying to find you so supportive of my feelings to reestablish the family," the professional wife of a former student later thanked her. And for "coming to talk and enriching our lives. I do hope you will get well very rapidly for yourself and for the world. You have been so instrumental in shaping my husband's world, his career, his life. We all still need you so very much."

Late Saturday morning, a representative of a local organization, Research for Better Schools, Inc., picked her up at the Civic Center Hilton. He took her to the University Museum, a place through which she and her siblings had roamed as children.

"It would be the greatest possible shot in the arm," the anthropologist dean of the Graduate School of Education at the University of Pennsylvania wrote her previously about plans for a conference on ethnography and education to be held there at a date when she would be available.

> The general theme of the symposium is to be "Child and Pupil"—ways of understanding youngsters both as children outside school and as pupils inside schools. At the moment there appears to be a division between kinds of work that are done: some intensive studies of classrooms, some studies in communities, the two not often being linked. I personally believe that the two ... have to be integrated. But any direction you want to take would be fine.

She lunched with the group in the Upper Egyptian Gallery at noon, gave a keynote address entitled "New Levels of Consciousness of Community" at 1:00 p.m., and was on the way to the nearest depot before 3:00 p.m. She boarded the Metroliner for Pennsylvania Station in New York City. At the end of the run, she met caring, eager-to-please Mary Elder.

In these last months of Margaret's life, Mary provided her with unlimited taxi service. From 6:00 a.m. to midnight on a sometimes daily basis, Mary chauffeured her to and from airports, appointments, classes, and depots. Margaret, in return, kept almost daily contact with her advisee's videotaping and juggling two or three generations of informants for her doctoral research project—primitive barter, pure and simple, which brought immense benefits to both recipients.

On this particular late afternoon, Mary's traveling adviser felt much too tired in general and cantankerous in particular to take the time for a formal restaurant meal. So they stopped off at a Horn and Hardart Automat for a quick bite en route back to the Beresford.

Margaret deplored her discovery that medical specialists have become so narrowly preoccupied that patients have to figure out what is wrong on their own. Because she was experiencing so much trouble with digesting foods like meat, she suspected her diverticulitis might actually be anorexia. She thought it wiser to cancel a talk on identity and sexuality at the University of California in San Diego the next weekend and consult with a nutritionist at Tufts University instead.

Totally sympathetic nurse–midwife Mary assured her friend that she would be on hand to get her to and from LaGuardia Airport for the Boston shuttle. Margaret started Sunday, her first day home again, with a 9:00 a.m. treatment from Carmen. Then she visited with members of her sister Priscilla's grown family until 5:00 p.m. At that hour, someone from Temple B'nai Abraham came to take her to Livingston, New Jersey, for dinner and a speech. Her lecture, part of the Community Forum Series, was "The Future as a Frame for the Present."

For the next few days, outside of her classes and a luncheon meeting for the Scientists' Institute for Public Information, she kept to the apartment and coped with the gastric complexities of her newly identified malady. Never one to put all her faith in one doctor, she phoned a friend in San Francisco two days before her Thursday, April 13, departure to see the nutritionist in New England. The physician on the West Coast promised to forward a medicine calculated to supply the proteins she would have absorbed were she able to digest meat. He recommended that she stick to "bland stuff like rice and pasta" and cautioned her to be with someone when she downed the first capsule. "Especially as you are on a semi-starvation metabolism," he said. "When the gut is avid for food, it soaks up all medicine too quickly."

In an early appointment the morning before she was to leave for Boston, Margaret asked Carmen to tell the story of how she came to know she possessed healing talents. "I was only three years old," Carmen remembered, "when my mother lay dying of cancer in a bedroom in our home in Chile. Relatives came and sat around the table. They cried about her. I crouched under the table and heard them. I wept and ran into my mother's room. I climbed on her bed and straddled her. I cried, 'No! No! No!' Each day I soothed her and prayed for her. My mother got better. I was only three years old, but she knew I was the one who helped her get better. My mother lived until I was fourteen years old. You are either born with healing ability or you are not. The rest is energy and experience and clean chakras."

Margaret told Carmen about Mary's giving her a backrub after her speech at Sienna College and seeing bruises on the skin of her midsection. "Ohhh?" The remark piqued Carmen's fancy. "The bruises your friend says she saw on your skin are not on your skin. They are inside. Your friend saw underneath your skin! That's what she saw! Who is this person? She sees with the eyes of a born healer."

"She's a practical nurse–midwife who came to me for help on a doctoral study she's doing on birthing and bonding behavior between Puerto Rican parents and their newborn."

"I should very much like to meet her."

"Good," Margaret said. "She's coming to pick me up and take me to the airport tomorrow morning after our next treatment. Come down to the car and meet her."

Mary drove up just as healer and patient emerged from the elevator. She wriggled out of the Blue Lemon and hurried around to the front to greet them. For some time, Mary had been as curious to meet Margaret's healer as the healer now was to meet her.

Carmen, middle-aged, straight, strong, auburn haired, surveyed the younger woman up, down, and through. Mary, thirtyish, a grown-up version of the robust and rosy-cheeked Dutch cherubs on old-time Campbell soup ads, returned the inspection. They knew each other without having to go through the formalities of an introduction.

"How are you?" Carmen spoke with an accent, soberly, and with serious concern.

"Never felt better in my life," Mary laughed as she opened the door on the sidewalk side.

"She's been doing fieldwork in the South Bronx," Margaret volunteered, "and I've never known anybody who didn't pick up some bug during fieldwork."

"You do look well," Carmen persisted, "but I'm sensing negative energy. Is there something wrong? How *are* you?"

"In the peak of health." Mary tossed her head up and smiled as she held the door open to ease Margaret's getting in and sitting down.

"See you tomorrow, late," Margaret called to Carmen as Mary hustled to the driver's side. They sped off toward the airport without a minute to spare.

Margaret began the conversation by telling Mary the tale of Carmen's childhood realization of her inborn healing powers. "I'm studying how Carmen thinks," Margaret confided. "Some day I'd like to have you ask her how she became a healer. Then we can compare the stories and see how they differ."

Margaret mentioned nothing about either her health or lack of it. They shared talk about the families in Mary's study, the traffic, the weather, and the lack of taste of fat women who venture forth in hugely patterned floral prints.

Mary got Margaret to the shuttle on time. Forty-eight minutes later, Margaret landed in Boston. She hailed a cab that took her to her sister's rooms near Harvard in Cambridge. Margaret and Elizabeth ate a hurried lunch at a corner drugstore across the street and down a block from Elizabeth's apartment. They ordered egg salad sandwiches on white bread, slightly toasted, and vanilla milkshakes.

In no less than ninety minutes, Margaret left by cab for the first of two appointments with a woman specialist at the Francis J. Stearn Nutrition Center of the New England Medical Center of Tufts University. Elizabeth intended to relax until Margaret's return. She leaned back in a comfortable overstuffed chair, put her feet up, and fell asleep. She awakened when she heard her sister turn a key in the front door. The door opened. She saw Margaret with one foot in the hallway and one in the living room, twisting both knobs impatiently. "Elizabeth, *when* are you going to get this damn lock fixed? I've been asking you to get this done for years and it isn't fixed yet."

"Someday," Elizabeth said as she sat up. "I keep hoping it'll fix itself but maybe I'll move first."

Margaret had no real news to report on prospects of a shared apartment in New York City. She had put her sister's name on the waiting lists of a number of places within walking distance of the Museum. All they could do was wait. "We should have thought of this three years ago," Margaret said. Elizabeth agreed.

The next day, Friday, April 14, Margaret left for her second appointment at the Nutrition Center. It would be over at 11:30—plenty of time to return to Elizabeth's for a quick bite and visit before heading for the shuttle at Logan Airport around 2:00. Except for Margaret's substituting tea for a milkshake, they ordered a repeat of yesterday's lunch. The two women sat side by side on barstools at the drugstore counter. For the first time in years, a stranger could have guessed they were sisters. The thinner Margaret grew, the more apparent became the family resemblance.

They talked about health foods and diet. "Carmen introduced me to health food stores," Margaret said. "I'm not supposed to eat wheat in any form, spinach, lamb, onions, or chocolate. No fried foods. No oranges or grapes. No coffee. I eat out so much it's difficult, but I've been trying to stick to her restrictions.

"Now look at this new diet here," she spread it out on the counter between them. "For breakfast, I'm allowed oatmeal or cottage cheese, toast, apple or cranberry juice. That won't be too difficult. But a broth with tofu and barley for lunch and two small slices of not fresh bread! Where's there a restaurant in Christendom that'll admit its bread isn't fresh, let alone that they've got barley or tofu on hand!"

Her eyes scanned past small helpings of meat and certain vegetables for dinner to the avoidances listed at the end of the sheet. "Avoid bananas, beans, broccoli, cream soup, ice cream, and onions," she read aloud.

"Diets contradict each other." Elizabeth sipped through the straw in her milkshake. "But I do avoid blueberries. I'm careful about foods that might rile my liver."

Margaret continued reading and familiarizing herself with the specifics of her Tufts University Nutrition Center diet. "Well, as far as I can see," she summarized the main points, "Carmen's diet and this new diet do agree on forbidding onions."

She sighed as she folded the paper, tucked it into a side compartment of her purse, and stood up to say good-bye. "It's all very, very discouraging to say the least." She reached for the check. "I've lost absolutely all the weight I can afford to lose. I needed to lose some, but this has gone too far. My appetite's no good and hardly anything stays down anymore."

She'd be in New York City by 5:00 p.m. Despite heightened traffic at that hour, Mary would meet her and see to it that she arrived at Carmen's at 7:00 p.m. Since February, Margaret kept an appointment with her healer every possible day.

Slightly more than a full week of geographically scattered speeches stretched ahead. In whatever time she had to spare over the weekend, she intended to check her most immediate scheduling folders. She presented "A Cross-cultural View of Child Abuse and Neglect" at an annual conference for social workers and counselors on Monday morning, April 17. On Tuesday, Mary Elder got her to the Eastern terminal at LaGuardia Airport in time to catch the 7:00 a.m. shuttle for Washington, D.C.

At 8:30 she walked into an executive committee meeting of New Directions. New Directions was a comparatively new organization of American citizens concerned about worldwide environmental deterioration, hunger, poverty, social injustice, and war. Members worked together to influence policies in both governmental and nongovernmental organizations in order to plan ways to alleviate these circumstances for the future good of our planet and everybody on it.

Margaret served as council chairperson for the group. She collected roles in organizations like this one because she believed that "liberated women have a major part to play and a wholly new place to create for themselves in public life as professional persons." She considered her presence and her vote at meetings with international goals so important that to attend this particular meeting she canceled her appearance as the keynote speaker at a seminar for senior citizens in New York City. "We women working in new kinds of partnership with men should be able to bring fresh thinking into law and administration of justice," I had heard her say. "I learned when I was a child that one little vote can make a very big difference." She prided herself on putting such convictions into action.

She caught the 1:00 p.m. shuttle and was back in New York City at 2:00. Mary met her, dropped her off at a friend's for a short rest, got her to her Methods class at Columbia at 4:00, to Carmen's at 6:15, and to 211 Central Park West by 8:00, where another doctor would be calling on her. She had an appointment with yet another doctor and her healer again on the morning of Wednesday, April 19, before she took off on a three-state lecture tour of the Middle West at 1:00 p.m.

At 8:00 that evening, Margaret Mead, migrant college lecturer, regaled students and citizenry in Bloomington, Indiana, with her thoughts on ending the sex-based division of labor. "The real difference between men and women," she declared emphatically, "is that women have babies and men don't. Any other difference is superficial.

"The population explosion makes it so every woman doesn't have to produce children. For the first time in history, some women can be freed to do something else.

"The consequence of ending a division of labor based on sex will be, and is, terribly rough on everybody," she acknowledged. "The worst is what it might do to the family. The image of a family with a father and a mother and a home is terribly strong. It predates ideas of marriage, kinship, and paternity." She held her hands up in front of her as though she were embracing her listeners. "We need to be sure that we keep something about that image intact."

She got to bed late. Since Chicago is so close to Bloomington and she had no obligations until the next afternoon, she was able to catch up on some rest Thursday morning. She arrived in the Windy City at 2:00 p.m. A porter waited to help her to her room in the O'Hare Hilton just in time to participate in a call-in talk show for station WIND.

At that time Illinois legislators were arguing a proposal that would permit grown-up adoptees to search for their biological parents. It wasn't hard to guess where Margaret stood on this matter. In predawn sessions at her typewriter, she was readying two columns for *Redbook* on adoption issues. On the radio broadcast, she defended the rights of those who called themselves yesterday's children to unearth ancestral roots in order to become more sure of their real identities.

At tune-off time, someone from Grayslake appeared to chauffeur her to the College of Lake Country for dinner, a press conference, and a lecture. She knew her speech well enough to deliver it in her sleep: "The Changing Sex Roles."

After a lonely night in the O'Hare Hilton, she left at 7:00 a.m. Friday for Columbus, Ohio, where she faced a press conference before being given a ride to her quarters for rest and lunch. A friend at whose home she would be having dinner arrived to escort her to Independence Hall for a 3:00 p.m. lecture.

Wearing a cape and carrying her thumbstick, she entered and exited the auditorium to standing ovations from nearly nine hundred people. The overflow crowd stood outside quietly straining to hear. Her speech highlighted the Women and Poverty Lecture Series at Ohio State University.

"I've never combined the two subjects before," she announced, "but the relationship between them is inherent. For 2 million years, childbearing and rearing have been women's main achievements. Now, because of technology and awareness of the consequences of overpopulation, women don't have to just have children anymore." Her voice deepened when she reminded her audience, however, that "women will remain poor until their work is considered as valuable as that of any man."

By 8:15 Saturday morning, she had found her seat on TWA flight 426 heading for the National Airport in Washington, D.C. The taxi driver who took her to the Dupont Plaza Hotel on New Hampshire Avenue stopped long enough for her to register and leave her bag before proceeding to the American Anthropological Association headquarters a few blocks away. She had come to attend a weekend meeting of the Ad Hoc Panel on Foreign Aid. Once she was in demand, Margaret Mead got herself to every possible discussion of this kind. "If you want to make any kind of impact on today or tomorrow," she thoroughly believed, "you've got to be where decisions are being made. Each person sitting at such a committee can, by his or her vote, help change the world."

When the meetings adjourned at 2:00 p.m. on Sunday afternoon, she taxied to the air shuttle for LaGuardia. Mary Elder picked her up and rushed her directly to Carmen de Barraza's for a special favor, a one-hour treatment on arrival.

Minutes after Carmen fluttered her hands over Margaret's forehead and planted a recuperative kiss between closed eyes, a buzzer sounded. Carmen opened the door into her waiting room. There stood the chairperson of the Plandome Forum, come to take Margaret to the North Shore Unitarian Church in

Westbury, Long Island. Her topic for the evening was billed as "Definitions of Humanity." The same person later transported her to the Beresford in Manhattan. At midnight, for the first time in five days, Margaret touched home base.

In the remaining week of April, Dr. Margaret, adjunct professor, discussed final exams with her three classes at Columbia. Margaret Mead, columnist for *Redbook* magazine, consulted with Rhoda Metraux on background research for an imaginary interview between the two of them and St. Nicholas for the December issue. The article was to be called *Talking to Santa Claus*. The idea for it had been inspired by Kate, Rhoda's granddaughter and Margaret's goddaughter, who at three was filled to bursting with Christmas questionings.

As anthropologist at large and earth mother, Margaret attended the annual meeting of the Scientists' Institute for Public Information. Peripheral to one of the major concerns of this group, she delivered two speeches supporting nuclear disarmament. One was at a cocktail party fund-raiser for an organization known as Artists' Mobilization for Survival; the other was at the twentieth anniversary celebration of the Women's Club in New Jersey.

Busy as all this was, the fourth and final week of April was more or less quiet, comparatively. Her rhythm for the year so far was to begin each month with a running start, taper down a bit for a second wind during the second week, pack the middle week with activity, and then brake for a supposed slowdown week of commitments closer to home.

During this month she had explained her digestive problems away as anorexia nervosa, a bug she picked up during fieldwork in the Pacific, diverticulitis, a touch of flu. These terms were not so much deliberate falsehoods as they were desperate rationalizations. She believed them as she voiced them. After all, specialists are only human and humans make mistakes. Specialists have been known to diagnose correctly too, but she spent precious little rationed time delving into that possibility.

So went April. Fate bequeathed her less than two hundred days. She behaved as though there were thousands. She was experiencing top potential. Life was too good to be true. Her teaching, writing, committee work, speaking performances here, there, and everywhere filled her with the elixir of usefulness and purpose.

"Terminality" as a fact never scared Margaret Mead. These days, always an optimist, she shrugged death off by the hour. Who was to say that this ailment might not pass? Many others had gone by the way, and she knew how people tune out the dying. She wasn't about to be tagged "terminal" until the last minute.

In the grip of an unshakable illness, Margaret Mead chose to be very, very tough. People whose egos didn't crush hers in too-close encounters during these last few months marveled at her grit. Audiences recognized her spunk and hailed her for it. The four-figure bonbons she received in payment for some of the appearances tasted sweet and digested easily.

Nothing is ever all bad. In the first four months of 1978, she accomplished something she had been hankering to do for forty years. Like most of us, Margaret Mead grew more nostalgic with time. As a child, she had fashioned paper baskets on the first day of May, filled them with violets, placed them on the verandah of neighborhood homes as close to the front doors as she dared, knocked, ran, hid, and watched excited playmates exclaim over them.

When she was a student at Barnard, she introduced this small-town custom to her big-city classmates. In May 1923, a coterie of Ash Can Cats rode the streetcar to Van Cortlandt Park to pick violets to stuff into a special May basket. Then they took their offering to the Greenwich Village apartment of a poet they admired. Her husband or her sister (stories vary on this point) answered their knock because Edna St. Vincent Millay didn't feel perky enough to do so. Jubilated by their gift of May Day whimsy, poetess Millay appeared in the doorway to extend her thanks and to hear their names. When Margaret's roommate, Leonie Adams, voiced hers, Millay recognized it and thrilled them all over again by association.

This May, fifty years later, she substituted visits for violets. Without putting anything into actual words, she was saying good-bye in one way or another whenever an opportunity presented itself. She sent birthday cards or made calls on friends in their apartments, which she hadn't done in years. She dropped in on Ruth Bunzel, who had been secretary to Franz Boas before becoming an anthropologist in her own right, and on Sula Benet, who told my class at Columbia what it meant to be a Pole. She and Sula posed for identification pictures in preparation for their trip in July with photographer and ex-student Ken Heyman to observe Russian centenarians for a book on aging that they planned to put together the following spring. She dined with June Goodfield, who had been her daughter's roommate at Radcliffe; with Frances Cooke Macgregor, with whom she wrote *Growth and Culture: A Photographic Study of Balinese Childhood.* In sympathy or in sentiment, she kissed some working peers at Columbia and at *Redbook.* She said "I love you" more often.

Her last classes at Columbia drew to a close. As her father had done before her, were she to retain her vigor, she would make employees of some of these latest students who would, in turn, become another batch of loyal supporters.

She made single appointments with five doctors and went to her healer twenty times. On her request, a tape recorder captured their conversation during each treatment. They planned to analyze and edit the tapes for a book on natural

healing. In Margaret's opinion, the behavior of many doctors had become so im-
personal and so apparently uncaring that she envisioned the warmly personal tech-
nique of faith healers someday gaining more of the respect it deserved. She was elu-
sive about her cancer, yes, but she wanted everyone to know about choices other
than putting oneself totally in the hands of the so-called medical establishment.

In this month too, just as Carmen had sensed on their meeting, Mary Elder
came down with the first signs of a rare intestinal infection, probably contracted
during her filming fieldwork in the South Bronx. All at once and altogether, Mary
became Carmen's patient, her student, and her sometimes aide during sessions
with Margaret.

In her running-start first week in May, Margaret flew to Chicago to attend a
Biennial Conference of the American Association of Retired Persons (AARP).
Two thousand of the 10 million members of an organization she refused to join
watched her receive the first Ethel Percy Andrus Award as an individual who
made "profoundly significant contributions to the world and public affairs."

She wore a loose-fitting jumper and a flouncy blouse with wide, long sleeves
that covered but did not hide the thinness of her arms and body. Her pallor and
fatigue shocked several officers who were unaware of her condition. They feared
their invitation may have created too much hardship on her. As she spoke and responded to their membership, however, she rallied and thrilled them by her presence. Seasoned retirees repeatedly referred to her as "truly great" and described
her talk "New Directions" as "the high point of the convention," which provided
them with "enough fuel for thought to energize constructive action."

Serendipity came in the form of a letter from an AARP member who also
happened to be a former student. In the late 1920s, the writer attended the first
anthropology class Margaret Mead ever taught:

> You made an impression on me when you lectured on Samoa and the culture of
> those people. Not that I was overly interested in aborigine culture, but you did
> compare all that with things that went on in America. What fascinated me about
> your anthropological ways were your opinions about so many subjects which one
> could read in many publications and I am sure that you will continue to honor
> America with your wise counsel and knowledge for many years to come.

Were there years ahead, Margaret would have showered her country with
the breadth of her knowledge and the wisdom of her counsel. All she dared count
on until the return of her usual bounce, however, was one day at a time.

She returned to New York City at noon on Thursday, May 4, the day after her speech in Chicago. By proclamation of President Carter, this was the second of a four-day environmental festival to celebrate the sun: what it does for the water, the land, and human beings. Sun Day was a national event that had begun in New York City at the United Nations at sunrise the day before with dancing, singing, and a speech by U.N. ambassador Andrew Young.

For her part, Margaret Mead joined actor Robert Redford and ecologist Barry Commoner Friday evening, May 5, at the Cathedral of St. John the Divine on Amsterdam Avenue and 112th Street. The three of them made individual comments on the central theme—a future with alternatives.

Dr. Mead's most immediate professional future, always dictated by her schedule, directed that she next fly south for a Sunday commencement at the University of Miami. At 8:45 Saturday morning, May 6, Mary Elder took her most frequent passenger to Carmen's for a quick appointment en route to the National Airlines terminal at LaGuardia Airport. At 10:30 Margaret greeted an older woman, whom she called the Baroness, who wanted to talk to her about a youth project before her noon departure. She had wisely arranged for Helen Reurs, a younger woman she had met eighteen years earlier at the United Nations, and her husband to accompany her to Florida. Margaret and Helen had cruised the Pacific together in 1974, and Margaret felt at home with her. Later Helen shared with me the experiences she had with Margaret.

"Our shared time was all very correct and old-fashioned. I didn't pump her. I never was a student of hers. I never was an assistant at the Museum or at Columbia. I was a completely free agent with no ax to grind," Helen said later. "She was Victorian enough not to talk much about personal matters, even to those close to her. As a result, I had no idea of the nature of her physical problems."

That she brought somebody along on this flight proved to be sheer good luck because attacks of dizziness and nausea began almost as soon as the plane left the ground. During the entire two and a half hours in the air, Margaret's malaise kept Helen hovering and hopping.

Bryce Dunham, a representative from the host university, and Helen's son, Robert Carlson, met their plane and transported the trio to a two-story cottage belonging to the luxurious Key Biscayne Hotel on Ocean Drive. Margaret chose an upstairs room overlooking the sea. There would be a reception and dinner in honor of the university's guests at 7:00 p.m. in the Rosenstiel School of Marine and Atmospheric Sciences, which left time for Margaret to squeeze in a recuperative nap. Helen excused herself to help Margaret settle down in new quarters. "This is too perfect a place," Margaret declared as she pulled clothes out of her suitcase and handed them to Helen, who hung them in the closet.

"Let's have a party." She lit up as she looked out over turquoise water lazily lapping a white, sandy beach. "When you go down to see Rob, ask him to bring a friend or two back with him in the morning. You and the kids can swim while I sleep. We'll have brunch here on the balcony. Nobody is coming to take us to the commencement until 2:00, so we'll have plenty of time. It'll be such fun and so wonderful."

At the banquet that evening, a doctor whose wife died of Margaret's malady earlier in the year recognized her condition. He rushed up to share confidences. "He's the first one to guess what's wrong with me," Margaret whispered to Helen. "And he hit it right on the head." Now Helen knew. And Margaret's knowing that Helen would keep her secret drew the two women closer.

Rob showed up Sunday morning with tanned and smiling friends. They brought their swimming gear and were set for several hours of watery horseplay. "You all run along and swim," Margaret prodded the Reurs. "Don't worry about me. I'm going to curl up and sleep. I'll have fun knowing how much you're enjoying yourselves." She fell asleep. Her guests tiptoed out to the beach.

"Life is so full of contrasts," Helen reflected. "Here I am, swimming around in this romantic setting and that woman up there is really, truly just plain dying. The rhythms of life, they supersede us, and mesh as relentlessly as waves breaking on a beach."

At the graduation ceremony some hours later, Margaret Mead received another of her many honorary doctor of science degrees. She waived her fee from the University of Miami (an institution catering to minority groups), provided she be allowed to repeat the speech, "A Future with Alternatives," that she delivered at the New York City Sun Day festival two days earlier. The subject was particularly timely because Miami planned a similar celebration for the middle of the following week.

"I'm very conscious of the difference between now and ten years ago when students thought they were pitted against the rest of the world, all alone on the other side of the generation gap," she began a speech of hope in the huge Miami Beach Convention Center. "You are inheriting a world in which, for many years, there has been much preaching of doom. But it's not like that anymore. Today, there's new hope in the world. Instead of talking about such crises as environmental deterioration, hunger, poverty, social injustice, and war, you young people are more likely to be thinking about solutions to these problems. And that's good news."

She stood in a cap and gown supplied by the university as she sipped from a glass of water and watched her words sink in. "Today we face a more promising future, one based on greater sharing among all people everywhere. Solar energy is on the side of every community, every nation, not just superpowers. We are beginning to develop the sun! That means we won't be living on the borrowed time of fossil fuels anymore."

She concluded her remarks with expressions of serious concern about a subject she had harped on for more than two decades: the need to stop the spread of nuclear weapons and the nuclear technology that can produce them. "I was chatting with a ten-year-old the other day," she said, challenging the class of 1978 to make thinking globally a habit, "when I asked him what he thought he'd be doing in the year 2000. He said he didn't expect to be alive anymore. Out of the mouths of babes. Think about it. Truly, none of us will be here in the year 2000 unless we take great precautions to halt nuclear proliferation now."

She was not feeling up to extra words, nor to taking more than half of her allotted twenty minutes. She got her message across without a witty one-liner. She asked to be taken back to her bungalow at the hotel as soon as possible after the ceremonies.

She was scheduled to leave Miami for New York City the next morning, Monday, May 8. Between these events, she managed to accommodate Professor Hazel Weidman, a social anthropologist who worked in the Department of Psychiatry at the university. Prior to Margaret's visiting Florida, Professor Weidman had written Margaret's office, requesting time to discuss strategies associated with a multiethnic mental health program. She also wanted to hear Margaret's views on the possible future of transcultural psychiatry as an academic discipline. The two women did not know each other well, but they shared similar professional interests. Margaret remembered complimenting the younger scientist when she read a report entitled "Family Patterns of Paranoidal Personality in Boston and Burma" at a conference. "You can find out more just listening to a person who reports on her research in a few minutes at a meeting than you can learn in hours of reading," she used to say.

As scheduled, Professor Weidman appeared at her cottage on Margaret's last evening there. The little trouper had fallen asleep after her return from the commencement exercises. Helen went upstairs to awaken her and remind her of the appointment. Margaret felt that she had to get up. She couldn't interview Professor Weidman in bed. She feared that her whole world would crumble and all her relationships would change were anybody to find out how sick she really was. Professor Weidman must not be allowed to suspect it.

So the proverbially hale and hearty Margaret Mead got up and dressed. She looked wan and weary, but she wouldn't let fatigue stop her. The show must go on. She put in an appearance downstairs.

She was a bit short-tempered during the visit, making no attempt to disguise her obvious discomfort. Nevertheless, she objectively discussed the problems involved in applying transcultural psychiatric principles to social services in a community as ethnically diverse as Miami with Professor Weidman as if they were at a transoceanic conference in the middle of nowhere.

10

SHE NEVER SAID GOOD-BYE

"Are you afraid of dying?" Helen Reurs asked Margaret flat out when they relaxed together in the privacy of their roomy first-class accommodations on their way back to New York the next morning, May 8.

"Of course not," Margaret snapped. "What on earth gave you that idea?"

"It's not my idea necessarily," Helen replied. "I just wanted to make sure."

"We bargain for death by being born," Margaret said matter-of-factly. "We never know exactly when either event's going to happen, and I've taken many notes on both in my lifetime."

She hailed a passing stewardess and asked for a glass of ice water. "You know," she whispered, "cancer's a crazy disease." Now that Helen knew what she had, Margaret could share confidences about it openly and honestly.

"You can survive it for years or succumb to it in hours. I deliberately operate on two levels these days. I keep working as though I'm going to live longer than I expect and, at the same time, I'm well aware that I could die on this flight— or tomorrow." The stewardess returned with the water. As she placed the glass on the tray, Margaret thanked her most graciously.

"I've told you about the wonderful aunt for whom I was named," Helen began. "Toward the end of her life, after a series of strokes, she came to live with us. She was really sick in 1972. During the next four years, until she died, I learned what was helpful and what was not. She didn't mind losing her intellectual skills. She let me know in her own way how she wanted to be treated—and trusted. No one imposed on anybody. No one dominated anybody. My kids came and went. They loved her as much as I did. It was a family scene. Absolute perfection. She taught me how to help someone die."

"My grandmother Martha died on a visit to the home of a favorite niece in Columbus," Margaret's voice took on a pensive quality. "I've been told that three generations of relatives drifted in and out of her room, holding her hand, stroking her forehead, feeding her, talking to her. My father came by train from Philadelphia during a heat wave around the Fourth of July. He fashioned a primitive air conditioner by having a fan blow across a tube of ice in her direction. Both of my parents died in a hospital, but they were taken there when they were too far gone to fight it. I want to die like my grandmother, in the home of someone who loves me. A hospital is the last place I'd want to die. They sanitize death too much."

"If you're being well taken care of." Helen hesitated to venture into so personal an area but her vibes said go for it. "Ordinarily I would not feel that I had a right to ask, but, unless I do, I won't know if there's something you might need. Is Rhoda being good with you?"

Margaret's eyes flashed. "She's doing everything absolutely wrong. She's even told me I'm already dead! And I've told her, 'If I am, I am, but I'm not going to predead myself.'

"Rhoda's living in a dream world," Margaret continued, "and she knows that my death will bring her dream world to an end. She's trying desperately to get and hold on to everything she can. She wants me to die in a hospital because that's where she could maintain control. She's jealous of every outside friendship I have. Anybody around me she can't manage, she hates. She wants to control every avenue to me, you see."

Margaret directed a hurt-dog look at Helen. "In fact, she hates you more than anybody."

"Me?" Helen gasped in amazement. "I've never done anything to her."

"Yes, you." Margaret turned and looked directly at Helen as she spoke. "The friendship you and I have has always threatened her. Now, more than ever. You're a free agent so she has no way of controlling information input from you or of monitoring what happens between us."

Helen nodded her head in disbelief.

"I tell you, it's hell. I'm going to move out and live with Elizabeth as soon as we can find a place," Margaret confided. "Rhoda doesn't know anything about this yet. In the meantime, I've only got four good hours a day to work without pain or exhaustion. I must organize my time tightly so that I'm able to meet my responsibilities. There are so many distractions at the office that I prefer to stay in the apartment and conduct my business from the phone. Anytime you want to get through to me, call me at exactly noon and I'll know it's you!"

"Okay." Helen agreed to the noontime talks.

"I've always admired your ability to discipline your life as diligently as you do," Helen said. "Here you are in the very process of dying, and you discipline your life as much as ever. When you continue to do that as sick as you are, I think of our young people. I wish more of them were half as responsible or disciplined."

Margaret curled her fingers around the glass on her tray. "There have been some interesting Danish experiments on how to motivate wayward boys to accept discipline. Out in Arizona, they're teaching kids responsibility by getting them to train dogs. A remarkable idea.

"I learned the habit of discipline as a child. My parents and grandmother scheduled lesson time and play time every day. When I look back on it, that was the most peacefully ordered time of my life. I've never been able to reproduce anything quite like it, but I try. Remember our trip to the Pacific on the Norwegian line four years ago? I've always liked shipboard life because it is so disciplined. None of the distractions that bombard me in New York. I should cut down on them, but I'm not so sure I can afford it. If we're running out of money, I can't quit. We need the income."

The plane gained altitude.

Margaret put her elbow on the armrest and her head in her hand. She closed her eyes. She began to retch. Helen shifted uneasily from the role of friend to parent.

"It felt a little strange on my part at first," she recalled later. "The only way I could do it was to think of Margaret as one of my kids. I don't know much about how to handle pain. I held her hand to reassure her. She seemed to like it, too."

At 11:28, they landed at LaGuardia Airport, where faithful Mary Elder waited to take an unwilling Dr. Mead back to the Beresford.

In her slowdown second week in May, Margaret visited her healer every day; she also visited an endodontist and an eye doctor in their offices. She phoned a local medical man, who was also a longtime personal friend, to demand relief from pain. She read through her final examination papers and turned in her grades. She attended one anthropological research foundation meeting and a reception honoring Ambassador Andrew Young at the United Nations.

On Mothers' Day, Sunday, May 14, a very subdued Margaret Mead gave a speech billed as "Parenthood." She spoke of family, of love, of parenting, and of death. She read some letters dated March 25, 1947, that husbands, fathers, and sons trapped in a coal mine in Centralia, Illinois, wrote to their relatives while they waited for a rescue that came too late. For the first time in the memory of many a museum auditorium regular, her words and herself drew tears.

At 6:00 the next morning, Mary Elder stopped at the Beresford for Margaret and then went on to pick up Barbara Sperling, a former assistant, who was to accompany her on a two-day committee meeting and lecture trip to Washington, D.C. On arrival, Margaret took a taxi to the Carnegie Endowment for International Peace, where she attended the first of two full-day meetings of the New Directions governing board.

After these discussions on the first day, she entertained a full house of local Barnard alumnae on the question, "Where is the horizon?" After the meetings on Tuesday, May 16, she addressed the Anthropology Club of Washington on "The Viability of the Village as a Continuing Form of Human Settlement."

People tend to send others reinforcing letters when they recognize inroads of illness. More of these filtered into Margaret's mail after her appearances. "The evening was a tribute to you in several ways," one of the members of the Anthropology Club wrote her afterward. "Quite a few of us brought our sons and daughters to hear you. While groups of students and their instructors from the various universities around also came. We should have had an auditorium three times as large." Letters like this one egged her on.

She was back in New York City Wednesday morning at 9:00. Mary Elder took her to the healer immediately and then to the Beresford for a short rest. Three and a half hours later, her day continued on a second itinerary. Mary Elder sandwiched in another interview with her adviser as she raced to the airport for Margaret's flight to Mankato, Minnesota, via Minneapolis.

At 8:00 p.m., May 17, Margaret delivered her third formal lecture of the week, this one simply called "Aging." She walked on to the stage of Mankato State University's Centennial Ballroom carrying a "branch of a tree with a forked end that looked like a dousing rod." She reportedly felt rotten. From May on, transcontinental airplane trips had taken a terrible toll. Deeply appreciative of her traveling so far to be with them, the members of the audience who packed the place applauded her before she opened her mouth.

"Aging," she announced, "is a new problem in the United States. When I was a child, I never saw helpless old people. They were all hale and hearty, riding bicycles at eighty-five and tatting without spectacles. With longer lives made possible with drugs and pacemakers, and earlier retirements, older Americans must find a way to make the last twenty years of their lives bearable. If they do not have gainful employment, too many people have nothing to live for. What can you give a retired U.S. Navy admiral as a substitute for a fleet?" she asked.

"The British have the right idea in their gardening." She thought of her friend anthropologist Geoffrey Gorer who won prizes for his rhododendrons. "When they retire, they just garden more.

"It's best that young people make good choices now about what they are going to do when they are old. One solution is to have definite patterns that need be continued after their work is taken away. More women live longer than men because their patterns of cooking, cleaning, and shopping give their lives purpose.

"American communities with suburbs that segregate old from young and rich from poor are not designed to help senior citizens become involved in anything in their last twenty years.

"American homes, no matter how expensive, are not built to accommodate an extra and older person. In the past, there always was room in front of the fireplace for grandmother to sit darning socks. Americans will not go back to the three-generational household like the one I was raised in, but they are beginning to realize the value of having grandparents near enough to be able to walk over and play with the children or let the plumber in while they're at work.

"By the time you reach my age," she spoke with a certainty that reflected the role her paternal grandmother played in her own early development, "you've seen it all and the best thing left for you to do is to provide a sense of proportion to your grandchildren."

She remained on stage afterward and responded to questions with lengthy and thoughtful answers. The general consensus was that her talk "couldn't have been better."

Thursday morning, she focused on the other end of the age continuum when she met with the students and faculty of a child development seminar. The class adjourned at noon. Immediately after a meal and minimal socializing, she flew to Minneapolis to make connections for a late afternoon flight to Michigan. A friend met her at the Detroit airport and took her to her room at the St. Regis Hotel in time to go to bed.

The planned activities of a spring conference on the future of the family at the Merrill Palmer Institute, where she once tried to find me a job, were to occupy her next two days. Early in the afternoon on Friday, May 19, she led a discussion on the ways in which a city supports the functioning of its families. A reception in her honor followed at the Ford Estate in Gross Points Shores, after which she was taken to the Wylie Groves Senior High School in the suburb of Birmingham. Here she introduced like-minded and long-admired Robert Coles of Harvard for a speech somebody else was to give for a change. Through Saturday, she alternated appointments with periods of rest until evening, when she gave the keynote lecture named for the conference. A friend took her to the airport Sunday morning, where a wheelchair relieved her of walking to the plane. Mary Elder waited at the New York City end of the line and transported her directly to the Beresford.

True to form, Margaret stuffed the third week of the fifth month of 1978 very full. After recovering from jet lag and general weariness, she visited her healer daily and saw two different physicians, neither of whom was able to palliate her pain.

An ominous sense of impending death seemed to pervade the air when she sat behind her cluttered desk in her office in the tower of the American Museum of Natural History these last days of May. The members of her staff felt a difference. They tried to underplay their puzzlement, but Margaret neither flinched nor missed a trick. She called them together and talked to them squarely. Yes, she did indeed have an undetermined illness for which she refused exploratory surgery or any medications that might alleviate pain at the expense of clear thinking. She intended to continue with business as usual. She preferred not to discuss the matter any further and she expected them to do likewise.

She shuttled to Washington, D.C., early Thursday morning, May 25, to attend a National Town Meeting at George Washington University. Here she made an opening statement, "Public Policy and American Families," and then joined in fifty-five minutes of dialogue with the audience and a moderator.

After a lunch of plain yogurt and canned peaches, she returned to New York, where Mary Elder met her and gave her a ride home. Four hours later, the two arrived at Carmen de Barraza's for a 7:00 p.m. appointment. Following this, Mary made a second trip to the airport with Margaret in time for a 9:30 p.m. flight to Boston on the Eastern Airlines shuttle. Mary's passenger brought her academic robes along as well as a present for her sister Elizabeth from Marie Eichelberger.

She stayed overnight with Elizabeth. In the morning, Wheaton College anthropology professor Ina Dinerman drove down from Norton to Cambridge with two of her students to escort Margaret to their College for its 143rd commencement. Because of tight parking near Elizabeth's building, Professor Dinerman kept the car running while one of the students ran up the stairs to summon their commencement speaker. She was greeted by a wan Margaret wearing a gray-colored dress. As they left her sister's apartment, she picked up her black purse and the package containing her academic robes.

Realizing that this was a ride her students would remember the rest of their lives, Professor Dinerman elected to let them carry the conversation while she focused on that foggy morning's freeway traffic. Margaret's mood reflected the weather; she was not as vivacious as the students expected her to be, nor did she seem to be overly impressed by either one of them. Nevertheless, she leaned against the front door so that she might face the driver as well as the young woman in the backseat. While she obligingly autographed their copies of *Blackberry Winter,* she learned that the younger of the two aimed to go on for graduate work and the older, a single mother of three, presided over the Wheaton College Anthropology Club.

She recalled the early 1920s, when most anthropologists were as close knit as such a club. Everyone knew everybody else. There was give-and-take. They helped each other. When one of them went into the field, the rest kept contact with the family that was left behind. They exchanged letters. Ruth Benedict, her professor turned personal friend, for example, corresponded with Margaret's parents while she was away for the first time. When a hurricane hit Samoa during her stay there, Margaret cabled Franz Boas the one word "well." He telephoned Benedict, who telegraphed Margaret's parents. These days, fifty years later, expansion of numbers within the profession had narrowed the range of mutual support. There were simply too many anthropologists for many of them to get to know each other very well, let alone their families. "And that," she declared, "is a lamentable loss."

When they reached their destination, Professor Dinerman parked and locked the car. Margaret inadvertently left her purse, which in her illness amounted to a first aid kit, in the car. This temporary inconvenience put another pressure on her before she got up to inspire the young women who witnessed her receiving her last honorary degree on the morning of their graduation.

She had been asked to talk about what educated women might look forward to in the next twenty-five years. She began her speech with a backward survey. She traced the history of humankind from the discovery of fire, agriculture, and husbandry to the beginnings of civilization when some men were finally freed to become educated and follow other than pure subsistence pursuits. Until modern medicine saved greater percentages of all babies born, however, no woman other than an occasional queen escaped a consuming preoccupation with childbearing.

During these eons, whatever men did was always considered achievement, whereas women's activities were casually brushed off as just "something women did." Mothers and grandmothers in her audience smiled at their peer's succinct audacity. "We are now entering a world in which it will not be necessary for anybody to spend their entire lifetime being a parent," she startled her total audience into taking special notice of a development she described as going on under their noses.

"For the first time in human history, humanity may be splitting occupation from gender. The definition of being human will still include whether one is a male or a female, but what one *does* for a living will not be a part of that definition. We have been wasting enormous talents right through history by limiting any activity to gender and we are now trying not to do it."

Her words would have pleasured the educated mother and grandmother responsible for imprinting Margaret Mead herself in her earliest years. "This is going to be a tremendous enterprise in which we are going to be able to say to children, a boy or a girl, 'Try anything. You want to be an engineer, you want to be an astronaut, you want to be a dressmaker, you want to take care of children? Okay. Try it and see what you can make of it.'" Proud fathers and grandfathers mentally applied her positive remarks to the possible futures of the bright young graduates who filled the reserved seats in front of the stage.

"For the first time in history we are going to be asking for equal shares between men and women in the productive world and in the home, because you can't ask women to spend a lot of time outside the home unless you ask men to spend a lot of time inside the home." She licked her lips and looked warily up at an overcast sky. "So men for the first time since very primitive days are going to be taking care of small children, and children are going to be reared by both sexes. We are going to be able to open to children every possible use of their gifts, regardless of which parent they got them from or whether the society has called it 'male' or 'female.'"

In direct contradiction to a Wheaton College tradition that it never rains on commencement, Margaret felt sprinkles on her hands and squinted through some that splattered on her spectacles. Clearly, this was no time to be wordy. She frowned slightly at her last batch of graduates as her voice assumed the somber tones of prophecy and challenge.

"We are going to have a lot of difficulty because all of us have been brought up with a lot of prejudices as to what makes me a woman and someone else a man. They are all here and we are going to get over them, but it's going to be exceedingly interesting and exceedingly exciting and you are the generation that is going to make a breakthrough. So I commend it to you."

Her view of the next twenty-five years stirred several generations of present-day New Englanders. "In twenty minutes," one of the faculty congratulated her as the academic procession disbanded later, "you summed up what I've been trying to teach for the last twenty years."

Within an hour, Margaret was back in Elizabeth's apartment. Her younger sister may have had other plans for that last weekend in May, but she ditched them when she learned Margaret was scheduled to come up to the Boston area for the Wheaton ceremonies. For over fifty years, Margaret Mead invited herself to the homes of relatives and friends, whatever their prior plans. As she felt increasingly uncomfortable toward the end of her life, her disposition became more noticeably impatient and irascible, sometimes straining the best intentions of willing hosts.

From May on, Margaret flew first class whenever possible. At least one companion came along to help her with the unforeseen and often shattering difficulties of traveling alone when ill. Carol Zwack, her appointment secretary, forwarded detailed dietary restrictions to conference or college hosts. As far as humanly possible, Zwack also made sure that a wheelchair was waiting for Dr. Mead's arrivals and departures at airports. Margaret began to spend more time in her hotel rooms than out of them. She turned in fewer claims for meals on her expense account.

In her lectures during this month, her mind spurted out ideas at a steady pace in a voice that sounded as strident and strong as ever. Between her mind and her voice, she held the attention of audiences on subjects as varied as human aging and the viability of villages. Stoutly tenacious for life, indomitable and dogged, she fought to stand off an ailment that she saw no reason to broadcast by name.

Her struggle would grind on for five more months.

In June, she slowed down to a pace that even her livelier student helpers could keep up with. For the first few days, except for daily visits to Carmen, she stayed home. She sent Rhoda off on errands whenever she conducted her most pressing interviews or meetings in the living room of their apartment or by phone.

She was due to fly to California for a week. Frankly, she didn't feel at all up to a transcontinental flight. Just as frankly, she considered it counterproductive not to go. She had committed herself to give a very important speech in Berkeley; another, in Los Angeles. She looked forward to the pleasant prospect of a relaxing visit with confidants Barbara and Frederick Roll, who would in turn facilitate a second chance to call on Gregory and Lois Bateson. In preparation for seeing Gregory, whose cancer seemed to be in remission, she instructed her office to send him a copy of her friend George Land's book *Grow or Die*.

At 7:10 on Thursday morning, June 8, with Carol Zwack already in her car, Mary Elder stopped in front of the Beresford, where Margaret Mead stood waiting. En route to Kennedy Airport, Carol briefed her boss on last-minute details of the trip. She handed Dr. Mead a scheduling folder for each of her two speeches as well as a third for spare-time work on New Directions, a citizen lobby concerned with global responsibilities and relationships. At the American Airlines terminal, they met Helen and John Reurs, traveling companions who would accompany her to the San Francisco Bay area.

Margaret suffered throughout the flight. Neither of the Reurs knew quite how to handle pain. There were moments when Margaret thought she was finished. "There's my black book and my thumbstick," she moaned.

"I think this is the same thing that happened on the Miami flights and they turned out okay," Helen reassured her. "Your body's just trying to adjust to the shifts in air pressure."

Margaret asked for ice water. Helen suggested that the ice could be upsetting her stomach. Maybe her water should be at cabin temperature. "You're not going to take my ice away from me," Margaret growled.

She could fight for ice water but she was too weak to get off the plane when it landed. An airline attendant brought a wheelchair to seat 3H after the rest of the passengers disembarked. Helen walked beside the wheelchair through the airport. She looked down at her brave little comrade. Margaret looked up at her. "I never thought I'd get off that plane alive," Margaret whispered.

Two of Helen's daughters waited to take them to the Claremont Hotel in Berkeley. Margaret assured the Reurs that she would be perfectly able to give the speech scheduled for that evening once she got some food inside of her and took a nap. She had packed a protein drink. The Reurs foraged for yogurt. "I've got an afternoon ahead of me," Margaret said between sips. "You watch. I'll bounce back. I'll be my old self again. I'll be able to give that speech."

A student named Lisa Stephens, at once Margaret's goddaughter and her brother Richard's step-granddaughter, joined them after Margaret's nap and accompanied the group to the Wheeler Auditorium at the University of Berkeley campus. Margaret came to deliver the first of a series of lectures to mark the fiftieth anniversary of the Institute of Human Development. Her speech "Child Development and Public Policy" memorialized old friend Lawrence K. Frank, who figured prominently in the inauguration of the whole field of child development. Margaret slurred words as she rambled through her speech. There followed a token appearance at a reception in her honor. To the famous, compliments come easily. This time at least, Margaret Mead needed to believe hers. Convinced that she'd carried off a brilliant performance, she caught Helen's eye as they left the reception for the Claremont. "Didn't I tell you?" she beamed.

Lisa Stephens lingered to visit with her briefly. Time was precious to both women. Lisa held down two jobs while enrolled in summer school, and Margaret's schedule was the best example of perpetual motion that existed in her lifetime. While they were together, however, they called Lisa's mother, Janet, in Los Angeles.

"Are you willing to work?" Margaret asked.

Ordinarily, when in Los Angeles, Margaret stayed with her brother Richard's widow and Janet's mother, Jessie. Considering Jessie's very recent hospitalization for osteoporosis of the hip, along with her own sometime dependence on wheelchair locomotion, Margaret chose instead to accept the suite in the Beverly Hilton supplied her by the Somatic Conference.

Midlife housewife Janet Stephens's everyday routine revolved around running an unofficial animal shelter. Wheeling her great-aunt to speeches and cocktail parties, locating phones and toilets, keeping articles of clothing within her reach and autograph hunters at bay presented a welcome change of pace. Janet served as Margaret's personal girl Friday on previous visits to Southern California. She told me that she considered her kinship with her great-aunt "special and closer than blood." "Yes, I'm willing to work." Janet agreed to help Margaret during parts of the four days of her Los Angeles stay.

Janet later recalled the events of those four days for me. Margaret announced that she would be landing at 10:15 the next morning, Friday, June 9, and that she planned to take a limousine directly to the hotel. She wanted Janet to be waiting for her in the lobby. After the fright Margaret experienced on her flight to California, only something like the assurance of Janet's gentle companionship enabled her to face another trip alone. She was coming to an international congress, The Explorers of Mankind, which I had read about on my Holistic Healing cruise in March.

Outside of a one-hour reception with her fellow speakers and staff Friday evening and a dinner together Saturday, Margaret was to be free until 5:00 Sunday afternoon. Conference planners placed her talk and subsequent question-and-answer period last on their program to guarantee that a greater percentage of the two thousand ticket holders would stay to the end of the conference. Such an arrangement suited Margaret most conveniently. Her body required every minute of that time to garner strength for her appearance.

Janet knew better. She had pitched in when her stepfather, Margaret's younger brother Richard Mead, was dying of cancer of the pancreas. "She's got the same thing as Richard, only worse," Janet told herself. Nonverbally, she communicated her disbelief of the diverticulitis story to her stepaunt, but neither woman chose to put the truth into words. Instead, they talked about Richard, Margaret asking numerous questions, Janet answering them.

In mid-November, three years earlier, when Margaret attended the International Convention of Women in Grahamstown, South Africa, her brother had an operation on his pancreas. He died within the week. Margaret didn't want to be operated on, nor would she choose to die in a hospital.

Were she to die (but she had too much to do to die soon), she preferred that it be in somebody's home. She wanted to be surrounded by family (adopted or otherwise), of preferably three generations, exactly as was the case in the home of her childhood. She fantasized members of a family tiptoeing in and out of her sunny downstairs bedroom, meeting each other's grown children as they came to pay her their respects, having tea, saying goodnight, and promising to come back tomorrow.

In fact, the kind of death she planned would have been hers had she stayed married to the Lutheran who became an Episcopalian minister at her suggestion. She would have served out her years in the anonymity of Crossroads, America, in a rectory filled with their six children, the mates, and the grands. But she ultimately chose to marry humanity and now coveted a niece's devoted care in a spacious hotel suite on Wilshire Boulevard.

So fragile was Margaret after her flight that Janet literally peeled her patient off the floor whenever she impatiently attempted to do so simple a thing as solo to the bathroom. Margaret was restless between naps, and Janet suggested that using the bedside telephone to visit with various friends in town might help Margaret put pain out of her mind. "No," Margaret negated Janet's idea. "I don't want them to find out how sick I am."

Janet and her aunt attended the reception when the speakers met informally Friday evening before the conference opened Saturday morning. Were she more holistically healed herself, the presence of these particular holistic healing leaders might have kept Margaret talking into the night. She had been seeking out men and women in this field for some time. Friends who were sympathetic to her interest supplied her with clippings and reports. She ran into flak in her inner circle, however, because so many of her oldest faithfuls pooh-poohed the movement as charlatan.

The Somatic Conference brought together such recognized pioneers as Moshé Feldenkreis, who developed the field of awareness through movement and from whom she'd taken instruction in San Francisco and New York. Also attending were contemporary Ida Rolf, who trained practitioners to align the human body with gravity, and biofeedback expert Barbara Brown. Karl Pribram's holographic theory of mind intrigued her, as did Alexander Lowen's ideas on energy fields, Carl Rogers's innovative encounter groups, and Hans Selye's studies of the effect of stress on disease.

Fellow anthropologist Ashley Montagu, who early identified the female as the stronger of the sexes, may have considered Margaret Mead one of the strongest of this country's females. He knew her well enough to comment on her very obvious weight loss.

"I have anorexia nervosa," she responded with a finality that cut off further discussion. "It has taken this affliction to show me how absolutely biased people in this culture are toward anyone who loses weight." Her eyes met Janet's. They pleaded for rescue.

"It's time for us to go." Janet rallied to the cause by excusing themselves shortly after their entrance. "Dr. Mead has had a very long day."

"I love you. Don't leave me. Stay with me," Margaret repeated as they returned to their quarters. "I have very bad nights." Their suite included a living room and two bedrooms. At Margaret's urging, Janet's room went unused.

"It wasn't like her to be afraid to be left alone. I sat beside her and held her hand all through the night," Janet reported to me later. "She wasn't asking for anything more than Tylenol and codeine for her pain. I said, 'Anybody can take them. They're not strong enough.' I wanted to get something stronger, but she said, 'These are all right.'

"We talked about a lot of things as she dozed off and woke up. She asked me about my smoking. 'I'd like to quit but I can't,' I told her.

"We had unlimited room service, but I didn't dare order even one drink for fear that it might put me to sleep. I told her about my cats and dogs."

Janet brushed back a wisp of straight blond hair with strong hands that had done a lot of outside work in their day. Then she spoke openly with me about Margaret. "Margaret loved animals. Her folks kept cats and dogs, chickens and horses when she and Richard were growing up. She thought that animals had as much right to this earth as we do. Not many people knew that she went to Save the Whales meetings every year.

"I brought along some snapshots I'd taken when Mayor Bradley came over to my mother's house to meet her during one of her last visits. They showed the mayor and Margaret standing side by side in Richard's yard. He, so tall and all in dark blue; she, so short and dressed in a bright red slack suit. She wore a fluffy white scarf with blue polka dots around her neck.

"Margaret held the pictures in her hands. She remembered that she and Mayor Bradley talked about the possibility of converting automobile factories into industrial plants for manufacturing products to help clean up the environment.

"I remember the advice she gave him, too. 'Don't ever waste any words saying you're the only black candidate in a campaign,' she said. 'That's unnecessary. Push issues instead. If you have to say something personal, identify as the tallest candidate who's running for this or that office.'

"She wouldn't be able to see him on this trip, but she did ask that I phone Father John Yamazaki. He's the pastor of St. Mary's Episcopal Church. She wanted to give him and his wife her complimentary tickets. Richard belonged to Father John's congregation and sang in the choir regularly. When she came here to visit, she always went to church with Richard. Margaret and Father John took to each other right away. She even delivered some sermons in St. Mary's.

"She mentioned wanting to go to Russia in July to gather material for a book on aging. She said some of the oldest people in the world lived over there. I take personal responsibility for talking her out of that one."

Janet lit a cigarette and looked over at me in her kitchen when I asked her about this stopover. "I told her to skip the whole idea and stay home and get herself well. 'Russia will do you no good,' I said. 'You could die over there. Just skip it.'"

As the hours of the night wore on, Margaret revealed something of her problems with Rhoda. The apartment was in Rhoda's name and Margaret's rent paid the mortgage installments. By mutual consent, Rhoda ran the place for years. This year, as Margaret lost strength, Rhoda gained it. She attempted to stretch her authority.

"She wants me to submit to her total control," Margaret confided. "She wants me to get into bed and let her do what she thinks should be done for me. I consider that absolutely wrong in every way. I've discussed the situation with Elizabeth. As soon as I can find an apartment to share with her, I'm moving out. I've got to. The stress is simply too much."

"There's nobody like Elizabeth," Janet answered, "and none of us have ever completely accepted Rhoda. We think she's too self-centered. But Elizabeth's something else. We're all crazy about her. She flew out here to be with us when Richard died, you know. You were off in Africa somewhere, and she helped us make the arrangements."

When daylight peeked through the drapes, Margaret informed Janet that she could go home and catch up on her sleep as soon as Hilda Brown, a healer recommended by Carmen, showed up. "Margaret knew her brother worked with a healer too," Janet told me later. "I didn't put much stock in the idea at the time, but, if a healer was what he wanted, a healer was what he got. I remember his healer was a man who sometimes played bit parts in the movies."

Healer Hilda Brown arrived. She was very attractive, dark haired, and a little taller than Janet's five feet four inches. Hilda freed Janet to go home and rest, shower, and change clothes.

Margaret and Hilda worked together uninterrupted until Janet returned late in the afternoon. Hilda embraced her at the door. "It was amazing," Janet recalled. "There was something so strong about her. When I came back still bushed from my first night's duty and the prospect of two more like it ahead, she hugged me. I don't believe in these things, but I got such a surge of energy I've never forgotten it. I just loved it. She gave me the strength to go on. Were I ever to get sick now, I'd call for Hilda before I'd call for a doctor."

Soon after Hilda left, Margaret and Janet took the elevator down to the lobby on the way to a scheduled dinner with the other conference speakers. It was the first time any of the conferees had been able to get a glimpse of her. "You wouldn't believe the numbers of people who literally worshiped her," Janet exclaimed. "I remember one young woman in a sari who bowed down in front of her as though she were a goddess and said a prayer of blessing. Margaret loved it. People followed us around like disciples. Women need models today and Aunt Margaret was one.

"I couldn't believe the number of autograph hunters I had to turn away at our door, either. I'd just say, 'Leave your book. We'll send it back to you.' She was in no shape to sign anything.

"Her ears were pierced and when she dressed Sunday morning, the day she was to give her speech, she couldn't get her earrings in. She asked me to try, but I couldn't get them in either, so I just placed them on the dresser and said, 'Why bother?'

" 'I bother because they're pretty,' she said, but she had to give up on them too, pretty or not."

The conference provided them with a golf cart to get to the Convention Center. Father Yamazaki, the son of a nisei displaced during World War II, caught up with her in a crowded passageway moments before Janet and Margaret reached the stage. A glance told Father John that this was perhaps their last meeting. He leaned down to embrace her. Their eyes filled with tears.

Janet stood in the back of the Los Angeles Convention Center with a glass of her aunt's coveted ice water in hand while Margaret made a short speech, "The Transforming Power of Culture." She described a New Guinea tribal people who jumped from the Stone Age to modern times in two generations. "Not because their genes changed, but simply because they had put at their disposal the accumulated wisdom and skills inherited from contemporary civilization."

When she made her field trip to study the mountain Arapesh, "they couldn't count beyond twenty and their heads ached when they tried to think logically for more than five minutes. Today their children's children have graduated from universities. The group as a whole belongs to one of the newest members of the United Nations. And their genes are just the same as they were twenty thousand years ago.

"A human being is a mosaic of genetic materials that represent the whole history not merely of human evolution but of the evolution of life itself. As human cultures have developed, they have ignored some capacities, overdone or cultivated others. Take psychic gifts." With these words, the Somatic Conference became the time and Los Angeles the place in which a former president of the Association for the Advancement of Science elected to acknowledge an unabashed interest in parapsychology as well as her support of its scientific investigators and everyday practitioners.

"When I went away to college," she disclosed, "I discovered that organized established science objected to the exploration of psychic abilities. Our culture suppresses them. It's just the opposite in Bali. The Balinese indulge every form of psychic activity: trance, prophecy, finding lost objects, identifying thieves, the whole range from trivial to important; but I've never found more cases of what I'd call real 'sensitives' anywhere."

The great-granddaughter of Priscilla Reese Ramsay (1812–1890), an acknowledged psychic, reached for her ice water. "In our own Appalachia, for example, children who have special gifts are taught, 'You don't have to tell everybody everything you know.' Which is a great protection because there's nothing more of a nuisance than a psychic child."

She didn't tell her audience that she identified with Priscilla Reese Ramsay as a psychic child so much that she went through a stage of signing her name Margaret Reese Mead. That would be too nostalgic. She needed a broader remark for a closing statement.

"Our task now is to look at all these [capabilities] like psychic gifts that we find distributed over the Earth, and which we may be able to actualize by our new inventions in all these sorts of ways that were unguessed at before. We may be able to keep individuals alive who, because they are so special and so fragile, have never been able to stay alive before. And this is one of the things I think is happening all over the world today with a bubbling up of interest everywhere in all the extraordinary and special gifts we find in some human beings."

"Are you a religious person?" somebody queried in the biographical question-and-answer period that followed her remarks.

"I think that's a very rude question to ask," she snapped. "It's like asking me if I'm good. What do you expect me to say?"

Even though she spoke sitting down, she bounced back answers to their questions as though they were boomerangs. The audience relished her spirit and her sass, her enthusiasm, her knowledge, her "go." This was the Margaret Mead they paid fifty dollars a ticket to hear.

"Are you a little astonished to find yourself the best-known woman in America?"

She grimaced. "I don't think I am the best-known woman in America, but I can tell you this: I have great faith in what the science of anthropology and its related explorations of the human psyche can do. They're tremendously important. They're not attributes of me; they're attributes of what an understanding of anthropology can bring to the world."

Her fatigue surfaced when she frowned, firmed her lips, and grimly muttered, "How many more of these nuggets have you collected for me?" They laughed and let her go.

In the morning, Margaret found a note from a member of that audience under her door. "Thank you for your remarks on the apprentice and the healer," it read. "I had a dream of healing for you. It was extensive and complete. The healing is there for you to reach out and accept."

She carried it in her purse when a conference staffer called to take her to the United Airlines terminal for the second-to-last leg of her journey, a short hop to spend a couple of days with physical anthropologist Barbara Roll and her husband. Janet went along to help her on the plane.

In their last few minutes together as they sat in the waiting room before passengers for flight 664 from Los Angeles to Monterey were allowed to board, Margaret assumed the role of beneficent godmother to Janet's daughter. "Find out what Lisa earns from both of those jobs she's got," Margaret said. "Tell her I'll match it each month. Summer school's too short. She'll get better grades and learn more if she can spend the time she would be working on those two jobs on her studies instead."

An hour later, Barbara and Fred Roll met their frazzled little friend and took her home to Carmel for a sampling of their "top of the line" hospitality. "Oh God, what relief it always is to come here," Margaret stalked into the Rolls' guest cottage. She always found privacy here, along with the silent companionship of a fireplace and a well-stocked refrigerator. This was the place in which she used to stay just before or after her sojourns at our house when I lived in California.

They'd met nearly thirty years ago when Barbara researched children's body types at the Gessel-Ilg Institute of Child Development at Yale. Twice they had traveled to New Guinea together. Between their trips, Barbara hosted (in 1969) the first visit of a Manus tribesman to the United States. Fred accompanied his wife on their most recent trip in 1975 in the capacity of photographer. The three of them planned to talk over another trip to New Guinea later in the year.

The Rolls, who dined with Margaret on St. Patrick's Day in New York City the day after her return from Mexico, could not help but be concerned about the speed of her decline from endo- to ectomorphism. She carried fifty-five pounds less weight than formerly. Their robust fieldworker friend with the cast iron stomach, who prided herself on eating anything the natives ate, could keep down nothing stronger than Pablum and pap, or similarly vapid substitutes. So honored guest and suffering husband, who was recovering from ongoing postperiodontal surgeries, challenged Barbara's anthropological ingenuity as a flavorful creationist in the kitchen.

On the only full day of Margaret's stopover, she and the Rolls drove fifty miles up the coast to Ben Lomond to spend part of it with Gregory and Lois Bateson. Theirs was a happy visit. Optimism ran high. Gregory's lung cancer had gone into remission. The news supported Margaret's conviction that cancer can be turned around. As was the case with her niece the week before, she didn't have to say anything about her disease.

Prior to her arrival, she had sent Gregory *Awareness through Movement* by Moshé Feldenkreis and George Land's *Grow or Die*. She reported having seen Feldenkreis in Los Angeles. She had taken treatments and Gregory had taken classes from him the previous summer. Both of them, as academics, acknowledged the worth of his ideas and, like their originator, were not overly inclined to exercise on a regular basis.

The message of George Land's book is the title. Margaret grew as she endlessly sought out new experiences, ideas, contacts, connections, and projects. Gregory paced his growth rhythms differently. He was the only one of her husbands too smart to put up with completing the maze leading to a doctorate. Increasingly respected for his synthesizing ideas, he did return to writing *Mind and Nature: A Necessary Unit* as soon as he came out of intensive care. At the end of the month, their daughter, Cathy, was due back for the summer. She planned to visit her mother in New York City for a handful of days and then fly on to California to help her father bring his book closer to publication.

Lois, who probably enjoyed Margaret's company more than any other of Margaret's ex-spouses' mates, invited her to come back anytime and stay with them as long as she chose. "You are such a nice lady," Lois explained when she followed up her verbal invitation with a letter.

Until this visit, the Rolls thought Margaret had diverticulitis. Sometime before the drive back to Carmel on the last night of her visit, she revealed the exact diagnosis: cancer of the pancreas. Their diminutive visitor, who spent much of her life trying to save the world as she saw it, now reached out to friends like the Rolls to help her save herself.

"It's impossible for you to lose a millimeter to whatever illness you have as long as your faculties are in such tip-top form," thought the otherwise distressed Rolls as they rallied to her rescue.

From the morning after she left on June 14 to brave a cross-country plane trip from San Francisco to New York, the Rolls reported results of their search for possible cures to Margaret by telephone and letter. She agreed to return after an engagement in Portland late in August and stay long enough for the three of them to experiment with what they referred to as "ploys for edible nutrition."

Despite jet lag on the first day back, Margaret met with former student Ken Hyman and longtime professional friend Sula Benet to break the news that she would not be able to accompany them to Russia from July 10 to July 30. She drafted a letter for Sula to present to the official of the Academy of Sciences who had set up the itineraries for their party to visit Abkhasian centenarians in order to gather material for a proposed book on aging. "I have been quite ill for the last six months," she wrote, "but I kept hoping that I would be well enough to make the trip, and I hope that I will be able to come sometime in the future."

She regretted having to give up Russia. She weighed the physical problems encountered on her last half dozen domestic flights and the possible consequences of a much more strenuous overseas trip against the good sense of niece Janet Stephens's advice, "Stay home and get yourself well. Russia will do you no good."

Ordinarily, Janet's saying the trip would do her no good would not have swayed do-gooder Emily Fogg Mead's oldest daughter. But the mental Margaret didn't make this decision: it was her body that balked. There's not too much a seasoned globetrotter can do when every nerve ending telegraphs, "Not this time."

There was a two-day jaunt to the nation's capital that she declined to cancel because the American Association of University Women planned to give her an award. Late Sunday afternoon, June 18, Mary Elder called for Margaret and Rhoda to take them to the Eastern Airlines shuttle terminal at LaGuardia Airport. The travelers, reminiscent of Tweedledum and Tweedledee in look-alike shoes, glasses, capes, and hairdos, checked into Washington's Watergate around 10:00 p.m. Once Margaret stayed at a hotel, she always tried to snare the same room. It was one way to establish a home base abroad.

For someone who could only count on four work hours at a time, Monday, June 19, turned out to be a stop-and-go, up-and-down, push, push, push day. She breakfasted with representatives from Dalton's bookstores about *Letters from the Field* at the hotel early Monday morning. Shortly after lunch, a reporter from WJLA-NEWS conducted a radio interview in her room. They talked about the ERA and reasons for society's sexual rules.

"Your thoughts and comments on the ERA were excellent and I am now more than ever supportive of it," wrote a local dentist fan. "I disagreed, however, when you said that, 'You can't run an army when the general is in love with the sergeant.' A remark like that rankles me because it does no good at all for the gay rights' cause."

Midafternoon she answered questions put to her by the press in the Williamsburg Room at the Watergate and then grabbed another nap before leaving at 6:00 for the AAUW Educational Center. Here, presidents from the fifty state chapters, members of the association's board of directors, as well as invited guests from government, Congress, and the local academic community, gathered for a formal dinner and reception. The event climaxed the four-day State Presidents Conference.

By previous agreement, a volunteer whisked her back to the hotel for another nap before the awards presentation at 8:30 that evening. A movie camera recorded her accepting the 36th Educational Foundation Achievement Award for mature accomplishment. It was an honor bestowed on one other anthropologist. Her friend and mentor Ruth Benedict preceded her in its presentation by thirty-two years.

As Marjorie Bell Chambers handed the award to Margaret, she cited the unselfish devotion of "her life, her thoughts, her energies, and achievements," which kept all of us "in closer touch with each other and with our brothers and sisters in the world community."

When she stood up before the microphone, Margaret wore her Phi Beta Kappa key and a button twice the size of a glasses lens that read "AAUW for ERA." She spoke on the obligations of privilege. "How can we maintain an open society with open access," she needled her audience, "and at the same time maintain excellence, [permitting] individuals to share with each other the responsibilities of privilege?"

The privilege she referred to was the education involved in earning a college degree. Margaret's ties to the organization began with her mother, who had also belonged to it. Emily Fogg Mead recognized the privilege of her status as a college graduate at a time when most women did not attend high school. Her diligence in promoting and supporting social causes throughout her life inspired similar commitment in her daughters.

Margaret tersely reviewed some of her own ways and means of serving humanity. She defined the association as "an organization of people who have had special privilege." In this, her final address to them, she challenged members "to use that privilege for the benefit of others. Privilege demands not only responsibility but also obligation to society at large. In this respect," she complimented her peers, "we can be proud of the American Association of University Women."

Three days later, Margaret welcomed the next generations of family membership in the AAUW when Mary Catherine Bateson arrived with her eight-year-old daughter for the last long visit grandmother, mother, and daughter would have alone.

On former occasions, overscheduling prevented maternal Margaret from spending as much time with Cathy as she might have liked. Now she was too full of pain to be available every minute, but she did intend to spend her four good hours per day with her daughter and with her daughter's daughter, Vonnie.

On their first morning together, Margaret introduced Carmen de Barraza to Cathy, who had attended a workshop on spiritual healing before migrating to Iran. The younger woman reportedly found the older one a warm, broad-breasted, amusing person with an intriguing Chilean-American personality, ready to touch and to comfort. The older perceived the younger as more like her British father than her American mother—taller, and chilly and distant rather than friendly.

Margaret and Cathy spent some of their afternoons together shopping for Vonnie's upcoming session at summer camp, admiring paintings at the Museum of Modern Art, and meeting people like environmentalist folk singer Pete Seeger. Evenings, they shared laughter at dinners with old friends or talked shorthand to each other while relaxing at home.

For Cathy's part, her 1978 forays to the United States must have put her in horrendous double binds. Each time, only briefly back from almost seven years in troubled Iran, she faced the reality of having both parents dying of the same disease in diagonal corners of the country. Her getting to see either of them as often as she, or they, might like couldn't have been more time consuming or expensive.

For either parent, however, the exhilaration of a visit from Cathy and Vonnie must have been poignantly precious. For Margaret, who was by far the more alone of the two, Cathy and Vonnie's end-of-June stopover amounted to an oasis of pure pleasure. It was just what she most needed.

Having to give up the July trip to Russia as late as mid-June must have been a real blow to Margaret. She had looked forward to meeting a group of the oldest people on the planet. These Russians were all well over one hundred years old. Some had probably come as close to death as she but had pulled through. They survived because they had meaningful work to do. She knew the type— she was one.

In the meantime, she would make the most of this latest disappointment by considering the necessary cancellation a blessing in disguise. She would stop racing around like a jet-set anthropological Paul Revere and stay put for a while. Give her body time to recoup energy loss so that she would be more able to take a trial-run third trip to the West Coast in August by way of testing her stamina for an even longer journey to New Guinea in December with Barbara and Fred Roll.

Except for morning notations marked "9:30: CdeB," the squares in Margaret's 15-by-12-inch desk calendar for July 1978 were mostly bare other than occasional reminders to phone someone or to expect a call from somebody at a specific time. A very few friends, professional peers, or students were due to come to the apartment to report on various projects or to pay their respects. She flew to Boston with the director of the Scientist Institute for Public Information for a day and a half on July 18. While he visited his brother she discussed alleviating her nausea and dehydration with a doctor familiar enough with current research on nutrition to be able to construct a satisfactory diet. Later in the month, she also kept an appointment with the endodontist who had capped her teeth. Best of all, she met Rev. Carmen de Barraza's friend, Dr. Charles Goodrich. After years of being disgruntled by a string of traditional doctors through the expensive and time-consuming process of trial and error, with Goodrich she stumbled on a warm and sensitive, holistically inclined medical man whom she felt she could trust. The end of her search for such a person removed a source of stress that had been plaguing her.

It was not until the second week of this month that I was officially informed of her illness. Dana Raphael and I exchanged a number of Connecticut-to-California phone calls during July, just prior to my departure for an end-of-summer trip to the Orient. On Sunday, July 9, the day before Margaret had planned to fly to Russia, Dana initiated the series to disclose something "not too nice."

"I missed Margaret at quite a few meetings lately," she broke the news. "So I went to see her and got the shock of my life. She's very, very seriously sick with what could be pancreatitis, and it may have spread to her colon as well. Someone said she's got diverticulitis. Whatever, it's so deep in her body that little can be done to ease her pain. She's lost over sixty pounds since Christmas."

"That's more than two pounds a week."

"She suffers from acute malnutrition, nausea, and dehydration. I could literally hear pain in her voice. She 'talks sick' if you know what I mean."

"Hmmm. I'm not surprised at what you say. There's been such a dearth of news items on her since the meetings in Houston last fall that I had a hunch something was the matter. If the newscasters announced the death of any anthropologists, hers would be one they'd mention, don't you think?"

"Most certainly. They'd even blab that she was sick enough to die. As they did with Senator Humphrey. Remember that? She doesn't want anybody to know anything about her, so don't breathe a word about how sick I say she is," Dana cautioned.

"It's strange, but she has been hovering gently in the back of my mind since I last saw her in Houston. I don't know if it's ESP or what, but it's a hunch that won't go away."

"She chooses to suffer in silence. She's proud of the picture most people have of her as a robust woman of great accomplishment and involvement. She'll maintain that image to death's door."

"I can understand that. It's certainly the way I picture her."

"She's the kind of person you can't play the usual games with," Dana continued. "She's had several doctors. When they don't treat her as a whole person, she lets them go. She's managing her own illness, if you can imagine that. Incredible."

"She's spunky and she's been sick lots of times," I butt in. "Nothing's ever stopped her yet. She warned us that anthropology is a profession in which one should expect to get sick. Whatever's the matter, she won't mollycoddle herself. Work's her priority. She's addicted to it."

"That's the kind of person who needs mothering the most," Dana hinted. "I wanted to let you know, hoping you'd be able to come and help take care of her. You're retired so you've got the time. You're one of her people, you know."

"Well, at least I've got the kind of bossiness she likes. Let me sleep on it. No use making Ma Bell richer while I mull over the decision. I'll call you tomorrow night."

"Such news explodes a routine firecracker very quickly."

I glanced at my watch: 3:30 p.m. West Coast time. I stopped sewing a slipcover that had to be finished before I left on my trip, cleared the cloth away, and sat and stared out the window in silence. An hour later, I warmed some leftovers for supper with son Laird. "Why are you so quiet?" he squinted his eagle eyes at me across the table during our meal.

"I've just heard that a dear friend in New York is seriously sick," I mumbled meditatively, "and the information burdens me."

"Do I know her?" He studied my expression.

"No," I lied and looked down.

"Is it Margaret Mead?" he asked without a pause as he helped himself to seconds.

No use trying to hide anything from this wise guy.

"Yes," I admitted, "it is. Please keep it to yourself though. She doesn't want anybody out of her network to get wind of it. Dana Raphael called today to see if I'd go to New York and help take care of her. For the first time in my life, I've got no pets, plants, pupils, or progeny to hold me back. The one big obstacle is that nonrefundable $2,000 I've plunked down for the trip that's in the offing."

"Sometimes we have to change our plans," he said simply.

"I've been awake on and off all night," I opened a conversation with Dana the next evening. "I've decided to go ahead and go. Self-sacrifice sucks, you know. There's no sense in giving up that trip without Margaret's asking me to come. It's

Rhoda's apartment. I can't invade that without running into static from her. Remember the opposition she gave us in Mexico?"

"That's right. Nobody else could take care of her at Rhoda's. Rhoda would want to do that herself."

"Can you get word to Margaret that I'll be free as a South Sea Islander come October? She'll raise hell when she hears that I've retired, but you can tell her that I'm ready and willing to help out whenever I know she wants it."

"That's good news," Dana sighed with relief. "I've been having nightmares about her. She's amazing, but I worry about her just the same. No matter how riddled with pain she may be, she still makes and keeps commitments. I'm going in to New York for a meeting with her on ecology in a few days. I'll mention that you're ready to come in the fall and then I'll let you know what she says."

A week later, Dana rang again. "There were so many people milling around and sapping her strength that I didn't get a chance to say anything," she reported. "I suggest that you phone her yourself. Don't write a letter. Phone. She's got the same habit you have of answering the phone in another voice so that she can say whether she's in or not. Remember that and identify yourself immediately."

"What does she look like?" I queried.

"She's a little jaundiced. She's lost so much weight. She had to get that weight off before I realized how small she really is," Dana answered. "She's wearing Rhoda's clothes because hers don't fit anymore."

"Margaret's illness must be tremendously disorienting to poor Rhoda," I mused aloud. "Her whole life will fall flat when Margaret dies. Does she show any signs of separation conflict?"

"Yes," Dana responded. "On the one hand, I feel sorry for Rhoda's having to face that death after so many years of faithful co-working and companionship. On the other, I'm annoyed at her. It's almost impossible to get past her to Margaret either by phone or in person. She's treating Margaret like a child. Margaret collects people, and Rhoda's cutting them off."

"Maybe that's how Margaret wants it. That happens in some marriages, you know. The good-time Charlie husband gets the wife to do all his dirty work. More than once Rhoda's answered the door to 16-J at the Beresford when I've brought a birthday or Christmas present to Margaret. Not once did she ever invite me in, but Margaret invites herself to my house every chance she gets."

"That's happened to all of us," Dana interrupted. "They've got a seven-room apartment with two housemates, two house cats, and a Haitian housekeeper. Margaret likes to describe herself as a 'boarder in a friend's apartment.' Rhoda runs the place, you know."

"There's bound to be both pluses and minuses in such a deal," I said. "A plus would be that Rhoda buffers for Margaret at the door and on the phone. And she maintains the place with Tulia's help. A minus would be that Rhoda might sometimes try to manage her star boarder as well. But the setup does free Margaret from most of the daily minutiae that bogs down the rest of us."

"Rhoda's closing the apartment any day," Dana went on. "She spends her summers in Vermont somewhere. Margaret went up there last year; this summer, no. She's going out on Long Island with a pregnant former assistant in a few weeks. She's going to fly to the West Coast in the middle of August."

"Oh, shucks. Right when I'm going to be gone. You know how interested she is in patterns?" I thought aloud. "Remember she said she spent the very first summer of her life near the sea in Lavalette, New Jersey? She came back there before she enrolled at DePauw and felt so nostalgic about that long ago. If this is to be her last summer, I hope wherever on Long Island or the West Coast she goes, she will stay where she can hear the sea. That would complete a circle for her."

"I don't know anything about that, but when she returns, she's going to rent an apartment with her sister. It's in a residence hotel just across the street from the Beresford. On the same floor too, if you can believe that."

"They were lucky to find anything in New York, as you very well know. It's about time Elizabeth enters the scene. Fits right in with what Margaret said in *Blackberry Winter* about siblings: You fight with them when you're kids and they're your best friends in older age."

"Yes. And she's also very close to a nurse–midwife she met last year. Mary Elder has a beautiful apartment in the Bronx, and Margaret stays there occasionally. She's welcome to spend time with us here in Connecticut whenever she wants as well."

"Or me when I'm home in Wisconsin," I echoed. "I've told her I keep my heart and my home open for her. She likes being taken care of, and many of her friends are habitually solicitous. She'd never stay long anyway. She likes variety too much. If she's dying, Old Man Death will really have to scamper some to catch up with her."

I dialed Margaret's number off and on through the rest of July without success. Finally, I ignored advice and wrote her a letter:

Carissima Makarita,
I have called you repeatedly with no luck. I'll be back in the USA from the Far East in four weeks. Dana has told me that you are ill; that you have found somebody who would treat you holistically. I want you to know that I have retired

and would be very much able to come and help out whenever you indicate you would like me to do so. I am capable, free to move on short notice, and a long time friend with plenty of experience taking care of those I love. All you have to do is beckon.

If I do not hear from you, I would like you to know that I'll be in New York City for Thanksgiving and will be calling on you at that time.

As is true of so many of your former students, I have great affection and sincere regard for you. Have missed your visits lately.

Love, and love from my four stalwart sons as well.

Pat Grinager

I slipped my letter to her into a mail slot in the San Francisco International Airport on the evening of my flight to Sydney, Australia. Some years later I looked for it in her papers at the Library of Congress. It was not there. She may or may not have ever seen it. Some letters she did see and would intend to answer. Then after several weeks of nothing but interruptions, she remembered that indeed she had written. As the years catapulted her into greater notoriety, with the consequent spiraling of calls on her time and attention, I began to feel that sending her a personal letter was as fruitful as airmailing one to the dead letter office—special delivery.

In the meantime at the Beresford apartment, difficulties between the two cantankerous housemates came to a head. Sister Elizabeth moved down from Cambridge. As luck would have it, they settled into another apartment on the same floor and facing Rhoda's apartment.

There are as many Margaret Meads as there are perceivers. There is some of her in all of us, all of her in none of us. She was our sister, our friend, our mother, our aunt or grandmother, our self. She was Everywoman. Bright and witty. Energetic and quick. Gruff and tough. Tender and tenaciously loyal. She could be thoughtful and thoughtless. She didn't mince words or overdo actions. She rarely lacked an opinion or a pronouncement, a sizing up or a calling down. She was impatient with little things, amazingly visionary with big ones. She was a stern taskmaster who drove her help, her friends, and her relatives as relentlessly as she drove herself. Very few, if any, of those close enough to work with her escaped her on-again, off-again temper. She screamed at assistants one minute and answered the phone with the dulcet tones of a receptionist in a mortuary the next; hung up and continued unabated. In the days before people put down or took up new jobs as casually as some do new mates, Margaret Mead's caustic tongue intimidated so many so often that her turnover of personnel exceeded the national average. But for her many stalwart colleagues and friends, she inspired respect, loyalty, and love.

And she never said good-bye.

INDEX

ABOUT THE AUTHOR

Patricia Grinager received her Ph.D. in Anthropology and Education from Stanford University in 1964. Over the years she has held positions as Associate Professor at the University of Delaware and the University of Wisconsin, and at Columbia as the Director of Admissions and Financial Aid and Dean of Students for the School of General Studies. She currently resides in Palo Alto, California.